THE DOOR IN THE NIGHTMARE:

FROM THE RUSSIAN REVOLUTION TO PAX AMERICANA

A Memoir

by Galina De Roeck

PRAV
PUBLISHING

2021

PRAV Publishing

www.pravpublishing.com

pravpublishing@protonmail.com

ISBN 978-1-952671-10-4 *(Paperback)*

ISBN 978-1-952671-12-8 *(Ebook)*

THE DOOR IN THE NIGHTMARE

ACKNOWLEDGMENTS

Because this memoir's range includes life on four continents and a hundred years of history, it owes much of its reflections to exhaustive readings to make sense of many of the things I had seen and felt. However, since this memoir is a tightly woven text of the personal and the historical, I have decided not to offer footnotes or even a bibliography, limiting myself to a few sources quoted in the text itself.

Just as important as any sources have been the comments of the several readers who kindly offered to read the manuscript. Margaret Fleming was the very first reader of the early chapters. Her suggestions have been invaluable. After all, English is not my first language, and her patience offered the encouragement I needed to keep going. My friend Nancy Diaz, whose friendship goes back to our days together in graduate school, read an early version of the manuscript. She too has been kind in her comments. At the same time, she offered extremely useful editorial advice. I have also received positive feedback from the historian David Gibbs, particularly on the Yugoslav chapters, since the subject is one of his specialties. After reading some 24 books on Yugoslavia, it was his book, *First Do No Harm: Humanitarian Intervention and the Destruction of Yugoslavia,* that I could finally accept as a fair and reasonable analysis of the turmoil that had visited the country in the '90s. I also turned for advice to Yuri Slezkine, whom I only knew from his writings, particularly *The Jewish Century.* He was kind enough to read the Russian chapters and responded positively. My friend Paula Wilkes also took the trouble to read the whole memoir and offer helpful suggestions. Finally, my friend John Mackoviak, who read the manuscript twice, commented on the liveliness of my writing style.

In contrast to these encouraging responses, my numerous attempts to publish the memoir have been a repeated failure. Most of the several hundred agents that I contacted stated that I wrote well, which they concluded just from my synopsis, but only one of them actually read the manuscript. I turned to Howard Zinn, whom I sent the chapters on Yugoslavia and who was kind enough to respond and recommend my memoir for publication. Sadly, however, he died soon thereafter, and I was left with the agents' collective judgement that my opus was not a promising sell. It was judged, and I can only speculate, a murky combination of the untypically personal and questionably political. And who was I to venture into such territory without the benefit of public standing: I was not, after all, Lady Gaga or Madeleine Albright.

This is why I would like to express my gratitude to Jafe Arnold, who long after I was resigned to my failure, expressed interest in reading my manuscript, and then offered to publish it. His willingness to take a chance on complex writing and challenging politics from a nobody is brave and unusual. Thank you, Jafe.

Last but not least, without the patience and skill of Steven Adger, I don't know whether I would have survived all the computer challenges involved in publishing in the 21st century.

- Galina De Roeck

Tucson, Arizona

29 April 2021

TABLE OF CONTENTS

PREFACE

My family has been caught up in the last hundred years of history: wars, revolutions, repeated migrations to unknown places like Africa, Australia and America... In short, what is known as "the nightmare of history" has been a very personal nightmare to us. However, as the title of my memoir also suggests, the presence of a "door" in the nightmare offers options. But then again, while some doors open up to the future, others remain shut. Thus, my memoir struggles to review and pass on the lessons of survival: what keeps doors open, or what shuts them up.

This is not easy. We have all experienced ordinary nightmares: you find yourself in a familiar place that is also strange, and one is going somewhere or looking for something, but things change around you and there is a sense of confusion, even impending danger... And what a relief it is when you wake up and the real world is just as you left it the night before. But when the real world turns out to be as inscrutable and dangerous as a nightmare, you have to, whether you like it or not, develop new skills: skills of observation, of making do, of understanding, of changing course.

My parents survived the Russian Revolution. Then together we survived World War II in Yugoslavia, camps in Germany, and colonization and decolonization in North Africa, followed by emigration to Australia. Going through all this, you do get a sense of "the way of the world." And because you don't want your kids and grandkids to repeat it all - all over again - you feel the urgency to share your hard-earned insights and reflections.

There is a perennial problem facing this, however, and that is the problem of finding a common language. I am aware that my language is that of an "outsider." I worry that to my American kids and grandkids my stories of wars and revolutions are going to appear strange and foreign and beside the point. But I have learned to sense impending danger, and I feel that I have to sound the alarm...

But first, by way of explanation, I would like to invite you to join me on my difficult journey of self-discovery, which is also a search for more general truths. Perhaps the most defining event in my life was the bombing of Belgrade in 1941, when I was three years old. Running from bombs and hiding in holes in the ground called "shelters" has made war a permanent, visceral feeling. I feel it even now just when planes or helicopters fly overhead. Call it PTSD, or call it the perfect makings of a peace activist.

Similarly, five years in refugee camps in Germany have taught me to live without: without food, without warm clothes, without school, without a future. Am I supposed to erase this from my memory when kids are herded into prison-like camps right here at the Mexican-American border, where I now live?

And then, there were the almost ten years of our life in Morocco, which was a French colony at the time. It was taken for granted that we, the Europeans, were "superior" to the locals, because their religion and lifestyle were unlike ours, but not for long, because they reclaimed their country and we had to move once again. Still, I had lived there long enough to figure out that just because we had some cultural differences, our common humanity made us eminently the same.

At the time, my understanding of the "Holy Land" was purely Biblical. Much later, I had the occasion to undertake a trip to Israel/Palestine with an interfaith group. This revealed the irreconcilable colonial situation I had known in Morocco. Since, unlike in Morocco, both the Israelis and the Palestinians have a historical claim on the same territory, they simply must develop a society of mutual understanding and resolve the unbearable state of exploitation and injustice inflicted on the Palestinians.

And then it was the time in Australia: I was twenty-years-old by then, and knew several languages, but not English: this made me a dumb immigrant and familiar with what immigrants face everywhere.

I met my life's companion and late Belgian-born husband, Rick De Roeck, in Australia, and he brought me to the United States. By that time,

10

my English was fair enough, and my American life took a reasonably stable, even comfortable course. And since motherhood is a woman's lot, raising my son and daughter became an all-absorbing task. But then again, opposing the nuclear arms race in the '80s to secure my children's future felt as "natural" as washing diapers.

Coming to terms with the nuclear arms race involved a more complicated issue. I had become an American citizen, and was determined to be a fully intentional one. On the other hand, I had absorbed something of my parents' Russian ways. For one, Russian was the family's language, even as I struggled in other languages during my spotty schooling throughout our international peregrinations. It never occurred to me to tell my grandmother, my dear Babushka who lived with us, that I would not speak Russian with her.

Then, of course, Russia was not Russia anymore, but the Soviet Union. I had heard plenty about how the Whites (to which both sides of my family belonged) and the Reds (the Bolshevik revolutionaries) had fought over the body of Mother Russia – and how the Whites had lost, which is why we had suffered all the hardships of exile. And the consequences of this loss were reflected in President Reagan's referral to the Soviet Union as "The Evil Empire."

My deep anti-war instincts, however, refused to settle for this "no exit" dead end. I joined some peace activists, and in 1983 traveled to an international peace conference in Prague. I had been extremely nervous about venturing into enemy (still Communist) territory, but found the experience remarkably liberating: 144 countries were represented, peace talks went on in all languages, and the whole experience was an international love fest. The real shock happened upon returning home: our vaunted free press completely misrepresented the events I had just personally witnessed.

I decided to pursue my war and peace education, and joined a Quaker delegation to the Soviet Union the following year. My parents warned me that I was flirting with the Gulag, but I decided to take the chance. We were joined by a group of Soviet "peace workers", and it dawned on me that while we Americans were a bunch of individual do-gooders, our Soviet counterparts actually represented their country's official policy. War had never touched

American shores: is that why they could not just afford, but thrive on the pursuit of the Cold War?

In the years that followed, I visited El Salvador and Colombia with Witness for Peace, and learned that we were training assassination squads at the School of the Americas in Fort Benning, Georgia. The Cuban Revolution, which I had earlier interpreted as a "red threat," now made some sort of sense. And the whole issue of who was entitled to be in the privileged class, and who was not, led me to question my own parents' anti-revolutionary assumptions. They had been born into the privileged class, and didn't know any better? Maybe. And I am infinitely grateful to them for salvaging kindness and common decency through all their trials.

But what about me? After all, my birthright had been the school of hard knocks from day one. Should I not know better? And now that I was an American, was I not automatically a member of the world elite? The tipping point for an understanding of the distribution of world power finally hit me when "we" bombed Belgrade in 1999. The circle closed in on itself: clearly, as an American I was now bombing some little girl whom I once was in Belgrade.

I decided to do my homework, but the "respectable" sources I had relied on for information now struck me as hollow. I stopped trusting the corporate media. I concluded that our endless wars in Afghanistan and Iraq and Sudan and Yemen and Libya and Syria, etc., are not humanitarian interventions and have nothing to do with democracy building. They are predatory resource wars. And where is the peace movement these days? Absolutely nowhere.

Instead, there is NATO. The Soviet Union had given up its "evil" ways, meekly broken into pieces, and joined the ranks of the "free world." So why is NATO inching its way up to the borders of the Russian Federation? And now Ukraine, the historical borderland, is in the sights of NATO as well.

My Dad was born in Russia, while my Mom's family came from Ukraine. I never heard a single word of argument about this between them. Poor Ukraine: no wonder a civil war broke out over the claims of contending powers. But no worries: Victoria Nuland, and now President Joe Biden are there to proffer a helping hand.

This scenario has all the makings of a nightmare in real time. And is there even a door in this nightmare? I am counting on the next generation to find and open that door...

My memoir is the story of a double life. It is the story of an immigrant who strives to become an American, and of an American who strives to claim her hard-earned membership in the world community. My American life, which I entered in my mid-twenties, was an unremarkable, pretty satisfied middle-class life. It was made of the joys and sorrows of family life and the successes and disappointments of career goals. It would hardly need special attention. But it was shadowed by a second life - events distant in both time and space which my unspoken goal had been to keep locked in the past.

The unspoken has a way of demanding a hearing. Thus, the course of this memoir becomes a tapestry of thematic cross-links. Events, encounters, and landscapes in the New World trigger childhood memories or motivate trips in real time, thus weaving together past and present, the personal and the historical, experience and political analysis.

I was finally willing to relinquish the pieties of my Russian family – which means that I must acknowledge that the Russian Revolution, however devastating to many, was fought in the name of the common man. And that its experiment in Socialism was defeated by deliberate economic containment, the horrors of World War II, and the resumed hostilities of the Cold War.

And what of the "American dream"? It is as if war, revolution, civil strife, hunger and desolation don't really happen when they happen somewhere else – when they happen to others. That was the hardest door to push open: that the American dream is built on the nightmare of others. How much longer can we maintain our military bases around the world to protect our interests? How many "new and improved" nukes can we produce in the relentless push for Capitalist growth? And what of the militarization of space?

This global nightmare is happening in real time to all of us. And what of our kids and grandkids: do they have a future? All I can do is sound the alarm, and be a witness. It is up to the next generation to renew the effort. May its mission be to shut the door to the excesses of human hubris, and to reopen the door to human solidarity.

- Galina De Roeck

Tucson, Arizona

20 March 2021

PRELUDE

"We must sleep with open eyes...
We must dream with our hands...
We must sing till the song puts out roots..."

-Octavio Paz

An odd whistling came through the car radio, then there was a sound gap, then something like a huge wave breaking. I doubled over, and when my husband Rick took his eyes off the road momentarily to glance at me in surprise, I was still unable to speak. He pulled the van over and brought it to a stop: he thought I was having a heart attack.

It took me some time to get the words out. "Did they just say we were bombing Belgrade?" Yes, our radio had been tuned to NPR. But what was the matter with me? My body had registered the news before I did, and there was a split between me and myself. There I was, a three-year-old in the Belgrade of 1941 to whom this whistling noise was intimately familiar, with its willed sound blank before the inevitable, earth-shattering explosion. And here I was, a late-middle-aged American woman on the way to the supermarket in 1999. We were raining missiles on Belgrade, I was a little girl in a cellar in Belgrade, and it felt like I was bombing myself.

Rick tried to comfort me, but it was as if I had disappeared into the gap between the whistling and its resolution on impact. All his assurances about smart bombs and surgically excised targets and Milošević and ethnic cleansing sounded familiar but odd, as if dubbed. Rick and I went on with our errands, returned home, had a meal, and went to bed. I kept tossing and turning, and then I found myself in this dream: *I was in a place I knew well, the house with the big porch in Belgrade... I was sitting on the rug in the play corner between my parents' bed and the glass door to the other room...And I was crying and crying... I looked up... There was someone crying out there on the porch... I moved in that direction, but Mom stood by the door, her eyes flashing... I hesitated, then reached up and began to turn the knob...*

I felt Rick's hand on my shoulder and opened my eyes. "You were making strange, choking noises," he said, "Bad dream?" I touched my cheek, but it was dry. I was glad he had woken me up before I could open that door. All the same, those missiles crashing in Belgrade had released old ghosts, and I became haunted. That dream, so familiar and so elusive, got mixed up with everything I was doing the next day: drinking my coffee, checking my e-mail, idling at the red light on my way to the dentist. But as I sat in the dentist's waiting room, I noticed that the night's visitation was beginning to fade.

Still, while I sat in the dentist's chair, and even as he poked and drilled, it seemed that I was still holding on to the comet's tail of my dream. Who was crying in the dream? But the new-age muzak, the bright poster of pristine nature, and the inordinate cheer of the good dentist were taking over. Then I remembered how George Washington was said to have ended up with wooden teeth. It occurred to me that I had worried more about the family's teeth than about our perishable souls.

Between the dentist's golf scores and the saga of his Caribbean cruise, I resolved that my gift of life to my kids was not enough. Tilted way back, my mouth gagged with cotton pads, I watched the dentist morph into the interchangeable talking heads of our brave new world. They were selling us down the river, with special discounts on tsunamis, famines, and massacres. And here I was repairing my own toothy smile, no longer bombed but bombing. The dream, like static or heartbeat, lingered on.

As I drove away from the dentist, I made a sudden turn toward home. The other errands would have to wait. It was high time to enter the gap between the middle-aged woman settled in the U.S. and the little girl sitting it out in a cellar in Belgrade. But those doors in my dream… Did I really want to open them?

Once home, I settled down and looked up at a portrait of Dad. An Estonian friend from the DP camps who had ended up in Australia had painted him some six months before he died in 1987. Dad sits on a park bench wearing a brownish suit which should have been passed on to the

Goodwill store long ago. His floppy hat bears witness to many a fishing trip around Sydney Bay. Dad had been a passionate fisherman and the memory of his fishing stories took me all the way back to Bihać, Bosnia, where I was born. Not that I remembered much, for we had moved to Belgrade around my third birthday. But in my mind there still lingered a certain angle of light playing over the water, a dim outline of people, and Dad's voice telling fishing stories. He had supposedly cast for trout out of a window of our house in Bihać, which stood by the river Una.

I kept looking at Dad: his body is trim and his back straight, though he leans forward a little, his hands resting on a cane. No one had spotted his glaucoma, and it was his progressive blindness which finally landed him in a nursing home. My friend fudged the troubled eyesight a little, placing the upper rim of his glasses across his downcast lids. But she did well with the half-smile, a little self-deprecating and tinged with irony. I had known that smile all my life. Even now, from the still canvas, it was telling me to go on ahead among the ghosts and open those doors.

I hesitated. It was like bracing myself to give birth all over again. Only instead of passing on the record of evolutionary life cycles compressed in DNA, I would attempt to pass through the birth canal of my memory big chunks of history, still raw and contested. Making history used to be men's work, but they had made a monumental mess of it. I prepared to enter the time gap.

Here it goes: Call me an American, gender female, classification Caucasian. But the American part entered my make-up when I was in my mid-twenties. I am foreign-born then, a hybrid American, politically engineered, and the shape-shifter and busy-body hyphen is the secret hero of my story. It's as if I had two lives - my adult life, familiar, ordinary, American - and then another life inhabited by a silent partner. And now she was demanding her day in court.

Let me start with my American story. My Belgian-born husband Rick and I arrived in the U.S. in 1962. We had met as students at the University of Sydney in Australia, and at first, our trip to the U.S. had been planned as merely a passage. Rick's father Frank, a Coca-Cola company man, had been transferred over the years between Belgium, the US, and Australia. In 1962 he and Rick's mother, Francine, were living in Stamford, Connecticut, while Rick remained in Sydney to finish college. Having graduated with an Economics degree, Rick's plan was to go back to Belgium, where the whole idea of the Common Market was beginning to take hold. On his way to Europe he planned to visit his parents. My plan was to follow him.

Am I an Australian then? Not exactly. I was what was then referred to as a New-Australian. There goes one of my many hard-earned hyphens. Only in Australia it proved to be a strictly one-way sign. Our past, it seemed, was perversely concocted for the bewilderment of Old-Australians.

Although both my parents had been born in Russia, the latest country we had lived in before coming to Australia had been Morocco – at the time a French protectorate. Did this make us Moroccan? The Moroccans didn't think so. But we had Moroccan papers, whose Arabic script no one else could read. On the day of my wedding this presented a problem. The mayor needed verification that I had not already tied the knot elsewhere. I can still see the puzzled look on her face as she turned the document with the mysterious script this way and that. In the excitement of wedding bells, we had forgotten that minor detail and now sat there sheepishly, wondering what next. The kindly mayor finally made up her mind that I was too young, and likely of the wrong gender to try bigamy. She signed our marriage license.

Now that I was married to a Belgian national, I tried on my new identity as one tries on hand-me-downs. I learned that Belgians subdivided into Flemings and Walloons, and that only the Walloons spoke French, while the Flemish spoke a form of Dutch. I was confused. Rick was a Fleming, yet Rick spoke French… But why look a gift horse in the mouth when it had been the French language which played Cupid to our romance? The French Department at Sydney University put on a play, and for lack of qualified Australians, Flemish Rick and "Moroccan" Galina were brought together as leading man and leading lady. The rest is history.

Travel was cheaper by boat than by plane in those days, so in 1962 we booked our passage on an ocean liner, which was to take us to the United States. Friends and family came to see us off. This called for Australian bubbly and a flutter of streamers. People still used to throw those long thin strips of colored paper across the divide of parting. I watched the streamers slowly stretch out and break off as the lumbering ship turned away. Individual faces blended into an indistinguishable crowd and finally the inanimate outline of a coastline left behind.

I turned away. Stepping onto that boat was like entering Noah's Ark – leaving behind a lost world – or lost to me… I just couldn't look back… And yet I couldn't look forward either. Can one really start over? So, I stepped on board, prepared and not prepared.

Our boat happened to be a Dutch liner. We were seated at the purser's table, and the occasion proved a crash course in the non-existence of Belgium. Placed between the Dutch purser and a French couple, Rick was completely outflanked. The fact of Belgium, created in 1830 by international agreement, was apparently still in question. The handsome Dutchman raised his eyebrows and mimicked astonishment, "Belgium? Never heard of it." The French couple was more enlightened, as the French tend to be. They merely deemed the border between France and Belgium in poor taste. Such is the fate of small countries lopped off the edges of mighty former empires.

As Rick parried these assaults, my mind turned to yet another facet of his identity, namely his religion. It remained unaccounted for. Due to lack of time and money, our wedding had been a modest civil affair. As a Belgian, Rick could be presumed to be Catholic. I had spent two years in a boarding school run by nuns in Morocco, so the Catholic environment was pretty familiar to me, even though my own birth religion was Russian Orthodoxy. Rick's knowledge of the faith proved so abysmal, however, that I concluded that only a Belgian of the Jewish faith would be ignorant of even the word "catechism." Since World War II and its concentration camps was hardly a distant memory, I refrained from probing any further. A third alternative did not occur to me.

But now we were on our way to America, and the prospect of facing Rick's parents was a potential iceberg floating closer and closer with each passing day. What did I really know about being Jewish? As the heavy sea churned below, however, we celebrated our postponed honeymoon, and this bride danced away above the waves. And thus dancing, we approached the shores of America.

***

CHAPTER 1

AMONG CONNECTICUT YANKEES

That first year on American soil was not what I had expected. I had worried about meeting Rick's parents, and I had looked forward to the thrill of New York. Frank and Francine's welcoming hugs reassured me soon enough. However, my encounter with New York proved traumatic.

As I emerged from Grand Central Station and looked up, the sky-scrapers huddled together and prepared to crush me. I looked ahead, but the crowd advanced caterpillar-like, filling the sidewalk five abreast. It was a thousand-headed monster, and its myriad gaze was unseeing. I was afraid to be mowed down by its motion - and I was also afraid, if I entered its ranks, to become just like them. There was a third option. A tall, powerfully-built man in Viking garb stood on a street corner, holding some kind of theatrical pike or lance. A horned helmet sat askew on his disheveled hair, and his eyes were wild. Gulping for air, I locked step with the crowd and began to march.

We had applied for Green Cards, and Rick had landed a job right away with an investment firm. It did not take too many days of following job leads for me to get an offer as well. The outfit was Radio Liberty, and they hired me as a translator. Their stated mission was to broadcast news, political commentary, music, and sports across the "Iron Curtain." It looked like Radio Liberty and I were made for each other. In my Russian émigré family, talk of Whites and Reds, purges, engineered famines, and labor camps in Siberia had been the background noise of my childhood. But things didn't pan out at Radio Liberty. It was as if my task was to collaborate on a painting by numbers. The colors were set and the lines rigidly drawn. Something in me felt the urge to cross lines.

There was something else. I had been uprooted many times, and a trip to yet another continent had not alarmed me. What I now found missing was the emotional soil no country had ever provided, but that my parents, it turned out, had represented all along. They were my portable fatherland and motherland, safe haven, home and heartland. I was terribly homesick.

What was the matter with me? Did the skyscrapers of Manhattan, still leaning over to crush me, know something I didn't? And if the crowd was still hydra-headed and eyeless, was it something about them or about me? And about Radio Liberty, why did I have such trouble breathing within its walls? The mad Viking haunting the streets of Manhattan began to haunt me too. My new family took me to a doctor. Lucky for me, he was old-fashioned, and offered no happy pills, but simply prescribed rest. Lucky for me, rest was an option, and I quit my job.

My recovery - I knew not from what - took the better part of that year. I would be hard-pressed to describe its non-events. All the action took place below the surface. My nights were haunted by a decaying ship – and, somehow, I am that ship. I wake up screaming. And when Rick tries to put his arms around me, my skin bristles into barbed wire.

On the surface, the sea is flat. Time doubles up, adding night to day, as I can't sleep. And eating is too much trouble. We sit at the dinner table, dishes are being passed, and I even put something on my plate. But when it comes to actually lifting my fork to my mouth, I lose interest. The good thing is they all let me be. Rick and Frank leave for work in the morning and Francine putters around. I sit in an arm chair, looking out the window. The clouds out there don't move.

And yet, when I look up again, the alligator with the bulging eye has dissolved into filaments of white vapor washing across pale blue. I turn my head and notice, laid out on a plate just next to me, a small bunch of transparent green grapes. I look at Francine. She is now sitting across from me, reading. The tempting grapes, the choice of the pretty plate, and the placement at my elbow just within reach happened by magic. I sense the magic coming from that quiet woman, Francine, my mother-in-law. My arm moves, I pull off one grape. It feels plump and cool to the fingers, it feels smooth to the lips, and when my teeth break the skin and my tongue touches the pulp, the taste is sweet.

I began to venture outside. The quiet, tree-lined streets of Stamford were not Manhattan. I discovered the Ferguson Library. Books had been a refuge as long as I could remember. Grandmother, my beloved Babushka, is reading fairytales to me at bedtime while she tickles my toes. Dad, sitting in magical isolation in the soft beam of light cast by the lampshade, is reading. Later, I enter a book store in Marrakech: I am eighteen years old, and I shell out my very first paycheck for the long coveted edition of Proust's *Remembrance of Things Past*. And now the Ferguson Library in Stamford is the focus of my early days in America. Its generous stock of French books is a long-deferred respite.

While I drifted among the fictions of the French New Novel, which repeats its own echoes and mirrors its own mirages, the rest of the world was on a different trip. People watched Khrushchev and Kennedy facing off on TV, their trigger fingers tense on their respective red buttons: the slightest twitch could unleash a nuclear holocaust.

I knew nothing of the "liberation" of Cuba from Spain by the Americans in 1898. Nor of young Teddy Roosevelt, the President-to-be, leading the famous charge up San Juan Hill. Was installing American-friendly leaders in Cuba an early example of "regime change?" Using cheap local labor, American investors developed the lucrative sugar can industry. And especially under Fulgencio Batista in the early part of the twentieth century, Cuba was also a haven for the usual mafia activities: gambling, drugs, prostitution.

In 1959, the Cubans insisted on a liberation of their own under the successful leadership of Fidel Castro. This was a very bad example for other Latin American countries. That the Soviets used the occasion to sneak in a few nukes took the cake. The missile crisis was in full swing in 1962, and the whole world was holding its breath.

I was not indifferent to the affairs of the world. If anything, I had been involved in them more than I had ever asked to be. For now, however, I was enjoying my break. Having touched base with the familiar French fare, I went on to play the field. The De Roecks were members of the Book of the Month Club: history, archeology, biography, Pulitzer prizes, bestsellers. No single title stands out. All that reading was like a landfill out of which I would one day grow my American identity. That whole year had the dry, brittle feel of paper. It turned on the edges of pages, passed with the passing of stories.

I may have been living in Connecticut, but the De Roeck apartment was also an outpost of Belgium. We did not eat hamburgers or Kentucky Fried Chicken. We ate *hochepot*, a lamb stew cooked in beer, and *chicons* (otherwise known as the Belgian endive), not as a few leaves lost in mixed salads, but by the pound, slowly simmered in butter. We listened to records of the popular Belgian singer Jacques Brel, who sang of his *"plat pays"* (flat land), which had always been a land of transit - for goods and ideas, but also for armies.

Rick was five years old when Belgium was invaded by Germany in 1939. He remembers being awakened and hurriedly dressed. His parents and a couple of relatives got into their old De Soto and took off, heading south to France. The roads were jammed. Cars and trucks were surrounded by people on foot, pushing carts, carrying children. Stray columns of the French army in retreat were tangled with the mass of civilian refugees.

As the mixed convoy approached a village, the population greeted the men in uniform with a hail of stones. A French officer jumped on the running board of the De Soto. Spreading the blue cape French soldiers still wore in those days, he attempted to screen from the passengers of the car the sight of the French army in disgrace. This memory of the officer hovering bat-like on the car's running board was the lasting memory of Rick's "Flight to Egypt," as the family subsequently called their journey.

Once in the south of France, Rick's father found a job, and their three-month stay in sunny Languedoc felt, on the whole, like a vacation. They were the lucky ones; they had left a few days ahead of the real exodus. Twelve million people hit the road then, suffering repeated strafing by German planes - and some 100,000 died. But the survivors found that they had nowhere to go. Northern France was overrun by the Germans and the south had capitulated and installed a collaborationist government at Vichy. So, Rick's family returned to rainy Belgium, and the miseries of German occupation. He developed a mild case of rickets from poor nutrition, and a life-long aversion to cabbage.

What best characterized the new world I had entered upon marrying Rick, however, were the paintings of the Flemish masters. The attention to detail so characteristic of this school is carried to metaphysical extremes in the unadorned domesticity and bourgeois contentment of its interiors. Somehow, my mother-in-law's unpretentious but immaculate home and Vermeer's homely scenes were a comment on each other. If you followed the arrow of perspective of his well-scrubbed tile floors, there, framed in the diffuse halo of the kitchen door, stood Francine, holding a steaming bowl of mussels. And if you looked long enough into one of Van Eyck's convex mirrors, you might see a miniature Frank bending over his coin collection.

Nothing had prepared me to enter this composition of a Flemish painting. My family of origin had always cultivated, by choice as well as necessity, a certain aura of genteel shabbiness. Dad had emphatically scorned Mom's attempts at sprucing up our makeshift surroundings. I subsequently found in Vladimir Nabokov the same stance of all-purpose dismissal. The writer was known to favor rented lodgings and impersonal hotel accommodations even after the commercial success of *Lolita*. Dad's ultimate insult, the Russian word "*uyut'*" which approximates the notion of "coziness," matched Nabokov's famous "*poshlust'*" in a minor key. I must have unwittingly identified with Dad's lofty stance, and was affected to despise creature-comforts as philistine.

But there was a kind of alliance between Connecticut, nicknamed of old "The Land of Steady Habits," and my Belgian family's *Biedermeyer* proclivities. The snapshots recording our first year in Connecticut reveal me positively framed in a collection of early Breughels, the series on the seasons where humans demonstrate a naive harmony with nature and its appointed activities. Rick and I, silhouetted against strips of blue sky and bluer sea, shoveling sand; Rick and I amid the blaze of foliage, shoveling leaves; Rick and I, sporting exotic fur hats, knee-deep in snow, shoveling same; Rick and I peering through flowering dogwood, shoveling nothing, for springtime is no time to shovel.

One of the many things that had attracted me to Rick was his sly and ready sense of humor. Meeting Frank, I could see that the chip had not fallen far off the old block. What shocked my untutored sensibilities, however, was the decidedly ribald streak in the elder De Roeck's sense of fun. I obviously had a lot to learn about the country whose emblem is the *Manneken Pis*, the little boy gracing a corner of the *Grande Place* (the main square of Brussels) reproduced in the act of peeing.

I had read something about *l'esprit courtois* and *l'esprit gaulois*, the two faces the Middle Ages show to posterity. There is a famous picture of a mask illustrating these two sides of the period. One side of the mask piously turns its eyes heavenward, the other side grins with gaudy merry-making. I had drunk in the magic potion of *l'esprit courtois* with its troubadours and love courts, and the endless ride of the knight who carries his lady's pennant like his heart on his sleeve. When it came to *l'esprit gaulois*, however, I remained clueless. I had found neither an echo of it in my girlish imagination, nor much confirmation in my immediate surroundings. Dad still kissed ladies' hands upon being introduced.

The unanswered question of Rick's religion was finally resolved as we sustained an invasion from Rick's Belgian relatives. Francine's peaceful home, so transparent with contemplative light, turned overnight into a Jan Steen reproduction. Our Belgian cousins filled Francine's shrinking space like a canvas crowded with rotund bodies and drink-flushed, grinning faces. It was on the very first such occasion that I finally saw the light. Rick was not, and could never have been Jewish. Not that Jews don't know how to party, but because it takes Catholics to tell hair-raising jokes about nuns and priests. My new family were all baptized Catholics, but their traditional credo was impenitent anti-clericalism.

My Belgian family, however, still bore the traces of a complicated history. While Holland had gained its own Protestant space in the Wars of Religion, what was to become Belgium had remained Catholic largely because Marie of Burgundy married the Catholic Emperor of Austria in 1477. From then on, its territory became so much real estate in the succession claims of the Kings of France and the Emperors of Austria.

And these squabbles over earthly goods grew infinitely when the infinite spoils of heaven became party to the disputes. Out of its crazy quilt of small principalities the German Empire fashioned as many religious strait jackets. If you happened to be a prudent Catholic and wished to buy after-life insurance, and your ruler was a worldly Catholic bishop, you went to Rome and brought back indulgences for your loved ones. And if you were Lutheran and you were lucky to live under a born-again Lutheran prince, you could freely express your outrage at Catholic corruption by running to the nearest church and smashing some saints' noses. But under no circumstances could you count on the solace of indulgences if your prince was Lutheran or on the redeeming power of iconoclasm if your prince was Catholic.

This made life difficult for those among the Flemings and the Walloons who had become Protestant under their Catholic rulers, and they were among the founders of New Amsterdam in New Holland, which is now New York. In 1976, Rick and I took the kids to Battery Park to watch the Tall Ships go by in celebration of the Bicentennial. It was then that we discovered a memorial to the Walloons, who apparently had been the first to set foot on Manhattan Island.

What a beautiful, bright day it was. A few puffy clouds tried to compete with the sharp-edged white of the sails, but gave up, and dissolved back into placid blue. Lady Liberty, in the distance, stood to attention, saluting the glittering, white-winged sea parade. All around us the crowd milled about, festive, relaxed, companionable. If you turned your back on the top-heavy city, you could imagine yourself in New Amsterdam with its dirt streets, taverns, and windmills.

But the Flemish pastoral where I had been content to graze was losing its luster. As I was watching Frank frame a poster of Breughel's *Fall of Icarus*, something happened. The plowman and shepherd and fisherman, and a ship setting off to move the life-blood of commerce – they were all oblivious to two tiny legs convulsed in pictorial rigor mortis, and a half-submerged object, a broken wing, representing Icarus drowning... As I stared at Icarus stuck head first in the glassy water, something moved. The wing stretched out, Icarus' head bobbed out of the sea, and he began to work his one wing like a paddle. Then, scooping up a big uptake of airflow, he took off. As he flew toward the sun, his wing caught fire and propelled him forward toward other worlds.

I was ready, it seemed, to push open the door of my Flemish interior, and to step out of the still life for which I had been sitting for some time now, holding my breath. As it turned out, I couldn't wait to turn my back on the sober Flemish burghers Frank was so diligently locking into gilt frames.

As our second wedding anniversary rolled around in February of 1963, we decided to celebrate it in New York. It was bitter cold as we ventured into the canyons of Manhattan. The wind blew through them like through the pipes of a giant organ, but the skyscrapers stood their ground, and so did we. The crowds scattered in all directions, and we too found our way. Unexpectedly, the sound and beat of Manhattan became the sound and beat of our own pulse. The spell was broken. New York was ours.

With Frank and Francine's blessing, we prepared to move to Manhattan. The final lap of our original trek, the one that was to take us to Belgium, remained in suspense. Still, I added my proxy relationship to Belgium to my treasure trove of hyphens.

***

CHAPTER 2

BETWEEN FATAL SHORE AND LAND OF DESIRE

It was in New York that our American journey began in earnest. Yet we still didn't know that we were immigrants. For one thing, we were college educated and our English, if not polished, was adequate. At least, it gave rise to comedy rather than to the more painful encounters of my early apprenticeship in Australia. Thus, when I tried to order "raped cheese" in a New York deli (grated cheese in French is *fromage rapé, n'est-ce pas?*) it merely provoked a quizzical look and a cryptic aside about cheeses with holes in them.

We rented a pocket-sized walk-up studio on East 66th Street, between First and Second Avenues. The trundle bed, which filled the place when we opened it, wouldn't snap together. So, we often ended up on the floor as the two beds slid apart: this only added fireworks to our love making and motivated us to go out for everything else.

That's what we did, walking up and down and across all of Manhattan. We would meet for lunch at Chock-Full-O'-Nuts in Midtown, where Rick worked, or go watch the skaters at Rockefeller Center, or just window shop on Fifth Avenue. Or I'd go down to Washington Square to wait for Rick: he had begun to take graduate classes at NYU. Movies took us everywhere. Our favorite was the Thalia on 95th Street. But most of the time we just walked, taking it all in raw, jumbled, indiscriminate. From Wall Street, ghostly and abandoned on Sunday, to Delancey Street, packed like a Moroccan bazaar. There were occasional spells in Central Park. A cold winter day, eerily still and white, stands out. My recollection registers an unlikely absence of people, just a squirrel hopping away, leaving its paw prints in the snow. Such a spectral New York, whitewashed of human static seems unlikely, but that's New York for you.

Our own neighborhood, however, was unremarkable. The occasional brownstone or two was wedged between nondescript four- to six-story brick buildings like our own, or between warehouse-like structures in transitional use. The latest aspirations to upscale comfort tapering off into penthouses were modest enough. In contrast, the massive structure which stretched between East 65th and East 66th Streets and all the way from Second to Third Avenue was a true example of territorial dominance.

Something about that building made it look like an ocean liner. Maybe it was the odd elongated shape, 12 stories high and a quarter of a mile long. Maybe it was the glazed white brick facing. Or maybe it was the fact that, unlike most apartment buildings in that area whose ground level connected to the streets through stores or coffee shops, it floated in a pool of greenery, cut off from the rest of churning, gurgling New York. There was nothing to see behind those windows, as sealed as portholes, or on those hundreds of balconies, vacant of love scenes and serenades, stacked up like life-boats.

At the time this fortress-like building awakened within me something I thought I had left behind in Australia: Andersen's match girl left out in the cold while the party goes on inside. Yet our current circumstances were hardly like the genuine immigrant experience - the disorientation, strain, and grit of purpose which had been mine in Sydney. Rick, on the other hand, had been a corporate brat. Once his father's tour of duty as a multinational employee was over in one place or another, he moved on, taking the shell of his comforts, turtle-like, with him. Not so for me. Australia had been a true school of hard knocks.

As my parents and I stepped ashore in Sydney on a sunny day in 1958, our past had already caught up with us in the person of a Frenchman we had known in Morocco, Maurice Jobert. He now stood on the dock with an armful of flowers. When it became clear that we could no longer live in Morocco because the Moroccans were reclaiming their country from the French, we started casting about for a new place to settle. France was the obvious choice. France, however, was overrun by her own colonial sons and daughters, who were being ejected from Africa and Asia with more violence than anything we had experienced in Morocco. Dad spent a summer in France, following various job leads, but to no avail.

But there was more to Dad's lack of success than politics or economics. It had something to do with Maurice Jobert. The little mining town in Southern Morocco where we had lived for the past nine years had been too small for secrets. That Mother and Maurice Jobert were lovers was quite an open one. I had first become aware of something going on during a vacation from my boarding school in Marrakech. I dimly sensed Dad's suppressed unhappiness. He had always been on the quiet side: now he grew quieter. He had never been much of a drinker. Now I noticed that his wine glass was always full at meal time. He had always been a voracious reader, and I used to look up to him for seeming to know something of everything. Now his reading was exclusively devoted to detective yarns, as if he had to nail down the ultimate "who done it."

Mom seemed equally subdued, and this was unlike her. Petite and blonde, she had always been quick to move, quick to laugh, quick to talk back. The two of them, Mom and Dad, had seemed to go pretty well together. Now there was something stealthy, almost feline in the way Mother moved her body or narrowed her green-grey eyes. This hidden energy isolated her from Dad, its source was elsewhere. I traced it soon enough to handsome, intense, discreet, devoted Maurice Jobert.

My hatred of the intruder flared up with the sullen, single-minded dedication of a fifteen-year-old. But it had no place to go. My parents slept in separate rooms now. Mom would disappear for a couple of days, then reappear as if nothing had happened. Babushka began to show the first symptoms of dementia. And all around us, war and rumors of war filled the air. A bomb exploded in a market in Casablanca; a car was held up on the way to Mogador. People began to make plans to leave. I held out the prospect of going to study at the Sorbonne.

There was, apparently, another option. The poker game was up. I was old enough to know what I already knew, and Dad laid his cards out on the table. I was free to go to France and study. Mother was free to make a new life for herself with Maurice Jobert. As to him, Dad was going to Australia. Going

WHERE? He could have said "the foreign legion," he could have said "the moon." We would have been equally dumbstruck.

I knew nothing about Australia, not even about the koalas and the kangaroos. Don't they speak English there? What about the Sorbonne? "That's right," Dad said, "The time has come to make hard choices." We turned to Mom, who sat there, saying nothing. Before I knew what I was doing, I threw my weight into the balance. "I've decided! I'm going to Australia with Dad!" Mother looked at us. "So, I am supposed to let you two go to the other end of the earth?" We said nothing. "You know I could never do that!" Those were the words we were waiting for. We hugged, we kissed, we cried, we contemplated the new life that was already unfolding before us in the far-away, mysterious land of Australia.

Next thing we knew, Maurice Jobert obtained his immigration visa ahead of us and was now standing on the landing dock at Sydney, his arms filled with flowers. And next we all moved in together. The standard under which we marched was "practicality." Mother was the one credited with practical acumen, so Dad and Maurice deferred to her the way "Jules and Jim" defer to Jeanne Moreau in the movie of that title. We pooled our savings, such as they were, and were able to scrape together a down payment for a house. We now had a roof over our heads.

Next, we marched out to look for a job. Maurice already had a job in a wool factory sorting wool. Dad, now 59, found a job in a furniture factory, lifting heavy wood panels onto and off a planking belt. Mom and I set out in response to an ad for seamstresses. We had been sewing our own clothes as far back as I could remember. The ad had mentioned car seat covers, so we presented ourselves, feeling fit and competitive.

To the short, balding man who stood at the threshold and shouted "Experience?" at us over the din, we shouted back, "Yes, yes, EXPERIENCE!" The place was a narrow, corridor-like room, where a couple of light bulbs seemed to absorb rather than diffuse uncertain light. A fan revolved unevenly, hacking at the condensed heat. About twenty or so huge sewing machines, the likes of which I had never seen, were placed together so close that we had to edge our way past. Women were bent over their work, and they didn't look up as we squeezed by.

The man took Mom further back in the room and motioned for me to take my seat at a vacant machine. When I sat down, the forward bent of the woman in front of me made her appear headless. The man came back, handed me two strips of heavy, unbending material, pointed to where the seam should be made, then left. I struggled to secure the two pieces together under the lever. O.K., here it goes. I put my foot to the treadle, the machine lurched forward, firing off like a machine gun, devouring one of the strips while the other one half-slithered away, refusing to be stitched. I realized I needed to hold the strips together more firmly, and place my fingers much closer to where the steel lever and needle waited, looking like Jaws. I glanced at the woman to my left. She was doing it somehow, her whole upper body jerking forward in sync with the machine's rapid-fire bursts.

Now the man was back. He lifted the tail-end of the ill-fitted strips as if holding a dead fish, and without a word, pointed to the door. Before I knew it, I lunged for the aborted part of the slip cover, and there was a brief tug-of-war between the man, me, and Jaws. I wanted to tell him that I was a quick study, that I would be the best synthetic car seat seamstress he had ever had… But the uneven staccato firing of the machines left no room for human speech. As I extricated myself from the line, I noticed that Mom was already at the door, waiting. She too had flunked out.

Those were not the kinds of jobs I had to face in New York. Having recovered from my stint with Radio Liberty, I found other translation work. My secret goal, however, was something else: I wanted to write stuff of my own. Rick was supportive. I began working on a novel, and the natural language at the time was still French. The novel slowly developed as a highly symbolic journey in the sands of Africa with two elusive heroes vying for the favors of a potentially fascinating but for the time being also elusive heroine. How I envied the transparent prose and how I despised the monumental success of the then famous young French novelist Françoise Sagan!

We had no TV to distract me, but we did have a radio. The programs gave full play to the invisible hand of the free market: the airwaves offered healing for the liver, the faucet, the car transmission, the soul. But the urgency of increased decibels failed to infect me with the intended optimism. And that's how, as I navigated my dial, I happened upon the island of Pacifica's WBAI: they ran no commercials. They talked in a normal tone of voice, and they talked about places called Tuscaloosa and Vietnam.

Actually, Tuscaloosa, pronounced with a lilting Southern accent, sounded more exotic than Vietnam to me. The latter was one place I had already heard about. I remembered people crying and strangers hugging on the street in Marrakech because Dien Bien Phu had fallen. That had been the battle the French could not lose, but had, unimaginably, lost in 1954. That battle had spelled the beginning of the end, the unraveling of the great French colonial adventure everywhere.

I couldn't tell where they kept black people in New York, but the sound of their marching feet could also be heard on WBAI. They marched in Montgomery, and they marched in Selma - and white people turned their water hoses and their dogs on them. In all that confusion, a man's voice came through to me on a Sunday morning. He was a Unitarian and/or Universalist (one of those mysterious American religious sub-subdivisions). He was saying, "Out of a race of beautiful white people and a race of beautiful black people, we will carry on as a race of beautiful brown people." Just like that.

I stayed tuned and discovered more: Joan Baez' *Kumbaya, My Lord* and Judy Collin's *Silver Trout* and Leonard Cohen's *Susanne* and Bob Dylan's *How Many Times* and Pete Seeger's *Where Have All the Flowers Gone*... These songs penetrated my psyche the way no commercials ever had. Theirs was the voice of America I felt in tune with.

But then I heard somebody Robeson, Paul Robeson's son. I had heard of Paul Robeson, and his trips and popularity in the Soviet Union. Wait a minute! This was a long way from Radio Liberty! But as I listened on, I heard no plugs for Red Redemption. Gary Null, on the other hand, was on a soap box, promoting "natural living" and tilting his lance at the giants of the health establishment. But some of his alternative discoveries sounded like my grandmother's home remedies, so he was preaching to the choir there. We also appreciated Andrew Sarris, who kept us on top of where, when, and what movies to see. Well, yes, some things did shock me, like the things Lenny Bruce said. At the same time, he had such a way with words, profane or not, that I simply had to keep on listening.

Words, words, words. Live, funny, thoughtful, irreverent, provocative words. WBAI became an addiction. And that's when my novel, still crossing the deserts of Africa, began to sink into quicksand. The trouble was with words - French words. But after five solid years of English and the final assault of the airwaves, I found myself in some no-man's-land between French and English. My own English, however, was still unborn.

Questions, U-turns, new starts - that had been the name of the game back in Australia as well. After our sweatshop venture, our job-searching paths, Mom's and mine, diverged for a while. I landed a job as a domestic in a Baptist young women's hostel. I now need to backtrack a little and confess that since my early days I had come a long way, religiously speaking. At that particular time of life, I was, actually, an Evangelical Christian. I had heard the call while still back in Morocco. I had renounced the errors of my birth religion and I was born again. At least, I was baptized again.

The first baptism had been pronounced null and void. It had been foisted on me in a state of defenseless babyhood, and from what I was told, under loud protest. I also heard that the priest had been drunk and that my parents had feared for my life. But that kind of gamy talk must be traditional among Russians when recounting solemn occasions. In *Speak, Memory*, Nabokov says that the arch presbyter, as he calls him, "bungled" the affair of his baptism, and that his parents had feared for baby Nabokov's life as well.

There is no record of Nabokov attempting a repeat performance of his baptism. In my case, the second time around was no occasion for flippancy or light-hearted bungling. Being washed in the Blood of the Lamb is no joke. Except that it was really a big tub. I only wish in retrospect it had been some river in the Deep South like in the movie, *O Brother, Where Art Thou*, and that the rejoicing had been voiced in the tunes one hears on televangelist revival programs. Those people sing like angels.

But the ones who baptized me were mostly Spaniards, and their innate fire had not yet kindled their Protestant hymn singing. There was, in fact, a large Spanish community in Morocco. Northern Morocco used to "belong" to Spain, and Generalissimo Franco had organized his onslaught on the Spanish Republic from this base, using Moroccan mercenaries. The rest of the Moroccan territory was claimed by the French and had offered a shelter for the vanquished Spanish Republicans and their ill-assorted and ill-fated allies. Some of them had evidently redirected their energies from political to spiritual regeneration.

I came into contact with them through a chance acquaintance. I was in typical teen rebellion against the hoary Byzantine traditions handed down to me by the Orthodox version of Christianity. I did not visit the onion-domed churches of Holy Russia until much later, and then as an American tourist. The church services I knew in childhood were held in makeshift quarters. In spite of this, or perhaps because of it, we felt about those homemade services the way early Christians must have felt about their secret meetings in the catacombs of Rome. These gatherings set us apart, gave us a special dispensation, and kept us connected to some mysteriously distant and fabulous heritage. This is not to say that my parents were demonstrably religious. Rather, the hazards of exile caused Russians to cling together in order to salvage their cultural patrimony. Thus, my parents sang in church choirs whenever possible, Father a pleasant tenor, and Mother a pleasant contralto.

My grandmother was the genuinely "pious" one. She taught me the prayers I remember to this day. Her faithful devotions would perhaps not have made such an impression on me if they had not been rooted in an inexhaustible gentleness of spirit. It was standing next to her during those interminable services, and looking into her sky-blue eyes at the words "Christ is risen!" which filled me with faith, hope, and charity.

I also enjoyed the spectacle of it all. The choir chants and the icons look down on you while the priests, with flowing hair and beard, bless and dispense clouds of incense. Yet this transcendental tension and exotic solemnity was also remarkably informal. People moved around, unhindered by rows of pews, placed candles in front of a favorite icon, stood or knelt at leisure, and prayed unbidden by bells. Things were so informal at times that I witnessed repeated mass exodus of the faithful for a smoke break at the time of the sermon. There seemed to be an unstated consensus that the most rational part of the service was also the most expendable one.

A time came when the most beautiful icons and chants, and my sweet Babushka's presence, became powerless to quench the inquisitiveness of adolescence. Things came to a head around the seventh commandment, which was already a conspicuous skeleton in the family's closet. My turn had come to wrestle with the injunction, "Thou shalt not be jerked around by your hormones," and I turned for advice to the elderly priest who traveled all over Morocco to serve his far-flung parish. The man sighed, hesitated for a moment, then passed the buck. He referred me to a woman, namely the Most Holy Mother of God and Most Chaste and Virgin Mary. But the ploy backfired. What qualified Her as teen counselor - She who didn't even get to taste of the forbidden fruit yet managed to get Herself with child? The whole thing stank of double jeopardy to this budding feminist.

It was at this propitious moment that I met the people from an Evangelical community. They introduced me to THE BOOK. Neither the Catholics nor the Orthodox encouraged the study of Holy Writ back then, and I entered its pastures full of hopeful anticipation. And then, miracle of miracles, the prophetic voice of Billy Graham himself, speaking to me in translation from a French record, found me among the barren hills of Morocco.

His sermon was on the subject of the "Unknown God." Apparently, there had been a monument to an "unknown god" in the Athens of St. Paul's day. And now the latest apostle, Billy Graham, was addressing the subtle French as the New Athenians. Their ornate Catholicism had obscured the simple faith of the early Christians. As the Good Book has it, "the scales fell from my eyes." Russian Orthodox services certainly qualified as "ornate." The God I had known so intimately as a child had indeed become an "Unknown God" to me.

What happened soon thereafter was an encounter with Him not unlike that of Moses with the Burning Bush. I was listening to a sermon in my community's little evangelical hall, whose walls were mercifully uncluttered by watchful icons. The only aid to worship were the words GOD IS LOVE writ large on a white wall. As the minister spoke of how sadly God walked through His garden, so empty after the Fall, and how He called to Adam, who was humankind, who was me… the words "God is Love" burst into flame. Radiating vivid tongues of fire, they reached out to me, and folded me into His molten embrace. That's how I was born again and baptized again.

And that's how I came to feel blessed working as a domestic in a hostel for young Baptist girls in Australia. The directress of the establishment, a white-haired lady of regal bearing, and her assistant, who made up in angular energy what the former contributed in poise, were both very kind. I was introduced to the traditional Aussie tea breaks. With their crumpets and scones, they offered a delicious interlude between mopping floors and changing beds. The only dark cloud was my dealings with the cook. She had a rather short fuse, and threw a tantrum if I handed her a pot when she asked for a colander.

There was another live-in maid, and we shared a room. Her name was Rhoda and she was an Australian Aborigine. She was diligent in her work, quiet and reserved, except when she raised her voice in song. The richly modulated intonations that were hers forever colored for me the hymn "What a Friend I Have in Jesus." Sad to say, she didn't seem to have any earthly friends and stayed in the hostel even on her days off. I was told that Aborigines lived in a distant suburb specially designated for them.

Black Americans must have also had a designated living space in the New York of the '60s, for as far as I could tell, theirs was a purely symbolic presence on the East Side of Manhattan. I once noticed a poster somewhere near 65th Street and Third Avenue. I recognized it as a Käthe Kollwitz print. She was a German socialist artist of the expressionist school who depicted the plight of the poor. But there was something odd about the poster I was looking at. It was a black and white print, showing the wide-eyed anguish of a mother clutching her child, but the menacingly hovering figure above her, which I recalled to be an allegorical representation of "Death," was darkened out to suggest an African American. The word "RAPE" was scrawled across the poster, and the caption read, "Vote Conservative."

But I had my own memories of black Americans. This was going back to when I was ten years old in our last D.P. (Displaced Persons) camp in Germany. World War II had precipitated yet another episode on my family's wandering lives, the five-year German episode between Yugoslavia and Morocco.

This particular D.P. camp was located near Munich, in a small town called Schleissheim. A stately baroque castle bordered our camp. Barbed wire separated us from the castle and its manicured grounds, and we motley kids were not allowed anywhere near the place. We had never seen an African, so when a company of black GIs relieved the white American soldiers, who had stood guard at our gate until then, the forbidden territory doubled in dangerous allure. Oscar Wilde's story of the children sneaking in to play in the Giant's garden became our story. With hysterical fear and trepidation, we crawled under the barbed wire to wander the enchanted alleys of the castle's grounds. We held our breath. A leaf rustling, a false step crunching on the gravel, and the black Giant guarding the castle would appear to eat us alive!

I myself had the occasion to test the ferocity of the black Giant at the gate. Of all my friends, I alone had to go to school beyond our enclave. Mother, who obviously marched to a different drum, felt that the improvised camp school was deficient, and decided that I should go to a German school outside of the camp. I tried headaches, stomach aches, open rebellion – nothing doing. The first time I faced the black Giant, I nearly fainted when he asked me in a stern, deep voice: "Your pass?" All I could do was shake my head. "O.K.," said the black Giant, whipping out of nowhere a WHOLE chocolate bar. "Here," he said, "is your pass." My pass was regularly renewed after that. In time, we invited him and his friends to our lodging in the barracks, and I remember Mom sewing a button on his shirt. Communication in sign language facilitated by much laughter was no problem.

As for Rhoda back in the Baptist hostel in Sydney, from the limited conversations my poor English allowed, I understood that she had been raised on a mission somewhere in the Australian Outback. It was only some thirty years later, when I got to explore the country again as an American tourist, that I was able to visit the famous Hermannsburg Mission near Alice Springs.

The Mission's founder, F.W. Albrecht, was among the first to observe that the Aboriginal population, displaced by the cattle-grazing practices of the White Man, was on the verge of extinction in Central Australia. Until then, the Aborigines had trod lightly upon the land. Having to dodge the ever-recurring droughts, they had practiced a strenuous nomadic life. Over the millennia, an intimate knowledge of every feature of the land had been recorded in memory and passed on in song lines called "dreamings." Instead of inheriting a piece of useless land, tribes inherited stretches of song lines established by the footprints of their totemic Ancestor. These name-identified, story-associated pathways led to game, water holes, and inter-tribal gatherings.

Thus, what may look like an empty waste to a European is alive with secret sources of life, both material and spiritual, to the Aborigine. As our tourist bus crawled among those ancient wrinkles of the earth's crust, the vacant spaces began to shudder with a secret tremor, the breath of song – mankind's dreaming, mankind's naming of the surrounding world. I too joined in the "dreaming" as the shadows of passing clouds animated sharp-edged crags into fantastic beasts. I saw crested lizards crouching against the horizon, and instead of dry river beds, pebble-spotted snakes looping their way among piles of gigantic boulders. And at long last Uluru appeared in the distance, the sacred stone cast down by the Sky God, the visible sign of a covenant between God and man, man and God.

F.W. Albrecht's circling journeys among Aboriginal tribes wove together the dreamings of Moses and Jesus with the dreamings of Aboriginal ancestors. He agitated for safe "reserves." These "reserves," always threatened, were but torn shreds of ancient song lines. Still, F.W. Albrecht worked hard to turn the mission of Hermannsburg into a haven and a training ground for his charges. They would need to acquire marketable skills in a white man's Australia.

The Hermannsburg Mission is now a museum. As I looked at their photo displays, I kept searching for a little girl who might be Rhoda - even though

I knew that she belonged to a later generation. Also, she would have been classified as of "mixed blood." A law had been passed in the early years of the twentieth century to promote the forcible removal of any part-white children from their matriarchal Aboriginal families. They were warehoused in state and religious institutions, and many of them later turned against the larger society which had inflicted this wound on them. Rhoda, however, seemed resigned to her fate, and to find solace in the friendship of Jesus. She and I thus found ourselves pretty much in the same boat. We were both destined to serve others and to praise Jesus for it.

Unlike Rhoda, however, I was getting restless. My English was beginning to cope with the cook and her unpredictable ways. I had wanted to become a nun at the school of Our Lady of the Apostles back in Morocco, and now, hearing much of missionaries, I wondered whether this was not the fate God had intended for me all along. I asked my kind employers about any chances of going to a Bible school, but nothing came of it. Maybe I was to draw the obvious conclusion that my missionary work had already found me among the mops and dirty dishes of the hostel.

I pressed the Almighty for a definite answer. Is it not said, "Ask, and you shall receive?" The answer came on a Tuesday. It was the day to clean all the bathrooms. I was working on my seventh bathroom, and down on my hands and knees straining to wipe up the inevitable strands of hair and other sticky grime that tends to collect behind the toilet bowl. Then I stopped. Still on my knees, raising my eyes above the toilet bowl, I called on the Almighty to give me a sign. How long, o Lord, how long? The white walls, white tiles, white wash basin, white toilet bowl were repeated, at a slight angle, in the bathroom mirror. There a white toilet bowl, white wash basin, white tiles, white walls repeated the white walls, white tiles, white basin, white toilet bowl.

God had given me a blank check and I intended to use it. Our immigration papers had stated that my French baccalaureate would make me eligible for tuition-free higher education, and I decided to apply to the University of Sydney. It turned out that to become eligible for free tuition, I first had to pass an English spelling test. I probably could have litigated my case, for there had been no small print about spelling bees in the immigration papers, but this never occurred to me. Instead, I tripped miserably over "wooden" and "woolen," doubling letters that did not need to be doubled or not doubling any of them at all. In short, I didn't cut it. Why not take another year to improve my English, said the man. Or else, be prepared to pay tuition, said the man.

But the salary for domestic work was not promising of savings toward tuition. When Mom's friend Panya alerted us that the fruit factory where she worked was hiring, Mother and I both jumped to the occasion. I went to bid my farewells to Rhoda and the kindly ladies at the Baptist hostel. The cook was irate of course, but that was to be expected.

We got up at the crack of dawn the next day and joined a large crowd of women outside the factory gate. A man came out, and climbed on a wooden crate. The buzzing in many tongues quieted down, the shuffling and shoving intensified briefly, and then everything froze. "You," yelled the man, "you," and "you," pointing at us, one by one. "You," he pointed at me. I took Mother by the hand, and stepped forward. He hesitated: Mother is rather on the diminutive side. I looked straight at him, praying silently. "O.K.," he said, "Go ahead." Hallelujah and praise be to the Lord of Hosts, we were in.

We followed another man up some unsteady steps. The place was old and rickety. He placed us in front of two conveyor belts moving in opposite directions and carrying a stream of apricot halves. Our job was to take the larger apricot halves on the lower conveyor and put them up onto the higher one. That was it? This was A-O.K. with us, and we went right to it. Mom stood next to me, which was a comfort, but a man came up and put a finger to his lips to signify that we were not to talk. After some lapse of time, a dull gnawing pain visited the small of my back and decided to move in. I looked at Mom: it occurred to me that her small stature must make it even harder to lift her arms to the upper conveyor. But she smiled at me, and all I could do was smile back.

When the five o'clock whistle blew at last, we started for home. We were all bent out of shape and could have competed for the ministry of funny walks – perhaps the reader is familiar with the *Life of Brian* movie and sundry British sitcoms where John Cleese demonstrates "the ministry of funny walks." Now we could see why Father came home, as they say, "on his last legs," and why Maurice put his feet up and read the paper after work. Besides, they didn't know how to cook or wash dishes or do laundry, poor darlings.

The next few days came and went, and so did we. We got the hang of it, by and by. Apricots were before me, apricots were behind me, apricots were to the right of me, apricots were to the left of me. They appeared in my dreams: *lit-up apricots float by on dark streams just out of reach... reach and reach, but they accelerate, they slant away, they reverse gear... they must be magnetized, you think in perfect dream logic... you have to lift your arms, lift your arms... your arms are heavy, you cannot move your arms, move your arms... the effort lifts you out of yourself, you cross some unimaginable time-space...* RISE AND SHINE! APRICOTS WAITING!

I tried to break the spell. I tried to comfort myself with a fairy tale Babushka used to tell me at bedtime. Vasilisa the Fair was the maiden who was always given impossible tasks. Baba Yaga the witch saw to it, she of the wooden leg who lived in a windowless, doorless hut perched on a giant chicken foot. One particular task, I recalled, was to sort out a mound of wheat kernels mixed in with sand. But Vasilisa kept faith, working away at the given task, and lo, an army of ants, to whom she had been kind earlier in the story, filed in and sorted out the grains of wheat from the grains of sand. Baba Yaga was foiled again.

Lunch breaks at the fruit factory were a godsend. This one time, our friend Panya suggested we take our lunch bags to the roof of the factory. While Mom and Panya talked about the days of their youth in Yugoslavia, I looked out over Sydney. There I saw something that took my breath away. Floating above a mass of trees in distant proximity rose the neo-Gothic spires of Sydney University. Like Parsifal approaching the Fortress of the Grail, I was lifted into a glorious, thundering clash of trumpets and cymbals, and the back-to-work whistle was barely a false note in my private Wagner fest. I returned to the ceaseless apricot stream with a barely suppressed smile. There was life after apricots.

***

CHAPTER 3

RITES OF PASSAGE

New York was pretty different from Sydney. It didn't have the harbor, not cutting into the city like Down Under, where land and sea are locked in passionate embrace. Instead, New York, especially Manhattan, seemed landlocked, turned in on itself, humming and boiling over like some mad scientist's laboratory. Sydney, in comparison, had been a "members only" club. Frightened at first by New York's relentless drive to parts unknown, we had finally stepped on board. No one came to check our tickets, and we were in for the ride.

I had been neglecting the wind-swept trails of my French novel, yet thinking of switching to English was still a non-starter. It was for this reason perhaps that I found myself haunting First and Second Avenues, which had not yet undergone their more recent face lifts, and were one non-stop flea market of Europe's collective past.

I peered through display windows at objects intricately carved, delicately put together. There was a painting of a woman with half-bared breasts and aggressive wings. Her left hand rested on a stone urn, her right hand held up a torch to some scrolled writing. Maybe I kept coming back to this shop, as if one day I would decipher the message. For now, I observed the containers, cups, tankards, beakers, mugs, ewers, chalices, flagons, flasks, decanters, basins, bowls, jugs - made in Germany, England, France, Holland, Bohemia, Denmark, Italy, Spain, Russia, - made of pewter, tin, silver, brass, porcelain, crystal, - made opaque, transparent, filigreed, embossed, engraved, cut, cloisonné, globular, vermeil, ormolu.

Did I know ormolu from *vermolu*, (worm-eaten)? My family's headlong flights across half the world were not exactly shopping sprees. And yet, the litany of inventoried objects was a familiar tune. When Babushka grew older, and ever more apt to linger in the memories of her youth, she became fond of lists, especially the long list of her dowry. There was the set of monogrammed silver cutlery and plate for twelve, which she insisted upon tallying with painstaking accuracy: twelve soup spoons, twelve regular knives, twelve fish knives, twelve fruit knives, twelve regular forks, twelve dessert forks, twelve tea spoons, two sugar prongs, a tea set and tray, four candelabras… "and a partridge in a pear tree," or a Russian equivalent, would be Dad's unkind intervention.

There had apparently also been embroidered linen and carved furniture, and fashionable clothes, and Oriental rugs, and objets d'art, and jewelry… But she would grandly abstain, only to start from the beginning again after a few moments of meditative silence. The exact enumeration of the cutlery, the recitation of their orderly count seemed to restore an essential link to an otherwise irretrievable past. It offered mathematical proof of its existence.

Among the bunk-beds, makeshift trestle table and odd chair which comprised our furniture in German D.P. camps, and the ubiquitous U.S. Army surplus blankets which served as dividers between us and other families, Babushka's stories sounded pretty exotic. Her monogrammed sugar prongs were as mythical as the gray wolf of her Russian fairytales, who sallied forth to rescue Vasilisa the Fair in the midst of her many trials. And yet, I was a believer. The monogrammed sugar prongs were a secret talisman and I firmly counted on the gray wolf to take me where I needed to go.

And after the arduous test of counting apricots at the Redfern fruit factory, Sydney University had been the place to go. Since there were no evening classes, I was to attend school during the day. As it happened, hospitals advertised nursing-aid positions for the graveyard shift: just what the doctor ordered. I chose Prince Albert Hospital for its proximity to Sydney University, and was hired. The position included room and board, and I prepared once again to leave my family to carry on its *ménage a trois*.

Sydney University in close-up appeared everything I had glimpsed from afar. It was a fair facsimile of Oxbridge complete with a Lockean quad and dons in black regalia. Earlier, in a different life, I had thought I would do

Sciences-Po (Poli-Sci) at the Sorbonne. The mix of stoicism and fatalism about politics modeled by my parents did not inspire me. Their world had repeatedly collapsed on them, and I intended to find out why. I had projected my Parisian dream not only onto the venerable flagstones of the Sorbonne, but also onto the smoke-filled cafés of the Left Bank. There Juliette Greco would be singing in the background, and at the very next table Simone de Beauvoir and Jean-Paul Sartre would be arguing about the latest book or the latest protest.

But Sydney University was a horse of a different color. Its flagstones were somewhat less weathered, and the smoke-filled cafés were beer dens. I never really had a chance to discover whether there was anything at the bottom of those giant mugs other than the subtext of regurgitated beer. My storied vision of a higher education dreamed from afar crumbled in the light of day. After all, my English still struggled with the many pitfalls of the language. In order to survive I took what I already knew, namely French and German, subsumed in a general Humanities Degree. Instead of drinking deeply from wells of knowledge I was reduced to treading water in order not to sink.

Another problem was the schedule at the Prince Albert Hospital. There was a nine-night stretch that proved a killer. The place itself, with its Victorian turrets and dark passages, resembled the Bates Mansion. Hitchcock's *Psycho* had come out just then, and I KNEW Tony Perkins to be lurking in the shadows. Actually, the head nurse was more like Frankenstein, large-boned and hollow-eyed, and I had never seen such large feet on a woman. The nurses in their striped uniforms and tiny stiff caps lined up for inspection, and Florence Frankenstein reviewed them like a duty officer on military parade. Behind this impressive front, however, the place was rather a jolly mess. The nurses ignored my lack of training and relied on me to hand out medications and even to give shots.

But I really came into my own as an interpreter, blossoming from mumbling idiot to indispensable polyglot. I handled the Latinate and Slavic patient population with consummate aplomb, but, general expectations notwithstanding, drew the line at Hungarians and Turks. All things considered, Prince Albert Hospital was a success. Frankenstein herself approached me with a proposal to enter their nursing program.

Was this the missionary work I was intended for? An incident with a French patient flown in from New Caledonia made up my mind for me. The woman was an interesting case, and attracted some luminaries from the faculty with their following of residents. They turned her over this way and that like a chunk of prime beef, and discussed her freely. The news was bad, and it was my job to break it to her. As I looked into her eyes and read the wild hope in them, I knew that the medical profession was not for me.

As it was, I didn't know how much longer I could stick it out. My circadian rhythms were shot. When the red light went on for a bedpan, I would take aim, close my eyes, and sleep soundly for the time it took to walk the length of the ward. It would be a little trickier once the bedpan was full, but practice makes perfect. As for classes, attending French and German was what I lived for, and slept through. Philosophy was more problematic. I could recognize polysyllabic words derived from Greek and Latin in my sleep, but the short connecting words beloved by Anglo-Saxons tripped me up. In English classes, Dickens' *Bleak House* proved to be the fitting title of a recurring nightmare. The early pages of the fog-laden allegory repeated on me until I was able to swallow the rest.

Dad observed my struggles and insisted I quit my night job at the hospital and move back home. I graduated to the career of waitressing. My first job was in a coffee shop in Downtown Sydney (known as "the City") near a courthouse. The latter seemed to have something to do with a regular clientele of attractive young women. The Hungarian coffee shop owner proceeded to enlighten me. His loud whisper, significant leers in the direction of the women, and obscurely allusive language succeeded at last. I finally caught on that they were "ladies of the night," and found myself staring at them wide-eyed.

Now that I knew their secret, would those beauties mirror back to me, as in Oscar Wilde's *Picture of Dorian Grey*, some sudden unveiling of unspeakable degradation? Would their eyes sink back into a web of wrinkles, their hair fall out in tufts, their breasts begin sagging immediately as a demonstrable sign of hidden depravity? Is that what is meant by "The wages of sin is death?" But if the soul is immortal, how can it be said to die? Is degradation, then, more like the chemical reaction that eats the gloss off pictures in family albums? How did pictures of little girls in their baby frills or footsy pajamas become the women sitting in my coffee shop? But I noticed the paleness of sleep deprivation under the makeup, and my pious shock gave way to something like recognition, even solidarity.

There was another waitressing stint in a Greek restaurant, and another in a Chinese restaurant, but the only enlightening life experiences there were aching feet. Then I got an early morning job at the main dining hall at Sydney's Central Station. The place was an imposing Victorian affair with ornate chandeliers and brass fittings. I was instructed to walk with unhurried dignity, British butler style. Coming, as I did, from the Continental breakfast tradition of *café au lait* and croissants, I also had to master the various possibilities of the hefty Anglo-Saxon breakfast.

I tried my rookie skills on a prim elderly gent who sat down in my section. I took his order, and returned with scrambled eggs and bacon. "Oh dear," he said, "I had so looked forward to poached eggs this morning." I panicked. Memories of typical French high-mindedness when it comes to food flashed through my mind. I remembered only too well how I myself had aped their ways, and sent back to the kitchen elderly waiters fit to be my fathers. As I apologized profusely and braced myself for the devastating results that would inevitably follow, the elderly gentleman took my hand, called me "dearie," and sweetly insisted on keeping the wrong order. This tempest in a teapot was a milestone of sorts, a reshuffling of cultural score cards, a small lesson in Australian democracy.

But I was also to find out that "Australian democracy" was made of local, homespun cloth, and did not necessarily include cross-cultural embroidery. The charming episode of the scrambled poached eggs order had a counterpart. Mom and I were in the City (Sydney's Downtown) on some errand. Pitt Street is narrow and very busy at peak hours. Oblivious to the fact that the flow of traffic, pedestrian as well as motorized, holds to the left in this far outpost of the British Empire, we were making our way on the wrong side of the carefully divided sidewalk. Unburdened by any sense of British decorum, we remained unaware of our predicament, and struggled valiantly against the thick crowd bearing down on us. As we did so, we suddenly found ourselves shoved off the sidewalk and into the gutter. A towering young man whose magnificent physique deserved to grace a Nazi poster of the superior race stood above us and said calmly: "Australians first."

I was sitting it out in our Manhattan studio now, pondering over my accumulated sorrows. I had reread Dostoyevsky's *Notes from the Underground*, and was astounded to find in it a version of our own encounter with the Australian *Übermensch* (the "superman"). On Nevsky Prospect, the main street of Saint Petersburg, a tall and handsome officer bears down on the crowd, which parts before him like the Red Sea before Charlton Heston in *The Ten Commandments*. The Underground Man, swept away with the rest of them, falls into existential angst: is he a man or a mouse? After much literary bellyaching he finally faces the officer down, and they bump shoulders for equality.

I too was now looking to assert a human space of my own. I decided that instead of trifling with love plots *à la* Françoise Sagan, I needed to write my own version of the *Notes*. But was bright, wound-up New York a proper match for the milk-white nights of Saint Petersburg? And was our apartment, however modest, even close to the Underground Man's dank cellar? Instead, New York was one big carnival. Back in Sydney, the museums had been pitiful, the famous Opera House far in the future. New York, instead, had it all: a hundred museums, concerts, lectures, poetry readings, movies, gallery openings, and Central Park too.

Would my precious fund of rebellion, what Dostoyevsky had interchangeably called "spite" and a "highly developed consciousness", not get diluted by so much fun? And even if my "spite" passed quality control, did I have the gift to turn it into literature? At least the language issue was coming into focus. Either I was writing in French, and we had better revisit our original plan of going back to Europe, or I was writing in English, and I had better spend as long as it takes "underground," nursing my "spite" the way one sits on long-term investments.

Rick also had his issues. He had realized that he wasn't enough of a gambling man to deal with the stock market, and enjoyed his M.A. program in Economics at New York University. As to his birthplace of Belgium, he had been back once and couldn't believe how small the place had grown. After visiting *tante* Berthe and *oncle* Pierre, and the *Manneken Pis*, what else was there?

The Common Market was still there, but that coat of many colors had already been craftily parceled out. Like the Biblical Joseph in his dry well, Rick was condemned to hear his brothers divvy up the goods as homebound Belgians had already filled the established quotas. If he had to prove himself elsewhere, he already knew the place: America was the new Egypt. Here Joseph's divining of the seven fat cows and seven lean cows of Pharaoh's dream as years of plenty and years of dearth, could be updated to business cycles. Rick decided to join the priesthood of economic forecasting.

And so, New York it was, this time for good. We were immigrants at last. Just about then, something happened which bonded us not just to New York but to the whole country: President Kennedy was assassinated. Like every other American, I know exactly where I was that Friday, November 22, 1963. I had been roaming the streets once more. Off Union Square stood seedy, trashy Klein's. I doubt anyone gives a single nostalgic thought to the memory of that bargain-hunters heaven, now replaced by an architecturally correct, post-modern complex. Yet inside those shabby walls now wiped off the map, amid the piles of shoes and purses and scarves long since worn and discarded, I heard the news, and for the first time, felt at one with America.

It's not as if we knew much about politics. It's just that Jackie flew over steeple chase barriers, wore sleek gowns, and spoke French. As for the Kennedy brothers, they were hunks, and we loved them. Now Camelot was mortally wounded, and we mourned what could have been. As the song goes, "The times they were a-changing." Leaving my unfinished French novel to its drought-stricken African fate, yet feeling unready for Dostoyevskian depths, I scaled down my first attempt in the new vernacular to a short story.

It was supposed to be a Christmas story, but nothing jelled. It wasn't just the language. What did the angels trumpeting toward the giant Christmas tree at Rockefeller Center, the garlands at Saks Fifth Avenue, the toys at F.A.O. Schwartz, the carols advertising the shopping season, have to do with the little girl back in Belgrade whose daddy had disappeared into the war?

Feeling cooped up and restless once again, I stepped out. Maybe the mess in my head, which found no outlet on the page, would find its rhythm on the streets of New York, and like a string of Jazz notes, cascade into syncopated order. I passed some gallery and went in. I might as well have stepped into a supermarket, the frozen meat section. Except that the meat display on these walls looked like a giant freezer after a major electric failure. It was a Francis Bacon show and it was crawling with life. It was all about the same man, the Pope, but in various postures: enthroned, his body amputated, his scream impacted, his mouth flesh-gorged and flesh-starved, gagged and nailed for all time on a few square feet of flat canvass. I saw what I saw and went home. When Rick came in from work, I put my arms around him and just stood there.

Rick had planned a night at the movies, but we stayed home. Instead, I had a dream: *I am in the apartment, alone. Someone is stealing up the steps. I know the door is unlocked and I spring to it.... Too late, the door handle is turning, the door is ajar.... I lean against it, bracing myself, I put my whole weight to it.... On the other side of the door, she is doing the same. We struggle back and forth, evenly matched. I can hear her breathing and grunting, I hear my own muffled voice...* as Rick shakes me. The sounds of my struggle had woken him. We talked. It was perhaps time for me to open that door.

If I didn't know what was on the other side, I also knew it only too well. Had I really forgotten that I had left Mom in a nut house, back in Sydney? Had I counted on the waters of the Pacific to wash away the picture of her framed in a window, clutching at iron bars? I had run away, then danced on that Dutch boat, then attempted a cakewalk on the gridlocked streets of New York. But the Escher landscape had tilted over and the skyscrapers had come after me. It had all been a Nabokovian *Defense*, his own record of exile, which he depicted as a headlong fall toward an up-rushing chessboard pavement.

But Francis Bacon had blown my cover, and behind his screaming popes, there was Mom, waiting. And now she had escaped, slipped up the steps of my New York apartment, and begun to press against the door of my nightmare, my conscience, my silent sorrow, my self.

It had taken the De Roecks' patient, unobtrusive care for a full year to put Humpty-Dumpty back together again. But could it be done? Could I face Mom now, and my running out on her? Was I ready to go back, as well, to that upside-down land where summer is winter, and Australians always come first?

Our problem - my parents' and mine - when we came ashore in Sydney in 1958, was that we were not convicts, or colonists, or settlers. Those were the historically sanctioned categories in Australia. We were immigrants. Yet despite all those years of enforced vagrancy, my parents had never thought of themselves as immigrants. The word in use had been *émigré*, the prefix "é" pointedly aiming back to the place of exit in contrast to the "im" (i.e., "in") which announces the place of entry. The French form also alludes to parallels of revolutionary terror and fatal aristocratic confusions. Where the French couldn't tell bread from *brioches*, their Russian counterparts wondered whether the peasants were revolting or disgusting. In short, the passive form of *émigré* underscored the acted-upon nature of our condition. We had been expelled and we were not heading anywhere.

My maternal grandfather had found his exile in Yugoslavia so provisional that he insisted that Grandmother prepare a daily ration of bread and boiled eggs in anticipation of imminent return. Even my otherwise unassuming father participated in his generation's dream of liberating Mother Russia from the scourge of Communism.

Nabokov records this dream in his novel *Glory*. The young protagonist, bouncing between Switzerland, England, and France, looks for some heroic gesture to escape from the trivial uncertainties of love and life. He entertains the improbable plan of crossing into Russia as a spy. There is a telling detail in Nabokov's novel. His hero, proud that his aristocrat's hands have been damaged by a summer as a farmer's hand in the French fields, counts on these workers' stigmata to "pass" in the land of the proletarians. I recalled Dad similarly showing off the calluses on his hands, and stating his chances in similar terms. But he did not cross back into Russia as a spy, and neither did Nabokov - sending instead a fictional substitute to his Russian doom.

In Australia the subtle distinctions between é-migrant and im-migrant did not apply. The country had its own hierarchies of social distinction. It had not occurred to us to aspire to the bloodlines of convicthood. Yet, as virtual prisoners of the Soviet Gulag, escaping by sheer chance the fate of remaining family members who ended their lives in its permafrost graves, my parents could make some claim to solidarity with the convicted.

Of course, the Australian penal system belonged to an earlier experiment in social engineering - for the greater glory of the industrial, not the proletarian revolution. As Robert Hughes puts it in his *Fatal Shore*, by absorbing England's petty thieves, drunkards, forgers, debtors, prostitutes and occasional murderers, Australia became its "geographical unconscious." Thus, waves upon waves of English thieves and Irish rabble-rousers laid their bones in the parched Australian earth, and under conditions of unspeakable natural hardship and human cruelty built what Donald Horne called *The Lucky Country*.

As we landed in Sydney in 1958, having just left the colonial experience back in Morocco, would we not have had a better claim to the status of colonist? But the colonial era was breaking down everywhere, and we had precious little to show for it: no stocks in diamond mines or oil fields or shipping companies. Only the not inconsiderable satisfaction of ordering about a few colored folks. But that was not transferable to Australia, for now we were the ones lacking the requisite grade of skin color. Except for Mom, our eyes and hair were brown.

But what about the status of settler? After all, nine-tenths of Australia, roughly the size of the United States, remains unpopulated. This is the case for a "bloody" good reason, as "fair d'inkum" Aussies know only too well. The fabulous *terra incognita* of early cartographers offered mostly arid soil, capricious weather of alternating floods and droughts, strange flora and fauna, and "unusable" Aborigines. Those who prospered did so on the backs of convict labor assigned to them through British government contracts in return for wool and meat for the home country. For others, Australian settlement is mostly littered with heartbreak.

The uncompromising nature of Australia's huge continent, and the harsh, controlled conditions of labor used to develop it are, in fact, more like the conditions obtaining in the development of Siberia. One merely needs to substitute extreme cold for extreme heat. This parallel comes to mind as I recall a casual remark of Dad's that one of his uncles had been governor of Siberia. REALLY? Yermak, a Cossack leader, had taken the town of Kazan from the Tatars with a mere handful of men, and set his victory at the feet of Ivan the Terrible. This launched the rush to the Pacific Ocean, leap-frogging the Bering Straits, claiming Alaska, and setting up Fort Ross north of San Francisco.

Unfortunately, any nuggets of personal history which Dad dropped now and then remained in my brain un-mined until it was too late to ask questions. I have read since that the gold and silver mines discovered in Siberia were the personal property of the Imperial family. Thus, looking to improve productivity, Catherine the Great's enlightened policies had added usury, debt, incorrigible drunkenness, wife-beating, felling trees without a permit, and habitual idleness to crimes punishable by exile to Siberia. Australians and Siberians have indeed a lot in common.

All the same, whoever Dad's uncle had been, whether in charge of convicts both criminal and political, or profiteering from waves of the gold rush, or struggling to build the Trans-Siberian Railway, there's no denying genuine settler blood in our own veins. At this late juncture, however, it seemed to have run its course. I wanted literary salons for my testing ground, not scrubbing toilets. But Australia, emancipated, colonized and settled, was hungry for people to perform those very back-breaking, menial tasks we had earlier so gladly delegated to the Moroccans.

However strenuously I might have presented my equivalency credentials to Old-Australians, even at Sydney University I was a gate-crasher. I felt like Ralph Ellison's hero - invisible. No wonder then, that when I fell in love, it was with a Russian who was not a student. Yevgeny (Eugene) Sheremetiev's father was a former count. Eugene was tall and athletic-looking. His strong, regular features were marked by an aquiline nose. His physical presence made itself felt from across a room. If this were not enough, he was also unimpeachable when it came to manners. And, of course, he spoke French, as a Russian aristocrat should. He was not well-off, but that came with the territory. Anything else would have been in poor taste.

We were both busy, and there was little time to spend together, to really talk. If we had had time to talk, perhaps a fleeting sense that he was conventional, that he was rigid in his ways, that his interests were rather limited might have surfaced… No matter, I was smitten and we became engaged.

As my Father had done so in the past, Eugene sang in the choir of a local Russian Orthodox Church – not a tenor but a very sexy bass baritone. I had walked away from all that, but was now more than motivated to give it a second chance. We were attending a memorial service, and here I was, in another ungainly building reminiscent of the barracks of Germany, staring at icons. They were somber and beautiful, really. So were the chants. Instrumental music had not found favor with Orthodox churchmen and the sole reliance on the human voice evolved over the centuries into pure magic.

I stood there and watched the object of my love as he towered over the meager crowd. The walls stepped closer, the chants and the incense swirled about, time collapsed, and the familiar lullaby of my childhood and my love-sick longing were one and the same. But then I began to feel as if a web of sticky threads, a cobweb of fine gauze was gently folding my arms and legs and bending my head until I was swaddled into a tight cocoon. One more chant and it would be all over. I pushed back, my legs moved, and I stepped out. When Eugene joined me after the service, he just stared as I tried to explain my misgivings. He had nothing to say. Our engagement broke off.

I first noticed Rick in the University's Fischer Library. He was above average in height, and on the thin, wiry side. He had a full head of wavy brown hair and I thought he looked like the heartthrob of my generation in France, the actor Gerard Philippe. When he turned his head in my direction for a moment, I wondered about the color of his eyes; they were a liquid brown verging on pale green. These eyes of his have been duly passed on to our daughter Muriel, "the girl with the golden eyes." Apparently one of his friends, who had no reason to be in the know, pointed me out as 'hot.' What else are libraries for?

When it turned out that we had the French language in common, our fate was sealed. He was an economics student, which sounded impressive, but alien. Still, this did not seem to stop him from loving other books, and movies, and dancing, and tennis, and beaches. We laughed all the time when we were together. To top it all off, he bought a Russian grammar book: who could ask for more? The famous grammar never left his book shelf, but then we had far better things to occupy our time. His rented room near Bondi Beach became our love nest.

Rick also had a pleasant baritone voice, but he did not use it to praise the Lord. By that time, I was in the midst of a religious reversal. I had been attending a philosophy seminar on linguistic analysis. Our instructor had been inducing us to examine the Argument from the First Cause (also known in its latest version as Intelligent Design) and I was thoroughly put off by the pedestrian word splitting. It was all very simple, I thought. Faith and reason could not communicate to each other their separate realms of experience. If the Argument from the First Cause was a 'categorical mistake' according to Wittgenstein, it was also irrelevant according to Paul of Tarsus. The cute young professor sucked on his pipe as he listened to my speech. He finally said that if my emotional investment in my faith sufficed to answer the question, this was my prerogative. I had braced myself for linguistic dismemberment in the arena of the faithless, and now felt strangely disarmed by what sounded like gentle tact.

On my way home, however, a distinct feeling grew in me that I had won a battle only to lose the war. If I had willed God into existence out of emotional need, then where was He outside of my own desire? I stopped and watched the imperishable flame of my religious quest burst into spontaneous combustion. As the smoke cleared, I was left hanging in the infinite spaces of not-God. I recalled Pascal's dilemma between the infinitesimal small and the infinitesimal large, and his "play it safe" gamble. And there was Einstein and a putative God of expanding universes and black holes. This was no consolation. They seemed no different from all the Jehovahs, and Allahs, and Jupiters, and all the sky-and-stone-and-fire gods who had risen and fallen in humankind's brave dreams. Other people's gods, not mine. All I had yearned for was a personal God, sweet Jesus, to walk with me and talk with me when I was mixed up.

But it was time at last to grow up, and I made up my mind to do so. The immemorial weight of God slid off my shoulders and Milan Kundera's "unbearable lightness of being" filled my newly scrubbed inner spaces. I looked up. The sun danced cartwheels in limitless blue. At my feet, in the cracks of the pavement, a bit of earth was all the life and death I would ever need. What a fool I had been, looking for unearthly missions in unimaginable places. I felt born again, again, this time to finite, intensely brief, material life.

Meeting Rick had been providential. Prince Charming appeared just as this heroine was about to fall off a cliff. On top of my own struggles, a familial crisis was brewing. Mom was still working at the fruit factory, and she seemed troubled. She would stop me as I was rushing off to work or school, and begin some long, complicated story full of obscure allusions. There was something in her eyes that gave me the chills. I talked to Dad and Maurice both, and we convinced Mom to quit her job.

This did seem to help, but not for long. She worried about money. Now that English was becoming less of a hurdle for all of us, Mom could look for a job closer to her actual abilities. We looked for openings for accountants, and I accompanied her to her job interview. They gave her a written test to work on. I glanced at the basic computations and expected Mom to find them laughable. She went at it, working very fast. When the interviewer collected her paper, he looked puzzled, and then handed me the test. It was full of random scribbles, words, numbers, symbols, the hieroglyphs of a mind wandering in its own, private, inaccessible maze. Mom looked at me the way a very young child looks, proudly displaying his first finger-paint masterpiece.

I put my arms around her, and we walked away. After that Mom seemed evermore disoriented. She would fall to her knees to worship the stars and the moon, and glory in her own participation in their cosmic travail. Next, she begged forgiveness for her sins and thought she deserved to be stoned. The fears she now also developed seemed to go back to her flight from Russia as a child, and had to do with the Red Threat. It looked like the screams and tears and whispers of those days filled her life again.

Father and Maurice were at a complete loss as to what to do. It fell to me to cope and so I tried. I tried to shield the broken person Mom had become, and to keep faith with the incredibly resourceful person she had once been. But increasingly I, too, was walking in a debilitating fog. After picking up my grade averages, I began to slide again. I forgot tests and deadlines, I suffered from nausea, I was visited by blinding headaches.

Rick alone stands out in sharp outline at this time. He picked me up at work and drove me to school. We became inseparable. We became engaged. Rick moved out of Bondi and came to live with us in Croydon Park. We began to plan our wedding. Rick's parents could not join us for the occasion, and to please my parents, we planned to be married in a Russian Orthodox church.

We figured getting married during spring break would give us a whole week for a honeymoon. With this firm idea in mind, we asked to speak with the Russian Orthodox priest at the Strathfield Church. We prattled on about our plans as the priest gravely listened to us. Then he shook his head in disbelief: "Dear child," he said at last, "don't you know when Easter falls this year? - "...?" - "Don't you realize you are asking to be married during Lent?" -"...?" - "Don't you know that no weddings can take place during Lent, which is a time of reflection, penance and contrition? You'll have to wait until after the glorious Resurrection of our Lord at Easter to celebrate your wedding."

Those were not the rhythms that structured our actual lives, and we skipped the church wedding. But we did have a party. No, we decided, we can't afford a wedding dress. No, we said to the caterers, we don't need a photographer - a friend will take the pictures. No, we said, we don't need flowers - we'll bring our own from the garden. No, we said, we don't need a wedding cake - a friend's mother will make us one... Our friends came, all of them "New Australians," and the pictures show a happy crowd of revelers.

The same pictures show Mom elegant and distant. Soon thereafter, a friend of the family who had practiced as a doctor once, came to examine her and urged us to take her to a hospital.

I managed to pass my finals. Frank and Francine were awaiting a visit in the U.S., and both Dad and Maurice promised to look after Mom. The Rozelle Hospital, where she was placed, occupied beautiful, park-like grounds bordering on one of the coves of Sydney Bay. The buildings, however, were old and gloomy, and have since been condemned. Their windows bore iron bars. When I came to say goodbye to Mom on the day of our departure, she did not seem to know what was happening. After we left her, and I looked up one last time, I saw her sitting there, framed in the window, each hand clasped around an iron bar. And that was the visual imprint of her I had tried to leave behind but carried with me into my new life in America.

Now the time had come to stop running, and I prepared to answer Mom's call. I never thought that landing at the Sydney airport in December of 1964 could feel like a homecoming. The pictures taken on this occasion are out of focus, as if to reflect the blur of tears, the overwhelming wash of feeling that engulfed this first reunion. Mom had shown improvement and had been returned home. Other changes were in store. To ease her unresolved sense of divided loyalty between Father and Maurice, Dad offered a friendly divorce, and Maurice offered matrimony. We decided to celebrate. Dad owned a small motor boat, and took us out to one of the bays. We hugged the oyster-laden rocks, helped ourselves to fresh oysters, and washed them down with champagne.

This return trip to Sydney was to be the first of many. For now, the ice was broken, the umbilical cord loosened, and I was sent back to America with a renewed sense of life's promises. The excitement of impending change was in the air. Rick had gotten his MA from NYU and was toying with the idea of further graduate work. Early in our relationship we had pledged to take turns helping each other chase our dreams. Rick had done his turn while I recovered from my stint at the bottom of the sea. My strenuous roles as daughter and immigrant could now be put to rest. As to the fledgling author, she needed to go into cold storage for now. It was my turn to play back-up.

Rick had been accepted into the Ph.D. programs of Economics at Columbia and Berkeley. We picked Berkeley, not because we knew much about the place, but because it was clear across America. We bought a car at last, an old station wagon, stuffed it with our belongings, and went to say goodbye to Frank and Francine. They shook their heads at this postponement of adulthood, as they saw it. Wasn't it time to settle down, start a family? One day for sure, but now we hit the road. California, here we come!

**

CHAPTER 4

THIS LAND IS YOUR LAND, THIS LAND IS MY LAND

Moving on, everything moving past as we slide northward on US 87. Manhattan breaking up, falling away in the rear-view mirror, patches of green showing up ahead, the distant gleam of the Hudson moving closer, brimming over with sunlight, filling the valley like a glassful of bubbly. There was something altogether too effortless about this gliding into the opening landscape - like birds, wings outspread, carried by invisible currents. Unbidden, trace memories of other migrations scoured the horizon, looking for signs of trouble. A forgotten child was still hurried and huddled and hushed in a forgotten nightmare.

Travel light, they say. Do Canada geese pack a trunk, do they worry about what lies ahead, do they mourn what's left behind? There is something in the air, clouds hang lower, morning mists linger on, a brittle film of ice begins to form at the edges of lakes: it's time. And that's how it had been for us. We had learned to sense the new chill in the air, to pick up on the changing winds, on the recurring storm cycles of history, we had taken flight, we had traveled light. But as in the fairy tale of the seven princesses changed into wild geese by a wicked witch, we always longed to regain human form.

This time the skies were blue, it was August 1965, and history had just made some happy turns. The Great Society was rising from the ashes of Kennedy's assassination. In time I would unpack, unravel, strip away, and reform the contours of understanding the way a river alters its course within its bed. But just then we were spreading our wings, gliding on a sunbeam, heading for the other end of the rainbow.

Ignorant of recent Beat Generation precedent and the call of Route 66, we set course northward, in obeisance to the more humdrum wish to see Niagara

Falls. Our un-hip literary tastes were still tethered to Fennimore Cooper's *The Last of the Mohicans* and teen memories of high drama among impenetrable forests, dark caves, and foaming rapids. There, helpless maidens were ravished and rescued in turn by a medley of redcoats and bluecoats and deerskin coats and Indians wearing no coats at all but plenty of paint. This haunting sense of a lost world lingered against a vaguely historical canvas of the French and the English fighting over the possession of America. We too wished to possess America.

James Fennimore Cooper's lost world has since been repossessed in film. The backwoodsman Hawkeye, a minor character in Cooper, has taken over from the gallant British officer Hayward, who is happily sacrificed to Indian revenge. As Hawkeye embraces Madeleine Stowe in the final scene against a backdrop of yet undeveloped real estate, there is little doubt as to who gets to ravish maiden America in the end.

Like the audience of *The Last of the Mohicans*, we too yearned not for historical accuracy or political insight, but for the romance of wilderness. After New York and Sydney, and Europe as well, where all of nature is a formal French garden, America held out the promise of a land still plentiful and unscarred, standing apart from the human anthill. We were, after all, nothing if not wild-eyed newcomers like so many others, driven by the myth of inexhaustible America.

We drove all the way to Niagara Falls on that first day of our trip, and crashed in a motel. The next day we jumped up prepared to view the Falls. We followed the crowds, stood on the lip of The Cave of the Winds, and listened to the statistics of velocity per minute of output. I tried to imagine the original Falls before bridges and towers and parking lots, and miles of railings. But the mighty roar of waters was now pierced by car horns and out-yelled by wired tour guides.

Somewhat sobered but unrepentant, we went on. Taking the Canadian side of Lake Erie, we stopped for the night at what we thought to be a campground. It was already dark, and there was no one to stop us from pitching our tent right on the edge of the lake itself. Next day we got up just as a huge fire ball rose out of the lake and spilled a trail of molten gold across the water. We looked down. Only then did the earlier presence of strong smells, which had bothered us during our sleep, reveal its source. We were standing on the edge of a dump. There was earth and even grass under out feet. Late honeymooners, we stood on the very frosting of civilization's cake, whose cutaway side exhibited the layers of time's latest accumulation. The sun, indifferent archeologist, picked over rusted drums and twisted chrome and translucent plastic bags. We folded our tent and moved on.

We were now on Route 90, and crossing Minnesota. Lake Woebegone was not yet on the map, and we did not know the place where all the women are strong, all the men good looking, and all the children above average. The pleasant landscape of rolling pastures and corn fields gradually shed all attempts at markers. The road straightened out, the sky became the main event.

I don't remember actually crossing into South Dakota, except that the compass needle of my attention began to point to small changes. Grasses became stubbier, patches of earth began to show up, and the color palette now ran to ochre and terra cotta. It wasn't until the rain-sculpted crags and gullies of the Badlands spread their desolation before us, that some inner timer set up by earlier signs and portents finally rang out: I was home, I was in Southern Morocco. As I surveyed the Badlands, I recognized the backdrop where, tiny and lost, I had roamed as a restless teenager.

When we arrived in Morocco in 1949, we headed for a place called Imini. It was a mining settlement located on the southern slope of the High Atlas Range, somewhere between Marrakech, the ancient Berber capital, and Zagora, the last outpost before the Saharan Desert. A nearby oasis, called Ouarzazate, is well known to the film industry. The crisp outline of its Moorish Kasbah against limpid skies, the river below meandering through palm groves toward endlessly receding horizons is a perfect backdrop to adventure, whether of the muscular or the spiritual kind. I have recognized it in *The Man Who Would be King*, where Sean Connery already quells uprisings in Afghanistan, in some extravaganza about Sodom and Gomorrah with Stewart Granger as the Biblical Lot, and even in *Lawrence of Arabia*.

As to Imini, it had no Kasbah, no palm groves and no river. Our family album holds a picture where Mom and Dad stand in front of the house they had been allotted. The squat reddish rectangle, not unlike Southwestern adobe structures but without a hint of whimsy, occupies the middle ground, surrounded by an amphitheater of stony hills. Mom and Dad, standing on either side of the door, look tiny and forlorn. The place had no running water: weekly truck deliveries supplied our needs. There was no electricity: we were given a couple of lamps used in the mines and fueled by some vile-smelling compound.

We did have an outhouse, and it became the bane of my existence. I was afraid to use it after dark. My overworked imagination slithered with snakes and shapeshifted with genies. Mother, as usual, believed in toughening me up, and I was ordered to step out and attend to my needs. When I did so, and my fear began to sculpt the dark of night into an army of virtual monsters, what rose from the shadows, instead, was an angel of mercy. Grandmother, sweet Babushka, the secret sharer of my childhood, had slipped out the back door and come around to stand guard over me.

It wasn't all terror and desolation. Behind us there was a dwelling even more primitive than our own, occupied by an extended Moroccan family. As new arrivals appeared from some distant village, their house overflowed and additional dwellings were carved out of the nearby mountain side. Gradually, the surrounding mountain slopes became dotted with caves.

Our Moroccan neighbors had a yellowish mongrel. One of its ears had been cut off and fed to him as a proven method to turn him into a fierce guard dog. He and I became best friends. The women in the family wove rugs. Unlike the women I had glimpsed during our brief passage in Casablanca, these Berber women wore no veils. I spent long hours crouching by their loom, watching their practiced fingers tie knots of bright wool, one at a time, onto the vertically stretched threads. It was as if they were plucking the strings of a harp, and the nasal, highly pitched chant they carried in turn and endlessly modulated, created the slowly emerging pattern of the rug. To this day no fancy Ormuz or Karastan bests those bold, uneven tribal rugs woven by time and song.

Leaving the Badlands behind, we pitched our tent that night in a campground of the Mt. Rushmore National Monument. When we walked up the wooded path the next morning, and the mighty profiles slowly came into view, I was astounded. I knew from my school days some of the basic historical facts about these men, but mountain peaks shaped to human form and humans towering like mountain peaks was something else. I looked at the giant presidents and pledged to become an intentional American one day. Anything short of that would be like shrinking Mt. Rushmore to fit inside one of those round trinkets you shake to stir up plastic snowflakes

As we drove on through the Black Hills, we knew nothing of it as a place set apart by First Americans for spiritual pilgrimage or vision quest. The spirit we encountered everywhere was the spirit of gold. Custer himself had stumbled upon the mother lode, and William Randolph Hearst's father, George Hearst, had transformed it into the Homestake Mine. This mining town had the self-contained, solitary aura familiar to me since Imini. The aura of stubborn effort, isolation, and the magical descent into the bowels of the earth to snatch a piece of usable ore from the underground hoarding spirits, at the risk of one's life.

Back in Imini, Dad's mechanical duties took him down into the mine only when some major equipment needed his attention. This was also true for most other Europeans; the actual miners were Moroccans. We heard constant complaints about their shiftlessness. They left at will when there was trouble in the home village – or just a celebration. The star miner Belaid was a big black man, a descendant of slaves. As he explained, what kind of fool would want to spend his whole life underground, when Allah created the light of day, and running water in the wadis, and fattened sheep for a feast? First Americans, delighting in their prairies and fast horses, must also have wondered about the White Man's urge to crawl into the black womb of Mother Earth before his time.

But even if Dad did not have to go down into the mines a lot, he always came home covered with the black dust. And when the sirocco blew, raising huge sandstorms, the contest between sand and black powder left mere humans holed up in our flimsy shelters, waiting to dig out again. Even so I longed to be taken down into the mine, at least once. But women were considered bad luck underground, and Dad was unwilling to challenge the taboo. So, I contemplated the huge mound of black manganese ore, and it looked like some heaving science-fiction beast as wagons crawling out of the mouths of tunnels poured the stuff from the top as fast as it was chewed away at the bottom by an ever-moving convoy of trucks.

In time we moved from our first house, which had stood some way off near our Berber neighbors, into a newly constructed one in the developing European section. We had running water and electricity now, an icebox, and a wood stove. Actually, the house belonged to the mining concern, but we paid no rent. Everything in Imini belonged to the mining concern.

As one approaches Imini, nothing gives away its presence among the barren hills. Then at the turn of the road there it is, all of a piece. The mountain slope is cut into layers and stacked with houses in a medieval allegory of the natural order of things. Each level displays houses whose architecture reflected the residents' social status, starting with blue collars at the bottom, then rising gradually to foremen, and white collars, and engineers. At the very top of the hill, crowning this hierarchy of life stations, stood the house of God, a beautiful little chapel graced with a bell tower. The mine's director had his habitation elsewhere, fifteen kilometers away, in Boutazoult. He lived in splendid isolation on top of his own hill.

Further along the road, and past the European settlement, the Moroccans had a settlement of their own. Unlike the houses of the Europeans, which were spaced out to accommodate small gardens, the much larger Moroccan section was made up of long rows of connecting cubicles. Paying tribute to Moorish style, arcades graced the front of these rows. The Moroccans had no running water and no electricity. Women prepared meals over little charcoal pits, and fetched water from a common well, as they had always done.

Our house happened to be on the bottom rung, signifying a lowly position in the social order of Imini. But the mine's director, Mr. Moulinou, had three children, and this turned out to have far-reaching consequences for me. There were no other children in Imini in those early days. Martine Moulinou, the youngest, threw across to me, with a shy smile, a working bridge of sign language until I could meet her half-way on my own shaky bridge of French. The director's chauffeur was sent out to pick me up, Mom checked that I was clean behind the ears, and off I went to the sacred hill. There servants attended at the table, napkins were properly folded, and conversation was far-ranging. And so, like the angels in Jacob's dream, going up and down the staircase to heaven while Jacob wrestled with the shadow of the Almighty, I bypassed the struggles of mere mortals.

Martine and her brother Bernard and their older sister Françoise spent the school year in Marrakech, where the family had a villa. Mme. Moulinou and a couple of the servants stayed with them, and Mr. Moulinou undertook the four-hour drive on weekends. It was decided that I should be admitted as a boarder at the convent school Martine attended as a day student. The mine management offered to foot the bill.

Mother sat me down and spelled it all out. She pointed out that Dad and she, in their present condition and foreseeable future, couldn't do much for me, and that my future was in my own hands. She said that if I applied myself and did well in school, I had a fair chance at some options in life. Her speech as well as the lifestyle I observed on the hill made an impression, but it wasn't going to be easy. Thus far I had had no reason to think of school as an established fact of life for a child my age; I had been more out of school than in. The only constant had been speaking Russian at home and scampering to function in some other language in the outside world. I had done it in Serbo-Croatian first, then in German, and now at the age of twelve I had to do it all over again in French.

Here too the mysteries of spelling tripped me up. Five errors in the dictation test disqualified you for the sixth grade, and it took me two years with the nuns to pass that hurdle. When I finally made it into the *Lycée Mangin*, there was little to celebrate. There had been some space and time for gentle extra-curricular activities: song, embroidery, storytelling. At the public lycée, instead, it was up at 6 a.m., breakfast, study hall, classes, lunch, classes, one hour of free play between 4 p.m. and 5 p.m., then study hall, dinner, study hall, and lights out at 9 p.m.

It was a depressing state of affairs, and I contemplated it with teen bitterness. My fellow boarders exploded into bouts of rowdiness on occasion, but I had taken Mom's warning seriously, and toughed it out. The teachers were good, and I got hooked on doing well. The situation afforded a thoroughgoing if merciless academic education.

There was one saving grace: the school's athletic program. I made the volley ball team and got to see a good chunk of Morocco traveling to meets. The available mode of transportation was still the railway, and the highlights of the whole experience were not the games themselves (we got clobbered by some school in Casablanca soon enough) but the train rides. And the highlight of highlights, the ultimate proclamation of swagger in victory or unyielding spirit in defeat, was chanting at the top of our lungs as the train slowly left a particular station: *"Il est cocu, le chef de gare"* ("The station master, he is a cuckold"). There is no accounting for cultural idiosyncrasy.

The way to get home when holidays came up was to use the convoy of trucks which carried the manganese from Imini, then returned for more. Those convoys usually made their trek at night, and I remember biking to the edge of the Medina, the Arab section of Marrakech, at 2 a.m. to hitch a ride with the convoy. I had outgrown my fear of lurking genies while any fear of people never took hold. The truck drivers I rode with were all Moroccans, and I slept soundly in their cabs, sometimes waking only at the very last turn when the chapel of Imini floated into view, ringing silently of home.

Much of my life depended on the kindness of strangers. Take my friend Rovida Levy. She was a well-off and popular Jewish girl at the *lycée* boarding school. She noticed the pitiful state of my wardrobe and offered to share her stylish clothes with me. After losing sight of each other after graduation, we reconnected some fifty years later when she managed to track me down in Arizona and came down to visit. We marveled at how we were able to pick up again as if a whole lifetime had not passed. She did not remember the sharing of clothes. What was the big deal? I had cherished the memory all my life.

I could now ask her about being Jewish in Morocco. The experience went back to the expulsion of Jews and Moriscos from Spain in 1492. True to Jewish tradition elsewhere, her family had been merchants, scholars, and financiers; she felt both Moroccan and Jewish. She pointed out to me that discrimination in Morocco had been exercised by the French and that King Mohammed V had refused to deliver his Jewish subjects to the French Vichy government during World War II.

Another set of kindly strangers turned out to be the small community of Russians living in Marrakech. The de Millers took charge of me during weekends. As with Martine Moulinou, their two daughters Hélène and Irène also became friends for life. Here we are in Nabokovian territory again. Mr. de Miller was the son of a famous Russian general. As a matter of fact, he had taken his family to the relative anonymity of Morocco, where he worked as a civil engineer, to escape the notoriety of the so-called Miller Affair.

That 'affair' had been a *cause célèbre* headlining the Paris papers in the late '30s. My friends' grandfather, who had been the head of an émigré veteran association, was kidnapped in 1937... by a Soviet spy ring? Vladimir Nabokov, in his debut as an American writer, took the story over in his *Assistant Producer*. Using his standing as a plausible witness, he relished in debunking the stereotypes of Russian émigrés as "villainous generals, oil magnates and gaunt ladies with lorgnettes." But because the principal facts in the Miller Affair remained elusive, he also relished in melding fact and fiction with his peculiar talent for verbal double dealing.

Since then, the unsolved puzzle afforded by the Miller Affair has attracted another master artificer. Eric Rohmer's *Triple Agent* presents yet another version of the same events. The focus of this story is not so much the unexplained circumstances of the kidnapping of General de Miller, or Nabokov's bitter-sweet depiction of the Russian émigré milieu, but the tortuous mental workings of a spy.

Well-mannered and genteel in the typical White Russian style, the main protagonist, Fyodor, is faced with multiple dilemmas. He has to deal with the pieties of the older generation of Russian émigrés with whom he is officially associated and at the same time, as World War II looms on the horizon, needs to manage the Allied rapprochement with the Soviets… But then the Soviet-German pact occurs, and Fyodor must revise his calculations yet again. We watch him get bogged down trying to justify his evasions and inconsistencies as he attempts to reassure his wife and impress her with the agility of his gamesmanship.

The Soviet archives under Gorbachev's *Glasnost* have since disclosed the fate of General de Miller, who was indeed kidnapped, tried, and shot for treason. The fate of Fyodor, the elusive spy, remains unexplained. With typical *Schadenfreude*, Nabokov's narrator had "recognized" him in Hollywood.

It was at one of Mme. de Miller's soirées, where she read her memoir, that I first heard the "original" version of the Miller Affair. At the time, its extravagant details and political undercurrents mostly went over my head. I focused on another episode of Mme. De Miller's autobiography. At the age of sixteen she had cut her hair, dressed in men's clothes, tied together her bed sheets to lower herself out the window of her parents' house, and ran away to join the Whites. My father had done the same, minus the disguise and acrobatics.

At the same time, my friends and I were just typical, self-absorbed teenagers. I introduced Martine and Bernard Moulinou to Irène and Hélène de Miller. All the girls of our group, including me, had a crush on Bernard. He had superlative good looks, a generous spirit, and innate tact, all attributes rare enough in adults, let alone in raw youths. Unfortunately, he had a crush on Hélène. The oldest among us, she was a beauty: blonde, slinky, green-eyed. Her nick name of *la môme vert-de-gris* was the French version of "Poison Ivy," the title of a British detective movie.

But my own nickname topped all others in shock value. It had to do with the fortuitous combination of my first name (Galina) and the last name of an aspiring boyfriend (Raymond Gallot), and the predictable play of French *esprit gaulois*. My name, Galina, means "chicken" in Latin, and therefore *poule* in French – and therefore also "hooker." My friend's last name, Gallot, sounds like "gallop" because the French don't sound out their final consonants. Since we were all into movies, and the title of one of them was "*la poule au grand gallop*," my nickname, in fact, proclaimed me as "the galloping chick," or more precisely, "the busy hooker."

This was, in a way, flattering, for what I really had to play down were my good grades. Hélène and Irène were doing poorly in school, Martine was doing well enough, Bernard was not. Their respective parents used me as exhibit "A" in their case for the prosecution of their offspring.

In addition to the de Miller family, there were the Mayranoffs, who lived in the Medina, the Arab section of Marrakech. They ignored the poor plumbing and enjoyed the magical inner courtyards with their tiled floors and murmuring fountains and pomegranate trees. And since the Mayranoffs took turns with the de Millers inviting me over, I spent many weekends in the Medina.

The Mayranoffs shared their lodgings with an unrelated elderly man. We kids loved to giggle behind his back. He was fair verging on albino, and made his living painting the standard view of Marrakech. On his canvasses the jacaranda and orange trees which lined Avenue Mangin were forever in bloom, the Atlas range in the background was forever snow-capped, and the sky it upheld was forever blue. And the Kutubia, the landmark of Marrakech, raised its stately square tower among the palm fronds.

When he was in the mood, this man would regale us with stories of his youth. He had, apparently, been an entertainer and the proof of his former glory was that he had worked with Josephine Baker. WHO? Oh yes, and while we looked over our shoulders to check whether the adults were watching, he showed us pictures of the black goddess in feathers and beads and little else. The famous star of song and dance, the toast of jazz-happy Paris, and her French husband had adopted an international array of kids. Sadly, however, beauty fades and fashions change. Josephine Baker had to scale down her lifestyle and eventually disbanded her early experiment in United Nations.

Thus, the eccentricities of my Russian acquaintances allowed me to explore the streets of the Medina. My bike and I learned to find our way among the twists and turns and blind alleys. Other streets were filled with wall-to-wall crowds. I learned to dart among the vendors and carts and donkeys with native aplomb.

This territorial claim of mine upon the dark mysteries of the Medina of Marrakech imagined by tourists caused a memorable fight with my husband Rick. This happened in 1981. Rick was the International Economist for General Motors by then and undertaking many business trips. When Morocco appeared on his list, I joined him.

In Marrakech we happened to stay at the Mamounia, a remodeled Moorish palace, and a place I had only known from afar. Among its reported titles to fame was that it had been the favorite vacationing spot of Winston Churchill, where he had pursued his hobby of painting, no doubt trying to capture the same North African light and vintage landscape featuring the Atlas Mountains and the Kutubia.

When we were offered an escorted tour of the Medina, I refused. I took it as a personal insult that the place where every nook and cranny had felt the tires of my trusty bike should now be introduced to me by some self-important guide. This made Rick nervous, but I dug in my heels, and won that first round; we sallied forth without benefit of solicitous guides.

The square of Djemaa El Fna is a true time capsule of medieval town life. Snake charmers play thin reed tunes to swelling cobras. Water vendors dressed in colorful rags carry water in large goatskin pouches and ring brass bells. Mountebanks and story tellers draw large circles of spectators and listeners. And there is the souk or covered market with its carpets, fine leather goods, and brass trays showing off the age-old designs derived from Koranic calligraphy... I was long since inured to the charm of these wares, and used to the gamesmanship of bartering. The occasion is typically used to get acquainted, to exchange news, to match wits.

I remember Dad practicing this fine art. The object of discourse in this case was rather esoteric. He was dealing with a soothsayer, whose wares, spread out on a filthy rag, were feathers, shells, a bat's wing, bone knuckles, and the dried head of a bird whose beak was ominously stuck open. I watched Dad parlay with the owner of these impressive items. He challenged the magic of that bird beak; the point at issue was the number of teeth. Dad and the soothsayer, both crouching on their heels, took turns counting the dead bird's teeth. The soothsayer gesticulated excitedly; Dad shook his head with considered deliberation; low tooth count, weak magic, no deal.

The Djemaa El Fna square hadn't changed much since those days except that now a throng of beggars haunted the place. Rick felt acutely put upon by urchins tugging brazenly at his clothes. That's when our dispute erupted once again, and Rick felt entitled to his "I told you so." In my frustration I reached back into my treasury of Arabic, and told the kids to get lost, at which point a young man stepped out of the crowd, doubled over with laughter. I had interlaced my Arabic with some choice Berber words, and his funny bone was terminally tickled to hear, as he put it, "the curses of my own mountain." After that we no longer needed a guide, we had a bodyguard. Our newfound friend insisted on escorting us, and the kids left us alone. Every once in a while, he would start laughing all over again, whack me heartily on the back, and declare that I was, in Arabic equivalent, A-O.K. When the time came to part, he refused any remuneration.

***

CHAPTER 5

COMING OF AGE IN MOROCCO

Our rescue in the square of Djemaa El Fna recalls another rescue. We are now in Arizona; the year is 1990 and I am stuck in my Sunbird in the middle of a raging wash. Just like the Moroccan wadis or oueds, the dry washes of Arizona are apt to swell in minutes during monsoon season. As I struggled out of the car, a woman on the opposite side called out to me; she had a truck and for fifty bucks would bail me out. Short of cash, I offered to write her a check for the amount, but she was unwilling.

While we were negotiating this at the top of our lungs, and I was holding onto the slowly sinking car, my feet freezing in the swirling water, a young and very big Native American materialized out of nowhere, and calmly began to adjust a chain between my car and his truck. I warned him that I had very little cash on me. He simply nodded, went on about his business, pointed me back to my car, and proceeded to pull me out. I whipped out my checkbook and asked him how much I owed him for his trouble. He looked at me briefly, barely shrugging his shoulders, and took off.

Standing there I thought of the first American Indian we had seen back in 1965, when crossing the country on the way to California. He stood dressed in full feather bonnet and tribal regalia, and his liquor breath was powerful. He was available for souvenir photos for a consideration. Embarrassed, we had walked past him the way we had walked away from the raggedy boys and girls on the square of Djemaa El Fna.

Just a few steps down the street there stood another Indian. He wore war markings and the obligatory feather bonnet. He did not smile: he was a Log Indian. We did not know then that the twin Indians, the real and the wooden one, represented a memorial of sorts just like the presidents on Mt. Rushmore. Much later, I learned to "read" their unspoken message. It was like an Australian Aborigine "dreaming:" the Log Indian opens up like a mummy's coffin, and lets out a ghostly procession of warriors. Red Cloud of the Oglala Tetons, Spotted Tail of the Brulé Tetons, Little Raven of the Arapaho, Black Kettle of the Cheyenne: warriors, buffalo hunters, wild men, free men... Lone Wolf of the Kiowas, Morning Star of the Cheyenne, Little Crow of the Santee Sioux, Black Hawk of the Winnebagos: warriors, hunters, traders... Standing Bear of the Poncas, Nacarat of the Utes, Joseph of the Nez Perce, Cochise of the Apaches: warriors, trappers, treaty signers ... Manuelito of the Navaho, Little Wolf of the Northern Cheyenne, Geronimo of the Chiricahuas, Dull Knife of the Northern Cheyenne: warriors, treaty signers, reservation men, hungry men... Big Foot of the Minniconjous, Crazy Horse whose heart is buried at Wounded Knee, Sitting Bull, dreamer of visions, Wowoka, the Paiute Messiah leading them all in the Ghost Dance: hunters hunted, trappers trapped.

But our notions of the Far West were vintage Hollywood in those days, and with that as our guide, we had proceeded. When we drove into Deadwood, we knew exactly what to expect. As we walked through the swinging saloon doors - there it was: the bar counter with the mustachioed barman and the tall cowboys downing shots of whisky; the card game was in progress in the right corner; the piano player and the tightly corseted beauty in red satin and black lace, singing, were also on cue... And just as in the movies, there was a critical moment: a cowboy threw a punch, the card game froze, the beauty's mouth staid open, voiceless, and the fistfight erupted, spilling out into Main Street... And there was gun fire, and people cowered, and glass shattered, and a man fell off a roof, and people applauded...

Actually, Rick was much more into it all than I was. Already back in the days of my French *lycée*, when I struggled over the original Greek of the *Iliad* and the *Odyssey*, I had had my doubts about manly games. What was the point of Achilles pouting in his tent, and what did "honor" have to do with ransacking cities and dividing the spoils? What was so glorious about dragging Hector's body before Troy's ramparts? And all that human toil of blood and tears for the dysfunctional gods on Mount Olympus! And then the longed-for homecoming scrupulously postponed until Odysseus, worn out by nymphomaniac witches, crawls back to Penelope on all fours.

78

And now the open skies and unlimited horizons of the American West also seemed to take us to some final showdown at high noon. Is life just a brief, unhinged, gloriously pointless race to the finish? In deference to this existential insight, we visited the presumed graves of Wild Bill Hickock, Buffalo Bill and Calamity Jane. Rick considered buying a cowboy hat, but it proved way beyond our budget.

We drove on the next day, and followed a sign announcing a ghost town. We parked across from a row of weathered clapboard houses. I stepped on the partly rotted wooden sidewalk, pushed a door that barely hung on its hinges and peered inside. The large room, probably a saloon, had been stripped of its contents long ago, except for a wooden stairway, broken off halfway up. A pool of light rested on the floor planks, and I followed the pale beam alive with dancing dust motes back to a hole in the roof. Pack rats or rock squirrels stirred among the debris, and I stepped away.

What was the story behind those meager traces of once riotous human activity? Maybe the town had been a trading post where mountain men had exchanged furs for tobacco and ammunition - until the fashion for men's headwear back East changed from beaver to silk? Had it been a fort where garrisons had whiled away their time between raids - until all the Indians were rounded up on reservations? Maybe it had been a cattle depot, where the herds had been loaded on trains and sent east - until the grass was gone? Maybe the hills had been covered with wood - now cut down and shipped away? Maybe an oil well had been struck nearby, and for a while the town had been flowing with black gold?

Yet no ghosts hovered over that town. Neither Clint Eastwood, nor even the Duke could have poured life back into its wind-rattled bones. The gods on Mount Olympus, and in New York, Paris, London, Frankfurt, Milan, Chicago, Dallas... suppressed a yawn and turned to other ventures in Katanga or Bahrain.

Imini was not quite a ghost town when Rick and I visited it on that return trip to Morocco in 1981. But much had changed. Rick's interview with the new director, a Moroccan who now lived in the Moulinou house on the distant hill, revealed that indeed the scope of the enterprise had been reduced by two-thirds. The price of manganese on the world market had fallen severely, and this explained the slow-motion feeling about the place. All Europeans had left except for three. Two of them I remembered as a young man and a pre-teen girl. They were now married, and they were the ones who put us up. They now occupied the doctor's house.

That house happened to be very familiar to me. Dr. Mandryka and his wife were Russian émigrés like my parents. I came across the name later as associated with the inner court circles of Nicolas II. All I knew then was that Dr. Mandryka had been raised in France by his grandmother, who had been an opera singer in her day. Her grandson had put himself through medical school stoking the furnace in the basement of the Paris Opera House.

Mme. Mandryka's father had been a naval officer during World War I. When things turned sour during the Civil War, he gathered up his family, and together with other refugees, sailed all the way to Bizerte in Tunisia. This was the only harbor where remnants of the Russian Northern Fleet had received permission to dock. Mme. Mandryka told stories of a happy childhood being lulled to sleep by the waves of the Mediterranean at night and playing pirates on the planks of the decaying fleet by day. Eventually the old ships threatened to sink altogether, and to her eternal regret, she had to adjust to life on solid ground.

The Mandrykas had three boys younger than me, and they sort of adopted me as the daughter they never had. Mme. Mandryka was a bluestocking, and she undertook to advance my education. I was three years older than my grade peers and, having caught up with the language, was now feeling unchallenged. She tutored me through the summer following sixth grade and thanks to her I was able to skip seventh grade.

Mom, on the other hand, took me hiking all over the rocky hills. She now worked as an accountant for the mining concern. When a swimming pool and a tennis court were built in Imini, because she had to be at work at 7 a.m., she pulled me out of bed at 5 a.m. to play tennis. That's when I found out that she had been a pole-vaulting champion in her teens in Yugoslavia, and gave up making a case for sleeping in.

One summer, when I was fifteen, the Mandrykas took me to France and dropped me off with some relatives of Dad's. The spa town of Thonon-les-Bains on the French side of the Lake of Geneva turned out to be quite a landmark in my life, and not only because of the spectacular Alpine landscape and passing crushes on local boys. Amidst days of bracing hikes, and boat rides on the lake, and delicious snacks of wild strawberries with *crème chantilly*, my hosts saw fit to take me aside and enlighten me about my family history.

This was a gift I was hardly prepared to accept. I remember staring at tante Natasha's herringbone parquet while she spoke. Everything in tante Natasha's house was perfect. She was a collector of antiques and *bibelots*, and they all blended into a discreet fugue of harmonizing styles. When I finally looked up, I was struck by the soft shape of her mouth, which dropped words so effortlessly, and the hungry look of expectation in her eyes. I wonder if bombardiers' eyes have that same sharp look of imminent gratification as their hands pull the lever or push the button.

She kept talking: "We all loved your father so much... the way he played the guitar at our gatherings in Belgrade... and his truly amazing memory for poetry... you don't look like your father..." (I don't?) "Your mother never told you?" (Told me - what?) "Told you about your real father?" (My REAL father???) A huge sucking hole opened up inside me and I went spinning down, trying to put ever greater distance between me and all those words falling on top of me. But it was too late. "Don't you know that your father was another man, a Montenegrin"?

Aunt Natasha had been visiting my parents in Bihać, and had observed the "situation." She was willing to tell more, but I just sat there, looking away, saying nothing. There would be no missile-to-target contact, no explosion, no scattering of cluster bomblets, no emanation of depleted uranium. I did, however, ask Mother upon returning to Imini. "Never mind that bitch," Mom said, "but she spoke the truth." So, Dad, my lovely, kind, wise, wonderful Dad was NOT my father? "Of course, he is your father," Mom said, "just not your birth father. It's true, the man who conceived you was a Montenegrin. A tall, dark, handsome, wild and wonderful lover and you can be as proud of him as of Dad." She was going a little fast for me, but I listened up. She told me then that Father (my Russian father) was not very interested in sex. She apologized for my having to face things in this untimely manner, and from the wrong party – "some relative, that bitch." Mom went on to say how those relatives had looked down their noses on her because she had come from money but not from blue blood like them. As if they were not, all of them, equally poor in Yugoslavia by then. Obviously, distinctions needed to be made even more strenuously for that very reason. So, all my elaborate fancies of pedigreed ancestry in Old Russia, the long string of repentant and unrepentant noblemen, the notorious great-uncle who had been the governor of Siberia, and the glamorous grandmother, the Smolny graduate who had starved to death in the Communist Utopia… and that we were related to the Tolstoy family… all those stories which had nourished my childhood - just smoke and mirrors? But what about the unsuspected new vista which had just opened up and was beckoning me to some totally mysterious place called Montenegro? That opening was quickly shut again as Mom dealt out a final blow, "Your father (your Montenegrin father) was a follower of Draža Mihailović and was executed by Tito as an enemy of the people in the newly formed Communist order in Yugoslavia." And that was that. I did not press Mother for more. If I had had a bone to pick with Dad, I would have latched on to the fantasy of the "real" father. But Dad was a good father. He had kept me fed and warm and safe - and alive. I chose to stick with the living and let go of the dead. I re-committed myself to my Russian father with fierce loyalty. As to the Montenegrin stranger who was my accidental father, I locked him in my genes and threw away the key.

When I returned to Imini that summer I found that the Mandrykas were planning to move back to France. And in Marrakech our teen gang was falling apart. Bernard was yanked out of the lycée and handed over for improvement to a famous Jesuit school in Toulouse. Martine's prospects were a Catholic boarding school in Meknes. Mme. de Miller died that year, and the de Miller girls were sent off to Paris to stay with relatives.

And then there was, of course, Mother's affair with Maurice Jobert. Mme. Mandryka had been the only person in whom I confided. She side-stepped all judgment, and tried to reconcile me to the idea that the doings of adults, bizarre as they might appear to me, were ultimately their own business. My business was, to use an anachronism, "to get on with my own life." But I had no idea how to do that.

It was also around that time that my grandmother, my beloved Babushka, began to slide into dementia. Delicious *borsht* and *pirozhki*, roasts, incomparable poppy seed strudels and walnut cakes, were a thing of the past. Her wonderful culinary talents regressed to spaghetti and meat balls. We now discovered that Babushka was hiding edibles in her room. Strange smells led us to stashes of moldy madeleines, rotten bananas, and sundry items too far gone to be identified. Then she decided that the appropriate language of the land was German, which delighted at least one man, a former German prisoner of war.

These combined worries and events made my stay at the boarding school even more restive than usual. I took it into my head to quit school at the end of ninth grade in order to take care of Babushka. I remember Mom's guarded tones as she tried to discuss this unexpected reversal of my studious ways. She and Mme. Mandryka put their heads together, and came up with an alluring compromise. Why not do both - take care of Babushka and pursue a course of studies by correspondence? An added twist to spice the bait was that, surely, working on my own I could cover two years in one, and attempt the first part of the Baccalaureate exam the following year? Mother's dubious expression about this made me guess that this bit of devious mentoring was Mme. Mandryka's parting gift to me, and I jumped at the chance to prove myself. Thus, a new phase of my Moroccan life was ushered in, where Marrakech faded out in favor of Imini.

During that return trip of 1981 I was hoping to visit our former house. The Moroccan company accountant lived there now with his family, and he invited us to drop by. As we came up the familiar slope, the expected, intimately known surroundings took on an air of remoteness, as in dreams.

The house was there all right, but where were the two apricot trees, the honeysuckle gazebo, the flower garden in front, and the vegetable garden in back? The ground was bare. It looked like nothing had ever grown on its well-packed surface. Yet surely this was the very dirt I had spent many a blissful hour digging up and raking down? We did have a gardener, paid by the mining company, who came for the heavy work once a week, but I was the one who supplied most of the trial and error.

My parents had not been too interested, and help came from an unexpected quarter. Maurice Jobert turned out to be the gardener. At first, I bristled with suspicion as he began to show up and join me in my work. His persistence and evident green thumb, however, won me over in time. He had come of real peasant stock; his family possessed a fair-sized farm on the river Marne. He had been the only one among his siblings to join De Gaulle's Free French Army assembled in Africa. He had been part of the long ordeal of recapturing the Italian Peninsula, where his entire company of Senegalese recruits was wiped out. Upon returning home he found his brothers doing well from black market proceeds under the German occupation. In a fit of high-mindedness, he took off for Morocco. There he met Mother and eventually followed her to Australia.

Our combined gardening efforts bore fruit. I recall the apricot trees in blossom posing like brides for a wedding picture with their trail of scattered petals. And soon enough there would appear tight, pea-sized balls, suckling on the stingy earth through every hidden root. The transformation of those tight green knots as they swelled, became sun-soaked with color, then transparent and fuzzy-drunk with collecting nectar, was miraculous. I recall waiting for the long-anticipated harvest, and consulting Maurice about the right time. He considered the situation with the full measure of deliberation the matter required, wagged his head, and decreed yet another few days of postponement.

I woke up on the appointed morning with the inner conviction that this WAS the day. I jumped out of bed and went straight to the trees. They stood there, spare and stolid, their leaves shivering in the morning, their branches entirely delivered of their golden weight of fruit. Somebody else had also known that this WAS, indeed, the day of harvest. Dad laughed heartily. We suspected the gardener, who rolled his eyes and spread out his hands in theatrical dumbfoundedness. "Not to take away from your contribution," Dad said, "but did the gardener not, after all, carry the lion's share of the labor?"

As I haul stones and pick cactus spines out of my hands in my Arizona patch these days, Maurice's peasant know-how and Dad's patrician insouciance continue their dialogue over my head in the passing breeze, the cry of birds, the rustle of creeping creatures. It urges me to dig and plant, and it allows me to sit back and leave things alone.

When the current mistress of our former house opened the door, I did not ask her about the obliteration of the fruits of my youthful labor. I remembered sententious voices about how Arabs were too fatalistic to plant gardens, their religion bidding them neither to add to nor subtract from Allah's creation. And I remembered that Arabs had turned the parched land of Andalusia into a garden of earthly delights until the Christian Reconquista let loose their sheep there and wrecked the place.

As these contradicting versions of historical record fought it out in my head, our host opened the door of my parents' former bedroom to show the whole room covered wall to wall with sleeping mats: "This is where our twelve children sleep," she said. The children had evidently been whisked away for the occasion, and I briefly stood there, trying to fathom life in this house with myself multiplied by twelve. My brain drew a complete blank and seems to have also blotted out the rest of the visit. Instead, out of that memory hole floats Mom's face, also blank somehow, or maybe just pale, just tired. She is lying propped up in a hospital bed, and they have taken me to visit her. I am about eight; we are in Germany, some place called Watenstedt.

Mom had disappeared for a few days, and now I was allowed to see her. She hugged me and smiled, but her eyes remained fixed inward. She explained to me that a baby had been "on the way," but that "war conditions" did not allow large families. Her voice was light and hollow; it was like a bucket, slowly cranked out of the well, and now emptied out and dropped back to the bottom. I did not want to be there with her at the bottom of that well, in the dark. I began to cry. I had so begged for brothers and sisters. If a baby had been on the way, surely, they could bring it back? I didn't care whether it had been brought by a stork or found in a cabbage patch or, as I suspected, had come from some even more improbable place since adults liked to be so mysterious about it. Only let them bring it back; no more adult stuff about "wars" and "conditions." I created a scene, crying disconsolately, and Babushka had to take me away.

I don't remember the word "abortion" crossing anyone's lips at the time, but there had been an undertone, a Greek chorus of sighs and whispers and murmurs that seemed to hoist Mother up on some stage or scaffold.

The word "abortion," however, became quite explicit when I was about sixteen. By that time my own stake in any siblings had faded and I understood, besides, that if Mom was pregnant, the child must be Maurice's. He was not around, however, to pick up the pieces: he was a Catholic. So, it was Mom and me again at the bottom of that well. Only I was a big girl now, and I grasped the rope with both hands to help her climb out. I took Mom to a doctor in Marrakech who performed abortions illegally. I waited until it was done, then took her to a hotel room.

It was a long night. Mom was still heavily sedated as I put her to bed. Her eyes wide open and staring, she kept getting out of bed and trying to climb, for lack of a bidet or a bathtub, onto a sink. She wanted to wash herself. I kept trying to restrain her and put her back to bed. After yet another such episode, she looked right through me with her unseeing eyes, and her voice, detached and urgent, was not her own: "Why are you trying to stop me? All I want to do is cleanse myself and then die on the cross like Jesus Christ."

The rest of that sleepless night the voice of the Almighty pursued me, commanding "to go forth and multiply," and then whispering *ecce femina* as Mother's hands were nailed to the cross. And lightening-wielding Zeus, the insatiable impregnator, paraded his multiple guises in the dark: as a white bull with Europa, as a swan with Leda, as a shower of gold with Danae, as a snake with Persephone, as an eagle with Aegina, as an ant with Eurymedusa. And the bounty of Allah was everywhere, his blessed, polygamous seed scattering far and wide. It had filled one small room with twelve children where just one child, with three adults hovering over her, had had such a hard time making it into adulthood. Where is He when they fix the price of manganese on the world market? Will He give those twelve boys and girls their daily bread, or will he send them begging in the square of Djemaa El Fna?

But there had been a time of careless flowering and secret ripening and breathless expectation of divine love in that house as well. My 17th birthday inaugurated a succession of spring storms. Because of the political unrest throughout the French colonies, the distant battles in Vietnam, but also the not-so-distant struggle over Algeria, Imini had become a military outpost. A fort had been built on an outcropping across the road from our house. Our little town did its best to welcome the soldiers, and dances in the recreation hall took place often. Women were in short supply, and I basked in the whirl of attention. "Rock Around the Clock" was no stranger even to our lost horizons, and I remember dancing through the night non-stop.

The mature gaze of Claire Denis in the film Beau Travail captures something I could sense, but hardly name at the time - the radiating pent-up sexuality of young male bodies cooped up together and far from home, biding their time and waiting for release in love or combat. Ignorant, virginal, I fluttered through the mist of hormonal ferment that surrounded me as through a pollen–filled spring day, taking as my due the assiduous courtship of young men. And, primed by some ancient cunning, I held back as if guessing that choosing any one of them would break the spell, spoil the game, end the party.

When I finally yielded to the advances of one man, it turned out to be a local boy. He was "a bad element," and I had fallen for the James Dean syndrome. He had come to Imini after a bout in jail. It was a complicated saga of cars bought and sold - somehow leaving my hero holding the dummy check. I neither understood nor cared about the fine points. He was obviously a wheeler and dealer, and I had never encountered the type.

More to the point, the mere mention of his name terrified my parents. How long, after all, could I be expected to be a picture of responsible maidenhood when Mom herself was such an ambiguous model? Her free and assertive ways fascinated me - yet I strenuously planned to be utterly unlike her... But then again, who wants to be plain, dull, and overlooked by life? Still, Babushka had been neither plain nor dull, yet Grandfather had left her all the same... I obviously had to test the waters on my own.

René's charm and bad reputation were made to order. I defied my parents' strict prohibition, and relished the thrill of meeting him in secret. Our trysting place was way up on the hill, behind the chapel. Racing breathlessly up a set of endless steps uphill was like growing wings. Watching him step out of the shadows and stand outlined, his features indistinguishable against the paling sky, was like rushing into the embrace of Lawrence Olivier as Heathcliff in *Wuthering Heights*.

But we were discovered, and the scenes that ensued yielded all the drama I could have wished. In the tragic tones befitting the topic, Mom mourned the inviolable nature of my virginity while Dad sat crushed on a chair, looking like King Lear betrayed by Cordelia. Nothing that radical had happened thus far and my parents' accusations could be dismissed as *"son et lumière"*: this expression refers to the sound and light animation of newly scrubbed historical landmarks initiated under De Gaulle. It had been appropriated by teenagers to characterize their parents' theatrics. It only succeeded in fueling my curiosity. It also illustrated how much leverage I had acquired over my *"gisants,"* (another teen expression to refer to their parents, meaning the recumbent stone figures on medieval tombs).

The story's climax was reached one evening. Words of unfair innuendo were passed at the dinner table again, which poisoned the food in my mouth. I simply got up, opened the door, and stepped out. It was a beautiful night. The stars pierced the sky with innumerable spears of fire. I walked the three hundred odd steps that led to the chapel with deliberate slowness, knowing and not minding that René was not due to meet me there.

I stood near the chapel, watching the full moon above the hills, which floated in liquid silver. After a while I began to feel the cold. The chapel was unlocked, and I entered the dark place. There was a reddish night light by the altar, and I sat down in the front pew. The once familiar frescoes before me were now hard to make out. To the left a wing jutted out of the dark, and a tiny foot was poised on a cloud. To the right an angel's head hovered in its halo, and a pair of sandaled feet showed the way. In the middle, above the altar, two naked feet were nailed together one over the other by a daub of dark paint.

Feeling cold still, and sleepy as well by now, I tugged on the rug at the foot of the altar. It wasn't fixed to the floor, and I proceeded to roll myself into it. Pretty soon the glowing feet of my silent companions led me to the blessed shores of oblivion. At some point, however, I was disturbed by a strange vision: Mom stood over me, peering at me at close range. Next to her stood René, also looking somewhat startled, probably, as I began to make out, because Father stood right behind him, his shotgun wedged between Rene's shoulder blades. And behind them still there was a large gathering of people, swinging those foul-smelling miners' lamps.

When I hadn't come home that evening, Dad took his shotgun from where it hung on the wall, and flanked by Mom, went to knock on René's door. My hero subjected himself meekly to a search of his premises, and when ordered to disclose my whereabouts, was clearly at a loss for an answer. Since Mom, on the other hand, was never at a loss for bright ideas, she convinced the men that I must have gone to throw myself into one of the disused mining pits. They roused the populace of Imini and proceeded to organize a search.

When the actual night of love did happen, it could hardly match the drama of what had anticipated it. Luckily, I must not have been too fertile, either, as we knew as little about protection as about any positions of the *Kama Sutra*. Then, unexpectedly, Bad Boy Rene popped the question. His attraction had been in the call of the wild, not in settling down to barefoot and pregnant. When Mom organized an exile to France at the Mandrykas', I went along. The Moulinous drove me there as part of their yearly summer trip to France. It really does take a village. Upon my return the troublemaker was gone.

In this struggle to weather my first love, Mother and Babushka had offered strikingly contrasting models of womanhood. Mom had given me life in one heroic push and continued to do so, pushing me out into more life with an outpouring of warnings and expectations. Babushka was not like that at all. She neither exhorted nor protested, she neither demanded nor beseeched. Instead, she had fed and washed and clothed me, and sung me to sleep, and kissed away my bruises. She was the one who tied me to life by myriad ties so ordinary that they were invisible.

My loss of innocence had less to do, during that year in Imini, with engaging the opposite sex than with the utter failure of rescuing Babushka. I tried to keep up with her as the reel of her long life rewound itself with increasing speed. In the restless old woman I could hear pacing and muttering in her room, I tried to find my way back to the Babushka of infinite patience and fun and stories about Vasilisa the Fair. But Baba Yaga was winning all the contests now. I attempted to fix Grandmother's mind on some favorite topic, like her famous dowry, but the story now passed through some secret tunnel of horrors and came out changed. Babushka shrugged it off with distaste. She had not loved Grandfather; she had loved a brother of his who had been killed in World War I, and now he came to visit sometimes. I felt like an intruder.

The story of her Caucasus adventures also failed. I reminded her about the time her horse had taken the bit in its mouth and carried her off. None among the young men in her party could keep up with her, except for the handsome Georgian guide. But instead of taking her back to her companions, he had tried to lure her away into the precipitous landscape, speaking of wild poetic love. But now the story changed. Babushka as a young woman and her sisters were taken over by her later self and her two daughters. The exotic trips to the Caucasus became the headlong flight, during the Civil War, in a cattle car with a crowd of terrified strangers. She put a handkerchief to her mouth at this point in the story, and I too could breathe the excrement and the fever, and the stench of their collective fear.

I felt like a failure. I watched Babushka sink into a pit while I stood on the edge, helpless. She had brief periods of respite, but they didn't last. Mom intervened. She said all the things people say in these circumstances: that I had done my best, that it was God's will, that Babushka herself would understand and forgive. In short, that we needed to find a "safe place" for her. There was no such place in Morocco; we would have to look for a nursing home in France. And so, we did. Some three months later Babushka died in that nameless place. To this day I cannot reconstitute the exact sequence of events, nor do I have any recollection of her departure.

Improbably, I did manage to cover two years in one and passed my First Baccalaureate. To prepare for the Second Baccalaureate I returned to the Lycée Mangin in Marrakech. I was offered the position of *pionne, i.e.,* supervisor to assist in keeping the routines of the boarding school going. This should have been a good year. I was eighteen, I had met my scholastic challenge, I had a room of my own and I was earning my first salary. And away from home, I had the freedom to come and go as I pleased.

But it was not a good year. I did not like my duties of disciplining the caged creatures of the boarding school, one of whom I had been not long ago. Most surprisingly, I did not do well in class. I just sat there, but failed to engage. I wanted to connect, but couldn't. This was also true of my love life. I dated a popular boy I had admired from a distance earlier. My friends thought this was quite a coup. I thought it was a non-event. All in all, it was a lost year.

My calendar, however, showed one item with a check mark next to it: I did pass the final exams. So, I wasn't braindead, but my brain had functioned on its own, detached from the rest of me. The part of me which had hoped to identify with Babushka mourned us both. I was left with the uncouth youngster who had been frivolous and self-absorbed, an emerging self who had chosen Mom's resiliency over Babushka's meekness.

***

CHAPTER 6

IT NEVER RAINS IN CALIFORNIA

As we approached the Bay Area, the University of California at Berkeley did not materialize on a dream cloud the way the University of Sydney had appeared to me some years back. Instead, as we looked for the Student Village at Albany, we passed an open waterfront area. The sun had just set and in the dimming light we saw some rough sculptures made of railroad ties, wood planks and assorted "found objects." They were large, and looked at home amidst the surrounding warehouses. Yet the presence of these vaguely cruciform structures on that stretch of vacant beach also suggested a sense of silent witness.

It was dark by the time we found our apartment. We made a last-ditch effort to unload, and then collapsed on our sleeping bags. When we woke up the next morning and looked out the window, we saw fairly ramshackle barracks-like buildings. To me, it rather looked like the D.P. camps we had lived in in Germany, and was therefore quite within the range of my coping skills. We discovered the Salvation Army and, emulating Mom's virtuosity with U.S. Army surplus blankets, we soon put together a home of orange crates and burlap covers that was infinitely satisfying to us.

Rick went forth to imbibe the wisdom of Berkeley luminaries on the subject of economic development while I proceeded to work toward my Ph.T. ("putting hubby through"). With that goal in mind, I had already secured the job of editorial assistant for the Northern California office of Prentice Hall. My interview had taken place back in Englewood Cliffs, NJ. I remember walking into a huge hall subdivided into a warren of cubicles. Every single cubicle was "manned" by a woman. They ranged in age from early twenties to late '50s. The maze through which I was walked terminated in a large, elegantly furnished office, where a handsome young man cross-examined me. I had the distinct feeling of being looked over by a languid sultan, whose appetite for yet another recruit to his harem was not easily roused. But my credentials for dealing with foreign-language texts must have looked adequate, and the sultan gave me the nod. So, I began my commute to Palo Alto, where the Prentice Hall office was located.

But editing French or German-language texts, or even hearing lectures on econometrics, was hardly where the action was in Berkeley in the fall of 1965. Telegraph Avenue and Sproul Plaza were the 'zone.' The ebb and flow of the crowd among display tables was ceaseless, regrouping around one speaker and then another. Flyers passed from hand to hand announcing meetings, happenings, rallies, protests, teach-ins. It was a kind of Djemaa el-Fna, whose hawkers peddled and snake charmers uncoiled like so many swaying cobras, one question mark after another.

We shopped around like dazzled tourists, unsure of our credit in the market place of ideas. I had been raised, after all, in a family whose allegiances were conservative. Dad had been the last of a long line of firstborn sons dedicated to the military profession. The word "Communism" made this kind man bristle with outrage, and thus far I had largely deferred to his experience and judgment. In Berkeley, however, my earlier dreams of Paris, and of getting to the bottom of things political, surfaced anew.

In the fall of 1965, Berkeley was in transition between the Free Speech Movement and the Anti-War Movement. We did not know how bitterly contested and hard-won was the gaudy spread of opinion before us. College President Kerr, in defense of "discipline," had drawn an analogy between the college and a "firm," and himself and a firm's manager. Mario Savio had seized upon that analogy to refuse, to wild cheers, to be the raw material of that firm, as well as any of its expected products. He had famously stated: "You've got to put your bodies upon the gears and upon the wheels, upon the levers, upon all the apparatus and you've got to make it stop."

And now protests against the administrative fiat were expanding to include the war in Vietnam. As a matter of fact, a peace march was in the works. We hesitated. I had heard plenty about how so-called coalition governments in Eastern Europe had been taken over by Communist minorities and Soviet military muscle after World War II. The domino theory transferred to the Asian situation seemed plausible enough. Still, we hated to miss the action, and decided to check out the march from the sidelines.

The marchers came along, with their banners and chants and slogans. As I looked on, however, a light spring rain replaced the California sun, and I found myself approaching Avenue Mangin, the main thoroughfare connecting the Arab and European sections of Marrakech. The soft drumming of the rain on the pavement was quite audible, and I realized that there was no car traffic. Instead, a mass of people was advancing in the middle of the street. I stood there, startled, as the endless column began to make its way past me. The marchers were Arabs. I looked around and registered with growing alarm that there were no Europeans in sight anywhere – but a queasy feeling kept me riveted to the spot. The marchers were walking past me in measured advance, the rain ran down my cheeks, and something was happening to me. I was coming to, waking up. All we had feared, hidden in the shadows, was out in the light of day at last. Morocco was not our country, and its inhabitants were taking their country back.

And now I stood watching another march under the bright California sun and it was the same march. And here too something was struggling into the light of day. What was our claim on Vietnam?

But something else happened shortly thereafter to monopolize our attention: I was pregnant. For about a month or so, while we thought we were just going to classes and commuting to work, my blood cells had been hoarding up for a new life. Driving to work the day after our big news, and passing the waterfront stretch with the group sculptures, I slowed down, raised my hand, and gave them the peace sign.

Morning sickness, I discovered, was a misnomer. It lasted all day, and it encompassed the universe. I came to relate to the world through my mouth, mostly regurgitating what it had to offer. The supermarket became one big lab experiment where I raced up and down the aisles, constantly running into negatively charged thresholds. Reading labels became a chemistry test. I yearned for something, anything that was unprocessed, unpackaged, uncanned, unlabeled, unsprayed, and generally unimproved.

I now also came to dread the long double drive to and from work. I had been driving since the age of seventeen, and the hairpin turns up and down the Atlas range had not fazed me. Now everything spooked me. My boss took me out of my misery by firing me. I never found out what my failings were. Was I overdoing the editing with a novice's zeal? Did they have a policy about pregnant women? Had they run out of foreign-language texts to edit? I was upset, and my pride was hurt, but I also felt immensely relieved. No more long commutes hooked up to exhaust fumes for oxygen.

Rick announced that he would get a teaching assistantship in the fall, when the baby was due. I freelanced doing translating and editing in the meantime, and we managed. I now had the option to organize my day, and actually to tune into the mysterious goings-on that had taken over my body. The relentless nausea now appeared in a new light, almost a friend. It was all about making my body a fit place to grow a baby. I wanted to tune my rhythms to the hidden hum and pulse of the universe; I wanted to join my song to the self-generating chorus of life.

But all was not well with the world. On TV monks in saffron robes were setting themselves on fire. Haggard women carrying screaming babies ran as their villages burst into flames behind them. American boys were coming home in body bags. Strain as I might to capture the music of the spheres, the static of war drowned it out.

It was like the time back in Morocco when I had been walking about on the hill near the chapel of Imini, watching one of those technicolor sunsets only deserts know to pull out of thin air. I felt lifted up into the light and, like a Blake illustration, transfigured into a rainbow spectrum of colors. It was in that moment of moments that a young Berber appeared out of nowhere and approached me with unmistakable intent. The unearthly scream that rose from the very pit of my being sent him scrambling out of sight again. But it also extinguished the sunset.

Which one of us had spoiled the show? The cosmic moment had bridged heaven and earth in divine coupling, but human intercourse is not unconditional. The young Berber may well have had suns and moons on his mind when he saw me on that hill. But all I saw was a Berber. Or maybe he had seen conquest and revenge, and I had been right to scream for my life. Humans have developed the sacred gift of tongues, but Europeans and Arabs used it only to confirm who was master and who was slave.

It was the story of Lahsen that finally opened my own eyes. I had been at my desk studying when someone knocked at the door. I opened it to a young Moroccan about sixteen years old. He handed me a note: it was from Mom, who worked at the mine's office as an accountant. She was asking me to give the boy some food and install him up in the room at the back of the house next to the laundry room. He had walked all the way from the Sous Valley, a hundred kilometers or so, to look for work in the mine. When asked about his age, he had claimed to be twenty-four, and was told to come back when he would, in fact, reach that age. Mom, feeling sorry for him, sent him on to me: maybe something could be worked out.

Things did work out. The boy's name was Lahsen, and he became "our" boy. He picked up French with amazing speed. Not only that, but he managed to pick up some of the Russian we spoke among ourselves. If that wasn't enough, since Grandmother's mind was beginning to wander by then, and she insisted on speaking German to him, he got some of that under his belt as well. I offered to teach Lahsen to read and write, and he took to it with relish. He cleaned the house, ran errands, and learned to make excellent *borscht*. He was a real godsend; we didn't know how we had ever managed without him. At first, we went through an elaborate charade of hiding our money. When it became apparent that we had managed to hide it from ourselves rather than from Lahsen, who kept finding it for us, we gave up trying.

Time passed, and Babushka passed away. Lahsen grew taller, and took good care of us. No one needed to tell him his business anymore. The fort across from us was full of soldiers: it was now a way station to Algeria. The civil strife there between Arabs and *colons*, the French settlers who had called the place their own since the 180s, made the situation much more complicated than in Morocco, which had been a French "protectorate" (actually against German interests) only since 1911.

Albert Camus, who was born in Algeria, was accused of "colonial collaboration" because he tried to articulate the complexities of the issue, while Jean-Paul Sartre wrote a book on the torture the French army practiced in Algeria titled *La Question* ("The Question"). This reflected the deep division in the French population on the "Algerian question." President De Gaulle suffered attempts on his life for "betraying the cause" when he finally signed off on Algerian Independence in 1962.

The Algerian case is especially complicated because the Arabic and French ways had interacted for so long. After their liberation, the Algerians experienced a period of Nasser-like national modernization under Boumediene, then a radical Muslim revival, which precipitated the country into civil war in the 90s. The contest between the secular influence of the French and the assertion of traditional Islam is played out in the remarkable novel of Kamel Daoud's *Meursault: contre-enquete* (counter-investigation). Meursault, of course, is the name of the protagonist in Camus' novel, *The Stranger*, who commits an *"acte gratuit"* (a gratuitous or purposeless act) by killing an Arab "because of the sun."

Kamel Daoud's stated "purpose" is to endow the anonymous Arab with "a life," i.e., a biography. But this proves to be problematical as Daoud borrows Camus' style and the French language to conduct his "counter-investigation." Instead of demonstrating the outrage of the committed crime, the protagonist of his novel becomes a kind of Meursault himself - a "stranger" to his own people, particularly in resisting the sweep of the society's religious revival. Kamel Daoud became the runner-up to the prestigious literary *prix Goncourt* in France - while condemned to death by the fatwa of a Muslim cleric in Algeria.

The paradoxes of the colonial situation are further developed in the work of another Algerian writer, Yasmina Kadra (the pseudonym of Mohammed Moulessehoul). He too writes in French, and extends the conditions of the Algerian situation to Afghanistan, Iraq, Lebanon, Israel/Palestine... The

French language is meant as a bridge to reach the West, to make them "listen" to the cry of the oppressed.

But my Moroccan experience belonged to the late 50s – ours was not the escalating Algerian conflagration, and we counted our blessings for the calm that still held on our side of the border. It was a tense calm, however, and when a hunting rifle went missing, people became alarmed. Then the rumors died down until somebody else's gun disappeared. Thefts of various firearms continued intermittently, yet the thief or thieves were eluding discovery. Father pooh-poohed the growing panic: no one had touched his hunting rifle, and we practically never locked our doors. Then one day the French police came to that unlocked door of ours and asked for Lahsen. They found the whole arsenal of stolen arms in our storage room.

Lahsen was sent to jail in Marrakech, and I went to visit him. I cried, he didn't. I looked into his eyes. What they said was, "I am not sorry and I would do it again." There was nothing much I could do. Clearly Arabs were no longer willing to impersonate picturesque fixtures in an exotic landscape created for our benefit.

Neither were the Vietnamese willing to impersonate pawns on the chessboard of international power games. When that connection hit home for me at last, all the familiar features of a colonial war emerged on the map of Vietnam, previously hidden in plain view. Up until 1950 there had been no question but that the French were fighting a bitter colonial war in Southeast Asia. But then Mao Zedong recognized Vietnam, and its war of liberation became a Communist threat. To the Vietnamese, however, it was the same war of national self-determination, only now against the Americans instead of against the French. And so, the Vietnamese ignored efforts at "pacification" and stuck with Ho Chi Minh instead of the succession of American-sponsored puppets in the South. They eluded established rules of military engagement, and suffered our relentless bombing until it became imperative to flush them out of their jungle with napalm - in short, to destroy them in order to save them.

This death dance which linked the U.S. to Vietnam was also trampling on the Great Society at home. Disappointed expectations led to Black riots and White backlash. And here I was, getting ready to bring a baby into this mess. My body, after its self-cleansing drive to welcome a new life, was experiencing a surge of energy. I decided to extend the detoxifying process to the body politic. I had come across an article by Bob Scheer which clearly articulated my own insight into the colonial nature of the Vietnam War. When he declared his candidacy for Congress on a peace platform, I volunteered to work for his campaign. Day in, day out, my big belly preceding me, I waddled along, ringing door bells for Bob Scheer and peace.

It was amazing to me, years later, that my teenage children should view the '60s as a golden age of sex, drugs, and rock n' roll. Sex was not as big a discovery to Rick and me as it might have been to others. We had already done our share of experimenting, and now we felt mellow and content with what we had together. The same for drugs: life had already taught us to hang on to every unclouded ounce of brain power we had. We got high, instead, on the rhythms of the Beat poets. A memorable "happening" at the Fillmore in San Francisco featured the Russian poets Evtushenko and Voznesensky. They represented the Soviet "Thaw" movement, soon to fizzle out, which was trying to move Russia forward. We danced and grooved to loud rock, flashing strobe lights, and the guttural alliterations of Voznesensky's poem Goya.

Sure, there were those who dissolved into drugs and thought "free love" was about love and freedom. And there were the more desperate, whose embrace of "the revolution" only played into the hands of "the system." They were the ones in the headlines. For the rest of us, the '60s meant the excitement of breaking through racial prejudice and stereotypical notions of patriotism. We were horrified by the casualties of the war and no longer believed its purpose. We breathed the free-for-all of ideas, the gathering of community, and the hope of making a difference. In the Beatles' words and tune, "We all live in a yellow submarine, yellow submarine." But riding on the backlash against "rioting Blacks, unpatriotic draft card burners, and godless hippies," Ronald Reagan was to sweep into the California Governor's office that November of 1966.

Frank and Francine came to visit us that summer, and the four of us went down the California coast together. We did some of the Missions, and it dawned on me then that California had been, once upon a time, "Spanish." Yet nothing around us on the roller coaster highways suggested the early beginnings of *El Camino Real*. I liked the Missions. They took me back to medieval cloisters and Mediterranean fragrances. The workmanlike layout of church, garden, and service buildings were knit together by some hidden thread, now frayed or broken. And yet - had such quiet arcades and peaceful gardens not been the pious hand-maidens of Spain's bloody conquest of the Americas?

As we visited, Francine astonished me by sharing that she too had dreamed of becoming a missionary of sorts. Self-effacing Francine had secretly harbored the wish to run away to the Belgian Congo to take care of lepers. Leopold II, King of the Belgians, had also been a man with a mission. A chunk of Africa roughly the size of one third of the United States had been the private property of this one man.

In the second half of the 19th century, the mega-race to secure every last bit of 'unclaimed' territory on this circular globe of ours was coming to an end. Leopold II had felt left out. He felt claustrophobic in little Belgium and terminally bored by the feuds of Flemings and Walloons, Catholics and Liberals. Sitting at the very center of the complicated web of European politics which crisscrossed over Belgium, Leopold II took hold of every available thread and worked it into his secret designs. He patronized geographical societies, propagandized to the 'civilized world' about the remnants of the slave trade practiced by Arabs in Africa, and raised funds for Christian missions - and military outposts to protect them. He was a master of deceit: the CEOs of ENRON and latter-day derivatives merchants are but epigones to this early impresario in financial wizardry. Juggling stacked investments within hair-trigger timing, he acquired vast lands and closed interlocking deals with multiple commercial interests.

Leopold II never bothered with a money economy in the Congo, imposing, instead, a 'tax' in kind on the population: they had to collect so much rubber per village. When people tried to tend their fields or to run away, they were caught and brutally punished. Investigators came across basketfuls of cut-off hands, and flower gardens ringed with human skulls. Sleeping sickness, preying on the weakened population, was estimated to have claimed several million casualties around the turn of the century.

Francine, of course, knew the story through the prism of partial and local interpretation. Despite the dark allegations against the King of the Belgians, there lingered about him an aura of entrepreneurial daring, even glory. And if some of the terrible things the press (mostly foreign) was saying about their king were true, Belgians like Francine could still do their part: hence the dream to serve in the Congo as a nurse.

But when Leopold II died in 1909, other Belgians and their international partners took over. And when independence movements developed in Africa, they were willing to pass on the game of politics to the locals – as long as the multinationals kept their hands on its mineral wealth. Congolese Prime Minister Lumumba tried to resist, and was assassinated in 1961. The Belgian military and the CIA collaborated to back strong man Mobutu, who was only too happy to do their dirty work for a cut of the profits. And now well-intentioned NGOs are the new missionaries. There is a hue and cry for "humanitarian intervention" while Africa is plundered of its riches, its women raped, its children enrolled in savage resource wars.

But these insights would come much later. As we progressed south on our Californian trip in 1966, we were in a typical tourist mode. High over the hills of San Simeon, there loomed the twin towers of William Randolph Hearst's "ranch." After the sober grounds of the Missions, entering "the castle in the desert" felt like entering the belly of the beast. (do not delete)I expected at any moment to bump into Captain Ahab's missing leg.

When I saw Orson Welles' dark vision of Xanadu later, his mastery of the film medium also failed to win me over. No tender memories of Rosebud could draw me into this world of outsized men and their unfathomable compulsions of excess. And later still, when I learned that William Randolph Hearst had created the media foundation for the "liberation" of Cuba in 1898, this only underscored the New York Time's compliance with the myth of Saddam Hussein's "weapons of mass destruction," which paved the way for the War in Iraq.

The promise of Disneyland on that Californian trip with Frank and Francine was much more in tune with the child-centered hopes I was carrying inside me. We drove on and eventually approached the City of Angels. It was veiled in mists and hard to make out, a giant body dismembered by the coils of its freeways. Disneyland did not disappoint us. I was unfamiliar with the Disney characters, and entered the spirit of their antics without reservation. As we drove up the San Jose Valley on the way back to Berkeley, vast flower fields streaked past in a blaze of lavender and purple. The baby stirred inside me, as if to acknowledge the message of the world's beauty.

Upon our return, Rick found that his assistantship had not come through. Instead, I was offered a scholarship to enter the Ph.D. program of the Comparative Literature Department. The offer was tempting, but not realistic in my condition. Frank and Francine left in the midst of these worries. Our vacation was quite over.

What happened next was our son Peter; everything else was just background. Rick pushed on with another term in his program, but the various jobs he now took on to put food on the table began to affect his grades. Yet I don't remember that he complained. What mattered was good check-ups, setting up a corner for a crib in our bedroom, and checking off days on the calendar.

Finally, the big day came and Rick drove me to the hospital. As a penniless student I didn't have a doctor of my own. Things took a long time. Despite my Lamaze exercises, words like "discomfort" and "pressure" had to yield to the time-honored word "pain." Time stretched and contracted. I heard a woman screaming somewhere across the hall. They told me she was Black, as if her blackness and the screaming explained each other. I listened to her screams, and after a while, tried screaming myself. We took turns screaming, and I found comfort in it. I was in my thirtieth hour of labor when all of a sudden everybody started running around like they do on the TV show ER. They wheeled me into the delivery room, and Peter made his triumphal entry into the world.

He looked the spitting image of Frank, all eyes and wrinkles and a bald head with just a tonsure-like ring of hair. He was gorgeous. When Rick took him in his arms, it was as if a big light went on inside and made him transparent. Whoever came up with the bizarre Trinity of Father, Son, and Holy Ghost? Surely the divine trinity is Father, Mother, and Child, hovering in a sweet halo of tenderness. The outside world fell away. It was all snuggling, and suckling, and dozing off, and handling those soft limbs when changing nappies. Rick was always near, enfolding us in his care. The price, of course, was that he had to give up on his Ph.D. Our thoughts turned back to New York.

We celebrated Christmas with Peter under the tree representing Baby Jesus, sold or gave away whatever could not fit on the top of our station wagon, and finally took off. On the way out, we passed the big waterfront sculptures for the last time. They still stood there in silent witness. If there was anything we had learned at Berkeley, it was to trust our own yearning for a world of peace and justice.

***

CHAPTER 7

LOST WORLDS

A new year, 1967, had just begun, but instead of moving forward, we were heading back. Our crossing westward had been all about setting forth, pioneer-like, into uncharted territory. Never mind that the territory had been traveled and claimed by others. It had been virgin territory to us, and we had been conscious of embarking on a mythical trail of discovery. And now we had come to the edge of America, and sort of fallen off. But we had also produced an American: our journey was beginning all over.

For our return trip we decided to take a southern route. We crossed the Sierra Nevada, followed its foothills south, then turned east toward Death Valley. Looking for yet another short cut to the gold fields, the people who named the place had wandered here, then staggered, then crawled, then died.

We drove on, and the sun was now behind us, throwing long shadows ahead. It looked like we were chasing our own car. At long last, we saw a settlement in the distance. As we approached, we found ourselves staring at straight rows of the same dingy house: so that's what an Indian reservation looked like. We refilled our car and ate quickly. I gathered up the baby and we got away, as if by lingering, we would be forced by some spell to remain forever in this dead zone.

It had gotten dark in the meantime, and the stars showed up in force. I must have dozed off, for Rick touched my shoulder to point to something ahead; the stars had competition. It looked like the aurora borealis and turned out to be the glow emanating, miles away, from the Queen of the Desert, Las Vegas. Like the proverbial moth attracted to light, we sped on and eventually entered the city. But it was late by then, and we left early the next day. It would take another twenty years before I would actually get a real look at the Strip. It must have grown exponentially since that early passage, but its Caesar's Palaces and Luxors and Venetians and Monte Carlos, familiar landmarks in history and geography elsewhere, exist here in parody.

We passed Flagstaff, Arizona, and sped on toward Santa Fe, New Mexico. But I did not see Santa Fe. I saw snow-capped mountains gleaming in the near distance, I saw adobe houses etched in sun and shadow, and I was instantly flooded with that mix of joy and sadness we call nostalgia. I saw Marrakech. The unformed dreams of my adolescence, forever stamped with Morocco's horizons, lived on inside. Yet in all that time, though I had come to speak French like a native, I never learned to speak Arabic properly.

The unstated assumption had been that Arabic had no riches of past, present, or future to offer. It was a shock to discover later that I had passed many times without knowing it, in the Medina of Marrakech, the place where Averroes was buried. He was the one who had rescued Aristotle from oblivion and passed on to the West the great Greek's essential writings. How did Averroes, or rather Abu al-Walid Muhammad ibn Rushd, end up in Marrakech? I had never suspected that the high tower of the Kutubia, whose claim to fame, as far as I knew, was to advertise Marrakech to prospective tourists, had once advertised a famous booksellers' market. That it had preceded its twin, the Giralda of Seville, simply stood the reality of colonial Morocco on its head.

I had read the Koran in French translation. The Prophet Mohammed used the Arabic dialect of Mecca to update the Hebrew and Christian scriptures, and in doing so, fashioned the supreme literary canon of Arabic culture. But poetry does not translate well, and I had remained tone-deaf to its magic.

Yet all around me the living tradition of Islam had been evident. A man would be saying his prayers, bowing to the east at sunset, alone among the hills. Once I passed an open door in the Medina of Marrakech: a circle of young boys sat on the ground, chanting in unison. Much of the Koran is evidently committed to memory. Another time I encountered a funeral procession. People made way in the narrow streets, murmuring words of blessing. Two men distributed coins to beggars along the way. And then there had been Ramadan, the month of fasting. People staggered in the heat, abstemious. Later we could hear, from the Arab village at Imini, the beating of the drums as they broke their fast, and late into the night, sounds of guttural, monotonous chants.

But if it had all been intriguing, it remained remote. Why keep repeating that God was One, and that Allah was His name? It had meant a lot to the pagan tribes of Arabia who each had been worshiping a different local spirit and fighting over every well and palm grove protected by one of them. Their unification under One God and His Prophet Mohammed had opened the way to the wholesale conversion of ancient empires.

The Persians and Byzantines had exhausted each other in rival struggle. The Prophet's message was timely. It streamlined the many beliefs competing for attention, and pared them down to essentials: pray to One God, Allah the Merciful; obey His laws as compiled in the Holy Book; practice charity and practice tolerance. But the missionary zeal of the frugal and egalitarian Arab tribesmen was only frugal and egalitarian up to a point. To hold on to their conquests they needed the looted wealth from more conquests. In time these conquerors were absorbed by the more advanced civilizations they encountered, while the conquered, though not forced to convert, often found it expedient to do so to avoid the poll tax their conquerors imposed.

One such place familiar to me was Spain. In my teens I had traveled through Spain three times on the way from Morocco to France. Those were the days of Franco's Spain, not the Spain of Almodóvar's movies. We took the ferry at Tangier to cross the Strait of Gibraltar, and ended up on the other side of the Pyrenees Mountains three days later. All that the adults ever commented on was the general disrepair of Spanish roads.

It took an adult trip with Rick for me to recover Spain and its historic connection to Morocco. Spain had been a prosperous Roman colony, then suffered decline under the feudal rule of the Visigoths. When the Arabs swept through Northern Africa, allied themselves with the Berber tribes of Morocco and invaded Spain, the pickings proved easy. Because the Visigoths had been Arian, i.e., had not accepted the Trinitarian doctrines of Rome and Byzantium, religious coexistence between Christians, Muslims, and Jews was greatly facilitated. They intermarried and shared worship facilities. New crops were introduced from the east, Roman mines were reopened, crafts and commerce were fostered, and a stable currency was maintained. Caliphs and viziers patronized the sciences and the arts.

It was in the Alhambra palace of Granada that I thought I could read, in the over-refined stucco adornment of its walls, the exquisite proportion of its halls, the fragrant breezes of its gardens, and the clear pools and murmuring fountains - the vestigial traces of the former brilliance and ultimate defeat of the Moorish experiment in civilization.

Why did this success story come to grief? It was overtaken by a twin movement of opposing fundamentalisms: Christian fundamentalism from without, and Muslim fundamentalism from within. The Christians were no longer a persecuted sect of the Roman Empire. Having recovered from the Barbarian invasions, they were now empire builders themselves. Crusades were preached to beat back the infidel in Spain, Sicily and, of course, Palestine.

Against this powerful drive the rulers of Moorish Spain, seduced by wealth and culture, proved incapable of rallying their forces. The common folk, feeling unprotected, turned back to the Islam which had served their fathers, and the extremist leaders who preached it. They turned on their scholars and philosophers and burned their books. Averroes, who had interpreted the Koran symbolically rather than literally, was accused of atheism, and his work was condemned.

No wonder then that his grave in Marrakech was not a crowd stopper. It turned out, however, that blaming Averroes and his fellow intellectuals did not save the day. Allah, as we know from hindsight, did not rescue the Faithful. The fighting was long and bloody. When it was over, Muslims and Jews had to convert to Christianity. But they were not trusted and eventually suffered expulsion in 1492.

The Mongol invasion had already destroyed the Eastern centers of Islam in the 13th century, razing Baghdad to the ground. Turkic tribes had been pouring out of the steppes of Asia for some time, converting to Islam, and staying to rule. Their conquering drive overran the Balkans, breached the impregnable defenses of Constantinople, and was only stopped at the gates of Vienna.

The 17th and 18th were thus a stand-off between Islam and Christendom. But the stakes involved had little to do with religion by then, at least not the old religion which had sent the Arabs on their conquests, or propelled Spain and Portugal and the English Pilgrims all the way to the New World. The European Renaissance, sidetracked for a time by the Wars of Religion, reemerged as the Enlightenment of the 18th century, and produced a new religion. It was variously called "Mercantilism" or "Progress" and evolved, by the 19th century, into the "white man's burden" and the French *mission civilisatrice.*" It had to do with access to raw materials for rapidly industrializing Europe and access to markets for her manufactured goods. European incursions around the world and into Islamic territory in particular were ceaseless from then on, ending in various forms of colonization.

ᙍᖾᔡ

But all good things come to an end. It was our turn to leave Morocco in 1958 the way the Spanish Moriscos and Jews were forced to leave Spain in 1492. We took the train to Tangier, for our trusty little Renault had become the property of Belaid, the black star miner, who also bargained down the price of the rest of our possessions. From Tangier we crossed over by ferry, this time not to Spain but to the Rock of Gibraltar, which was still British territory. There we boarded a British ocean liner on its way to Australia.

When our boat approached the Suez Canal, we were not allowed to go ashore. Aside from the attraction of its famous sphinxes and pyramids, we had personal reasons to be interested in Egypt. My grandmother had spent six years in Alexandria, and I still cherish the quaintly colorized postcards she had sent Mom of palm trees bending to the Nile. One of my maternal great-uncles had ended up there after the Russian Revolution. His wife had died, and having heard of my grandparents' divorce, great-uncle Theodore invited Babushka to join him to help raise his two sons.

As I stared at the arid banks of the Suez Canal, I tried to imagine the contours of the fabled city founded by Alexander in 332 B.C.E. Was it like the Hollywood sets of Anthony and Cleopatra's romance? She was, after all, the last of the Ptolemies, the Greek rulers of Egypt under whose tutelage Alexandria had become a beacon of contemporary civilization. At the time of our passage in 1958 my awareness of the truly astounding nature of the place was limited to Archimedes. My high school physics textbook had shown him running through unspecified streets, a token scrap of toga floating over his private parts, shouting "Eureka!"

There was, apparently, no dearth of others. There had been Euclid the geometer and Ptolemy the geographer; Aristarchus, who had figured out even then that the earth revolved around the sun, was accused of atheism; Philo, the Jewish philosopher, had synthesized Hebrew tradition and Greek thought; Galen the physician had already come to understand the body's circulatory system.

But the famous library which nurtured their efforts is no more; a Christian mob had destroyed the venerable institution. From then on, the ancient temples of Alexandria were transformed into Christian churches. But this in no way diminished Alexandria's love of debate, which now became theological. Was Christ entirely divine, divine and human in equal proportions - or entirely human? Perhaps memories of ancient deities, anthropomorphic Greek gods, and godlike Egyptian rulers, lived again in these speculations. Arius, however, a Berber from Libya who had come to Alexandria to study, famously challenged the concept of the Trinity.

All the same, Christian dogmatism prevailed in the end. Monks looked for salvation in the sands of Egypt, and famous paintings depict the unholy temptations they suffered there. Back in 1958, in those devotional days of my Bible reading, I had not heard of Hypatia. She had been a mathematician and a humanist philosopher. Accused of magic and sorcery by those very monks who were tormented by lurid visions in the desert, she was dragged into a church in broad daylight, flayed, and burned.

As we stayed marooned near Port Said, we had plenty of time to reflect on how big-time politics can intrude upon private lives. Yet ordinary people are remarkably resourceful. A fleet of rowboats and other small craft came swarming around our ship and pretty soon many ropes connected us to them. Baskets with offerings of local artifacts began traveling up by means of some pulley system, and containers with money were sent back down. Our huge ship, tethered by its myriad ropes must have looked like an illustration of Gulliver tied down by the Lilliputians.

The political situation of the day could have been similarly illustrated. President Gamal Abdel Nasser of Egypt was the Lilliputian upstart against the giant powers of France and England, who had been the colonial masters of Egypt and the Middle East for nearly a century. Napoleon had fallen in love with the pyramids of Egypt, but the English, anxious to guard a passage to India, stopped him at the naval battle of Abukir. Eventually the British and the French reconciled their interests, and together financed the Suez Canal, connecting the Mediterranean to the Red Sea and Europe to the Far East.

We were now stuck in our ship at the headway of the Suez Canal because President Nasser had nationalized the canal in 1956. These contests were all about the sharing of the profits of the *Companie universelle* which had brokered the construction of the Suez Canal. By 1956 it had amortized its investment ten times over, and was a blue-chip stock on the various exchanges. Its revenue, however, by the time it "trickled down" to the Egyptian government and the Egyptian people, was negligible.

Just the same, Nasser's nationalizing move caused a blockade of the Suez Canal by Franco-British forces. I remember how the name "Nasser" was bounced around in French headlines, giving off a whiff of fire and brimstone. He was an outspoken supporter of the Algerian rebellion; he was in sympathy with the revolution in Iraq, which overthrew the British-backed monarchy in favor of a republic with Abdul Karim Qasim as prime minister.

What I didn't know at the time was that Israel had been the third party of the 1956 blockade. As a matter of fact, the very name of "Israel" had never been dissociated from my Biblical understanding of the region. I knew nothing of the Zionist movement, or of the foundation of Israel in 1948 as a settler colony. Given the passing of the colonial period everywhere else, this was a late attempt at reversing the direction of history, and it would prove highly problematical.

To this day, the land that was the cradle of the three Abrahamic religions is unable to weave together these common roots. The memory of the Christian crusades would be revived during the presidency of George W. Bush. An even earlier Christian monument, however, built in Jerusalem by the Byzantine emperor Constantine, the Holy Sepulcher which presumably encloses Golgotha, seems an accepted part of the landscape: it attracts crowds of Christian pilgrims and is a profitable source of income for the locals.

But the Muslim tradition, and the majority Palestinians who have inherited it, is a challenge: the Dome of the Rock, built in 619, towers over the mount where King David's temple once stood. The only holy place for the Jews to worship is the West Wall.

This crowded territory was not, as has been claimed by Golda Meyer, "a land without people for a people without a land." The Palestinians, (the Philistines of Biblical times) are still there and the creation of Israel was their Nakba - their disaster. Repeated rebellions, wars between Israel and surrounding Arab states (in 1967 and 1973) and more rebellions known as intifadas, have been challenging the Israeli claims to the land.

But the Israelis have been remarkably successful in their bid for what they consider their historical patrimony, which they have reclaimed after their 2000-year diaspora all over the known world. They have been successful in negotiating the conditions of their state at the United Nations; they have confined the Palestinians behind ubiquitous walls and military check points; they have extended Israeli settlements into Palestinian territory; they have evacuated Gaza, only to turn it into an open-air concentration camp, which they periodically bomb.

The international community is divided between the Palestinian plight and the memory of the Jewish Holocaust. Repeated attempts at peace settlements have failed. Israel has a powerful lobby in the U.S. Among them, the Evangelicals are faithful supporters as they factor Israel in the Biblical prophesies of the end-times. Israeli technical knowhow on digital control of fences is useful to American efforts to secure the border with Mexico. Israeli president Netanyahu gets to address the U.S Congress. The U.S. is a staunch supporter of Israel at the United Nations.

Marooned off Port Said in 1958, I had no idea of this complicated situation and the developments it was to take. We awaited our right of passage, and it was finally granted. Even so, as we were gliding past the barren banks of the canal, there was an uneasy sense that the Arab world we were leaving behind was in turmoil. In the Good Book Lot's wife is forever left standing on the borderline, a pillar of salt. I like her for defying the prohibition to look back. Turning my back on the Arab world was like condemning them to another self-righteous destruction as in the Biblical Sodom and Gomorrah.

Back in 1981, when Rick and I undertook that trip to Morocco, I was tense with anticipation. There was personal sentiment to be sure, but I also wanted to see what the Moroccans had done with Morocco. The French had been shaking their heads at the time Independence was granted, prophesying that the country would go to rack and ruin without them. The going joke had been that the Arab world was rushing full speed from the 14th century into the 15th. I was hoping that they had been proven wrong.

As we all know, however, you can't go home again. I got lost in Marrakech, not in the Arab section, which hadn't changed, but in what had previously been the European section. I wandered around and around and never found the convent school of my fond memories. I looked for the familiar palm grove on whose edge the place had stood. I finally realized that the chaotic construction sites, those sprawling villas among plowed up streets and happy-go-lucky electric wires were the palm grove. The palm trees, rustling in the night outside our upper-story dormitory's windows, and in the morning spreading their waving crowns for miles like a dark-green sea, were gone.

At least it was good to see that the twenty-five-year lapse since my departure had raised a generation of brisk and businesslike and competent young people to take over from the Europeans. I thought back to the last headache I had given my parents before we left Morocco in 1958. I had fallen in love with one of the sons of El Glaoui, the Berber chief who governed Southern Morocco. What had impressed me was his masterful backhand in tennis. He had a casual, yet devastating way of passing his opponent at the net that was heart-stopping. Actually, we barely met, and my parents hastened our exit plans to keep it that way. They pointed to the mountain fortress off the road between

Marrakech and Imini, where El Glaoui was said to keep an international harem. They wondered whether they would be allowed to visit me once I was locked up in it. I shrugged them off. The object of my flustered fantasies was perfectly sophisticated. Aside from his irresistible backhand, he was studying law in Paris.

The story of Malika Oufkir in *Stolen Lives*, however, shows that circumstances in Morocco could be appallingly unsophisticated under Hasan II, who succeeded his father Mohammed V in 1961. Malika's story is of a woman of extreme privilege and impunity falling into the parallel universe of the rejected. Malika's father had enjoyed the trust of the King as Chief of State Security. In that capacity, and with the financial help of the CIA and Israeli Intelligence operatives, he had masterminded the kidnapping in Paris and killing of Mehdi Ben Barka. The Moroccan head of the National Union of Popular Forces, and thus opposition leader to the king, Ben Barka became an exile. He traveled broadly and became a leading figure in the international anti-colonial movement.

But then Mohamed Oufkir became implicated in coup attempts against the sovereign himself and ostensibly committed suicide. His daughter Malika and the rest of the family were jailed, and from that day they contended with rats for their meager rations. Improbably, after fifteen years of imprisonment, Malika and her younger brother Raouf dug a tunnel under the very nose of their jailers, and escaped. They were now "wanted" in what appeared to be a police state. They managed to outmaneuver its traps and finally approached a French reporter, who helped Malika, eventually, to freedom in France.

What strikes me now is that one of the locations where Malika and her family had been imprisoned was a place I had passed any number of times on trips between Marrakech and Casablanca. To associate a familiar place with pain and suffering is a shock. Something in us must know of such existential threats: there but for the grace of God go I. We attempt to deal with this as best we can. Like kids, we love horror shows because the thrill industry hypes them into sheer fantasy. And we buy into the hypnotic trance induced by high-tech effects because they cater to the illusion that we are in control of the power game. The reality of such power games is less glamorous: it's a dark basement where a human being wreaths in pain.

I have to wonder whether the U.S. program of "extraordinary rendition" uses those very same places that once looked so innocuous to me. Morocco is known to be a willing participant in the U.S. program. But surely Moroccan torture techniques must still be stuck somewhere between the 14th and 15th centuries and need to be updated by our expert advisers known as "safety officers" who are members of the American Psychological Association?

This was not what I had hoped to find in Morocco. What exactly are the options of post-colonial countries? In the early stages of post-Colonialism, the Arab world had not looked to Islam for its rallying cry. They had looked to ground their newly won independence in modernity. Turkey, after the disaster of World War I, had led the way. If both the dynastic rulers and the republican governments tended to impose their solutions with an iron hand, their models could be found in twentieth century Europe. Mussolini stuck out his square jaw back to the glory days of Rome; Hitler's cracked voice trumpeted some lost Valhalla of blond warriors unpolluted by the embrace of impure races; El Caudillo scanned the horizon waiting for the Spanish ships of the Golden Age to come in again; and Mother Russia hemorrhaged trying to give birth to a proletarian Prometheus.

What of the "liberal" model of the West? In the name of civilization and democracy and free trade, it always ended up taking over by force of arms. France had been deeply humbled in World War II, and Sultan Mohammed V, who had been loyal during the war, was now expecting to negotiate terms for independence. General De Gaulle, grateful for all of the Moroccan fighters in the Free French Forces, had promised as much. But De Gaulle was no longer at the helm, and subsequent French governments were not prepared to let go of their colonies. Morocco was overrun by brash fortune seekers, much land was seized for French *colons,* and the exploitation of the country's resources was in full swing. In 1953 the French exiled Mohammed V to Madagascar.

And now in 1981 Mulay Hasan II had been ruling post-colonial Morocco for some twenty years. Unfortunately, the fellahin still couldn't feed their families – and they still can't do so now. Many among them leave to swell the slums of Casablanca, but there isn't enough work. They go to France or Spain illegally, send remittances back home - and sometimes disappear altogether. Like Zacarias Moussaoui, some of them end up in Al Quaeda training camps. Young people are easily seduced by the siren song of heroic action in a larger cause. Is this any different from young Americans joining the Marines in response to September 11 in 2001?

The rulers of the Middle-East and North Africa have to deal with a global, neo-liberal world order on the one hand, and the rise of religious fundamentalism within their borders, on the other. Islam, because it unites the respectability of faith and morality with memories of past military and cultural glory, is a handy, all-embracing catalyst.

But the ideological battle cries of "jihad" or holy war against the Satanic West sound very much like our own announcements of "end times" and promises of instant "rapture." And the official language of "war on terror," magnified in the media and relayed on the internet, have since inspired Andres Behring Breivik to kill close to a hundred young people during their Labor camping retreat in Norway. As his Manifesto spells out, his anti-Islamic and anti-feminist crusade is urging us to go back to the good old days of Medieval Christendom.

Experiments with gradual change or rapid modernization have not been successful in the face of Western economic, cultural and military domination. What about the rash of Arab Springs, from Egypt, to Libya, to Tunisia in the 2010s? Did they not offer a promise of positive change? Egypt, which receives almost as much U.S. aid as Israel, is as much a police state as before, and the economic situation is as limited as before. Libya was attacked by NATO, its leader, Moammar Qadhafi, assassinated, and civil war is still raging in the country. Tunisia was hailed as more successful in implementing change and achieving a balance between Islamic and Liberal trends. Is this why AFRICOM, the African branch of NATO, has been welcomed to install its military bases there?

And then there is Morocco and the Western Sahara situation. The former Spanish colony, from which Spain has withdrawn in 1976 has since been claimed by Morocco. Despite UN censure, the U.S. has recognized this claim – in exchange for Morocco's recognition of Israel. The *quid pro quo*, as the deal has been characterized, has been lubricated by the sale of American and Israeli arms to Morocco.

***

CHAPTER 8

BIRDS

Two years passed after our return from Berkeley, or maybe it was eighteen months. One day I burst into tears and couldn't stop crying. We had been living in Rego Park, Queens, and even if that was nothing to write home about, neither was it something to push one over the edge. Our neighborhood was a real oasis of curved, tree-lined streets. We rented the top floor apartment of a two-family house owned by Hungarian immigrants. Shopping was just around the corner, and a school and a park were a short walk in the other direction along Ellwell Crescent. What was there to cry about?

Rick, after hesitating between several offers, had settled on a satisfying job with General Motors. They wanted him to do macroeconomic analyses on how many more cars the world could afford. This job pretty much swept him into the commuter stream, and in due course sent him to most of the world's capitals. He didn't even make a pretense of complaining about the long hours; he plainly enjoyed juggling the statistics and travel schedules, international conferences, and power lunches.

But one day Rick came home unexpectedly early and his hand still on the door knob with the door wide open, said, "They killed Martin Luther King, Jr." That April 4, 1968, I knew why I was crying. Ever since our coming to the States that man's voice had been soul food to us. It had put into words our deepest aspirations. It had been a moral compass. We grieved.

But I hadn't started having those crying spells right away. The years or months had passed in magical time, because they were all about our son Peter. He was an easy baby. He slept well, nursed well - his daily transformation was all-absorbing. Past and future converged on each moment, and the simplest things packed a wallop of significance, like the first smile that was not the muscular reflex of passing gas. The passersby, as I pushed him in his stroller along 63rd Rd, cooed and wagged their heads at him, and called him "bright eyes."

One morning I found him sitting on the floor of his room instead of in his crib; he had obviously managed to climb out, and looked not just unharmed, but ready for an Olympic medal. The day I left him alone for a few minutes playing with pots and pans on the kitchen floor, and then discovered him on top of the refrigerator, was the day I decided I'd better head toward the neighborhood playground. It was that deliberate stepping out that seemed to mark the watershed. We had been self-sufficient and self-contained until then, but now we stepped out of magical time. Like a sleepwalker out on a narrow ledge, I stopped midway, fearing an untimely awakening.

If something about the mother-child bond places one outside of measurable time, I now came to feel the slow grinding away of time – hours, days, weeks, months, years… Years spent shopping, chopping, scraping, peeling, washing, brushing, stirring, sifting, cutting, spooning, spreading, wiping, scrubbing, pulling, lifting, folding, washing, changing, shopping, chopping, scraping, peeling, washing - spooning - measuring - weighing - a life.

Maybe this shift occurred in me because the playground experience didn't prove very successful. Remembering the easygoing community of our not-so-distant days in Berkeley, where babies had seemed a natural part of the bubbling mix, I looked forward to meeting other mothers. But the young mothers who haunted the playground off Ellwell Crescent seemed of a different breed. There was something baffling about the language they shared, a language filled by brand-names and formulas and towering authorities and ready solutions and readier judgments. My own voice, which had been in tune in Berkeley, was off key in Queens. There was something edgy and uptight about those women. We were all cooped up in that fenced-off playground, darting here and there after our toddlers, like a cackle of birds in a cage.

Something in me balked at looking for a place in that pecking order. Instead, Babushka came to my rescue as usual. A faint echo of some Chinese tale and a nightingale singing in her cage recalled me to my long-buried dream of creating parallel word universes. That night, after dinner was done and the dishes washed and put away, and the baby bathed and sung to and tucked in, and Rick and I took some time to pleasure each other and he dropped off to sleep, I sneaked out of bed. I settled down in the living room, opened a notebook, and tried to find my way back to the earlier word journey I had begun in some fictional African desert.

I knew that Australian Aborigines found hidden water tables where others died of thirst, so I decided to do a mental *walkabout*. As I stared at the white page, the sand dunes began to shift; a sandstorm rose and then settled down as a swarm of birds. They came to contest the ornithological human specimens of the playground. They were wild and free, soaring into azure skies or glorious with exotic colors among leafy jungles, sounding off in full-throated cries, shrill or cackling or exquisitely modulated. I too looked to find my song as my journey progressed among Laundromats and playgrounds.

But the handles of the clock were already pointing toward 3 a.m., and I went to check on Peter. He looked quite comfortable with his legs folded under his tummy and his butt sticking out. In our own bedroom, Rick too was sleeping peacefully, his Belgian gray cells busy regenerating for another day of problem solving in the Big World.

I snuggled up to him and, before I knew that I was asleep, Peter was tugging at my nightgown. Evidently it was 6 a.m., and Rick was splashing in the shower already. I must have drifted off again, because Peter was now tugging at me with imperious insistence and Rick was gone. I don't know what I said to my child, but what I saw in his eyes was Little Red Riding Hood's terror at discovering that her grandmother was a snarling, ravenous wolf. That look in his eyes haunted me through the rest of that sleep-deprived day. I went through it the way drunks must deal with a hangover. I simulated heroic poise about the stuck coins at the Laundromat, and the mix-up and endless wait at the pediatrician's, and the inevitable stint at the playground.

That night, however, instead of looking to repeat last night's high, I went on the wagon. I put away my notebook as if it was a secret stash of booze, and hit the pillow as soon as Peter did. And if Babushka sent me the firebird of Russian legend to revive the ashes of my flight dreams that night, it wasn't the snarling, ravenous wolf in me that scared it off. It was the me that couldn't be that wolf. The days that followed were sunny and busy, spring was out in full force, and I believe it was on one of those bright days that my first crying spell burst out like a spring shower.

That spring of 1968, Frank and Francine were planning a trip to Belgium, and invited us to join them. They even suggested that I travel ahead with Peter to visit my old friends from Morocco, who now lived in France. I could join the family later in Brussels when Rick was due to arrive there as well. They didn't have to ask twice. Martine Moulinou was abroad just then, but the de Miller girls were both in Paris, and invited me to stay with them by return mail. I scooped Peter up and we flew out.

Irène was still unmarried, while Hélène was now Hélène Castinel and the mother of three boys. For the femme fatale of our gang, she now looked the very picture of settled domesticity. Hélène's husband Jean-Pierre and Irene left for work every day, leaving us to visit and reminisce. We had found out that Bernard Moulinou had been killed in Algeria. How could Bernard, so handsome, so full of promise – be dead? And what was going on with Algeria? We didn't know. Our focus was on our own families now. Helene's oldest boys went off to school while we took her youngest and Peter on our homemaker's duties. First, we went to the farmer's market for fresh produce and a seasonal bunch of flowers: lilies of the valley were everywhere just then. Then there was the stop at the butcher's, on whom Hélène's looks were not lost, and who saved the best cuts of meat for her. And last but not least, at the vintner's we discussed with the critical flair the matter required, which bottle of wine would best complement the meal we were planning. Here we were, two Russian girls bending to local custom and putting together French meals deemed essential by the locals for life's immemorial flow.

But the flow of French life can also be quite turbulent. While we were engrossed in our mellow doings of family and friendship, all around us the larger world was breaking up. It turned out that a general strike was on and all transportation severely hampered. Irène joined us at home. Jean-Pierre, however, who had finished one of France's *grandes écoles*, did not approve of strikes. When the demonstrators blocked his car, he tried to make it to work on his bicycle. But things were too chaotic and he showed up eventually with all kinds of conflicting news.

Apparently, the students had started it all. I perked up: it felt like I was back at Berkeley. Jean-Pierre complained that the French universities were woefully overcrowded and understaffed. The students, instead of buckling down to the traditional rigors of French education, had been left to run loose. Now they idolized Che Guevara, and worse still in Jean-Pierre's opinion, the idiotic pronouncements of Mao's Little Red Book. I, for my part, was impressed that students were taken seriously by labor unions. I did not remember any student-worker partnerships during our days at Berkeley.

The mix of excitement and discomfort all these events produced began to take its toll. School was closed, all four boys were now underfoot, and Jean-Pierre kept pacing up and down in the living room as he held forth on the state of the nation and the world. But when his discourse crossed over from the public domain into the domestic, tempers flared. I felt that I was overstaying my welcome - but how was I to get to my next destination? That was Strasbourg all the way across France by the German border, where the Mandrykas now lived.

Fortunately, all kinds of ad hoc information centers were springing up, and the patient voice of a volunteer directed me by phone. A bus was due to leave Paris on May 17 at 1 a.m. at such and such a corner, and it would be making a stop in Strasbourg. I packed my bags and grabbed Peter, and my friends took me to the unofficial corner in question. The bus filled up and Peter fell asleep in my lap. I looked out the window as we passed through the outlying suburbs of the ancient city. All was quiet, and you would never know that Paris was in the throes of yet another one of its revolutions.

When we arrived in Strasbourg the bus driver took the time to look for the Mandrykas' address and dropped us off in front of their apartment building. It was 6 a.m. When I rang their bell, it was Dr. Mandryka who opened the door.

He stood there for a second or two, his sleep-clogged eyes opening wider and wider. But soon enough the commotion that ensued had all the happy noises of a homecoming. There was, however, a slight hitch. Their spare room was still occupied. A baby-faced, husky young man with a blond crew cut emerged from it: he was an American draft dodger.

This whole trip was definitely not your typical tourist junket, but my stay at the Mandrykas' had a touch of the *folies bergères* just the same. Not the standard stuff: more *Cherry Orchard* with only a dash of French cancan. Compared to the rather measured tone of discourse prevailing at the Castinels', which consisted mostly of Jean-Pierre's soliloquies, there were no holds barred on radical debate at the Mandrykas'. They might be French bourgeois now, but as former Russian aristocrats they were not going to be caught again on the wrong side of a revolution, even a mini one. That was precisely the point. If their Russian forebears had had the sense to make small timely revolutions like the French, the former Russian aristocrats wouldn't have been caught with their pants down when the Big One came along.

The young American was mostly left out of all this, due to deficiency in foreign language skills. His activism confined itself to Alsatian beer. He was just a scared kid who didn't want to die in Vietnam. But how do you talk about that? He just sat there drinking his beer, looking homesick.

In the meantime, the French May Revolution was being taken in hand by the various political parties, who worked to rally popular support behind their various platforms. Daniel Cohn Bendit, the Mario Savio of the French student movement who had been born in Germany, was sent packing back to that country. Charles De Gaulle, harking back to the glory days when his eloquent voice, broadcasted from London, had inspired the French resistance movement against German occupation, called on the French people to stand by their elected government. On May 30, 1968, one million people marched down the Champs-Elysées to support law and order.

My stay in Strasbourg with the Mandrykas was drawing to an end. Rick was about to fly to Brussels from New York, and I needed to make my way there as well. France was still in the grip of transportation strikes, and the only way to get to Belgium was roundabout through Germany. So, our farewells with the Mandrykas took place on the Strasbourg railway platform, where Peter and I boarded a German train.

We watched my beloved Mme. Mandryka and France diminish and float away together. Soon enough, Peter was excited about the roller-coaster effect of our train rumbling over the bridge that took us across the Rhine. We settled in, and I began to tune my ear to the German I had once spoken fluently. It all now registered with a sort of delay, like keeping up with a foreign movie by reading the subtitles. As I was attempting to get a grip on my surroundings, a woman's voice said, "Robert Kennedy ist tot!" Somebody handed me a newspaper. It was dated 6 Juni 1968, and I had heard right: Robert Kennedy was dead. As with the assassination of Jack Kennedy, the news now of Robert Kennedy's assassination also fixed a particular place in memory, a moving train somewhere in Germany.

Once again, the rhythmic sound of German trains was associated with death. I thought of all the people packed in them not all that long ago, and wondered whether they knew that it was to be their last journey. My own first journey through Germany, started in 1944 when I was about six years old, had had a similarly uncertain beginning. But by a throw of the dice, it did not prove terminal.

We had packed rapidly. I watched my grandmother break the wooden frame and protective glass casing of the icon of the Virgin and Child which had blessed her wedding in Russia, but had failed to safeguard it in Yugoslavia. She wrapped the icon in woolen cloth and placed it gently among the other items in her suitcase.

Later they lifted me into a truck's cabin and I settled on Babushka's lap. Mom was already sitting next to Dad, who was at the wheel. The motor gurgled and whined, then settled into a steady growl, and we began to move. But first there had been a lot of fuss about settling in all the other people. Sturdy women and kids with rosy cheeks and a few old men, all dressed in rough dark clothes and carrying big bundles were hoisted up on the back of our truck. I sensed the special privilege Dad's warm cabin afforded, but secretly yearned for the excitement of bouncing around on top of the truck among crates filled with chickens and geese and even a pig.

These people were called "Schwabe," but the official name was *Volksdeutsche*, meaning ethnic Germans. Now that the Soviet troops were about to liberate Yugoslavia, they were opting to "go home" to war-torn Germany, and Dad had been requisitioned to drive them there. In 1944 Tito and his Partisans had the strongest following in the country. Joining Tito or being liberated by the Red Army was a non-choice for a White Russian like my father. Being rounded up by the Occupying Forces for forced labor in Germany was another. It happened that Mom had a Russian émigré friend who was married to an ethnic German. This man, Max Sengevitz, was now organizing a convoy of fellow returnees to Germany. He had some room for negotiating his terms, and Dad was allowed to bring his family along. Going to Germany was hardly "going home" for us, but at least it was "going west."

And so, we left. It must have been late fall, and getting chilly. I remember our first stop-over well; it was some small town in Hungary. Mother, Babushka, and I were left in a room filled with one giant bed. My teeth chattered as they undressed me in the unheated place. I had to climb to the bed by a stepping stool, and I thought the crisp white of the linen must be snow and then there was a free fall and the heavenly cloud of down never broke it. *Feather-soft, light snow everywhere, and Babushka is there too in the sled, and we drift happily... but the soldiers appear, they are "the Reds," their whips hiss like snakes AND THEIR FACES ARE BRIGHT RED, THEY GLOW IN THE DARK*, and Mother is shaking me, still clutching at Babushka. Quiet, we must be quiet, not a sound, get dressed, step out into the night.

We walked to the corner. Our convoy, which had parked on the town square, was gone. Instead, the square was filled with other trucks. Men in uniform stood around, and their cigarettes lighted up briefly like fireflies. We came closer: those men spoke Russian. Mom's grip on my hand was painfully tight. "Red or White" was the question. Mom's hand let up, they were "White:" I could see that for myself, even in the dark. These soldiers told us that our own convoy had been moved a couple of streets down. We walked on and eventually made out familiar shapes in the dark. The front had shifted, they said, it was time to move on. Dad lifted me into the truck's cabin, and I snuggled between him and Mom.

We crossed fields and rivers and mountains. The truck purred, Mom and Dad talked in hushed voices. The word "Vlasov" hovered about like a ghost; it had been "Vlasov's" men we had bumped into in Hungary. These men had been Red and now had turned White. Did they get the color off the way Babushka scrubs my knees before bed?

Who was Vlasov? Born in 1900, the ninth son of a poor peasant, he could thank the Revolution for giving him his chances in life. Just a year younger than my father, he fought on the winning side of radical change, and became one of the outstanding Soviet generals. It was in large measure thanks to him that the Germans were stopped at the gates of Moscow in 1941. And yet in time he made a choice similar to my father's: he organized a National Liberation Army to free Russia from Communism. But to do that he had to rely on German help. No wonder my parents were whispering about this enigmatic figure: a traitor to some, a hero to others.

He had been captured during the desperate fighting in the swamps near the Volkhov River. Stalin had ordered what looked to Vlasov's military judgment a pointless stand. Moreover, this was now enemy-occupied territory, and his soldiers were scattered in the countryside, trampling on foot in the forest, and suffering from cold and hunger. Vlasov entered a village, hoping to find refuge. A village elder, instead, delivered him to the Germans.

It turned out that some segments of the population met the Germans as liberators, or at least ambiguously. This is well known in Ukraine, where resistance had been mounted to Stalin's collectivization. It is well known in the North Caucasus, where a large proportion of the Cossacks had fought on the White side of the Revolution. It is also true for many of those whose families had been repressed or sent to forced labor camps.

Another section of the dissatisfied population was composed of the military. Vlasov, who had focused on his military duties and had avoided politics, had nevertheless observed at close range the "purges" of 1938 associated with the "Tukhachevsky affair." The sources on this issue are still at odds. Some reports state that the German Secret Service had "alerted" Stalin of plots against him by the military under the leadership of General Tukhachevsky. Was that true or a trick to induce Stalin to weaken his military leadership?

And now that Vlasov was a prisoner in German hands, how did it come about that he turned to them for help? He met a number of high-ranking Red Army officers in the prison camp. Some of them now felt safe to express their hatred of the Stalin regime. Rumors of popular uprisings were repeatedly confirmed. Maybe this was a chance to organize an effective political movement to overthrow the Bolshevik government?

Much would depend on the attitude of the Germans. But whether at Hitler's headquarters or on the ground, German policy was one of brutal exploitation and extermination. Germany, lagging behind Britain and France in colonizing the world, was now looking eastward for *Lebensraum* (living space): the Slavs were *Untermenschen* (subhuman) and subjugating them, not liberating them, was the plan.

A number of German leaders, however, saw this policy as utterly ill-advised. The Russian people, once disabused of their hopes of friendly relations with the Germans, would rally around Stalin and unite to defend the fatherland. There was still time, they thought, to convince Hitler to change policy. Thus, some of the Russian prisoners hoped to use war conditions to confront Stalin's regime, and some of the Germans (who would eventually organize a failed attempt on Hitler's life) found common ground.

Vlasov's capture made these projects seem possible. He was one of the ablest and best-known Russian generals – he also had a reputation for personal integrity and a proletarian origin. This made him the perfect rallying figure to lead a national liberation movement. Russian emigres everywhere, my father and maternal grandfather among them, rallied to the cause. It was agreed that the fight would not be about restoring the *ancien régime*, but about actualizing the democratic promises of the February Revolution, which had been "stolen" by the Bolshevik October Revolution.

The big question, of course, was about the conditions of an alliance with the German side. A number of proposals and proclamations composed by Vlasov clarified his aims: to defeat the current Soviet government, and to establish an independent democratic one; to have sole charge of the Russian volunteer army to achieve this; the release of the millions of Russian war prisoners starving in forced labor camps, so that they could join Vlasov's liberation army; and once liberation was achieved, the exercise of the privileges of a free Russian government as a German ally on equal terms.

Repeatedly, however, the hopes of Vlasov's German supporters to sway Hitler's aims of outright conquest were angrily rejected and ridiculed: how dare an *Untermensch* like Vlasov display such arrogance? And after the defeat at Stalingrad, and when the German army was visibly disintegrating under the Soviet advance, the Germans finally turned to the now significant Russian liberation movement – but only to use them as mercenaries.

Thus, Vlasov found himself in an impossible situation. There were suggestions for him to escape to the West. After all, his anti-Communist goals and the democratic traditions of the Western allies fighting Nazi Germany were related. He sent out delegations to the Americans, but refused to take the escape route for himself: this would mean abandoning all those who had shared his vision. As the Anglo-American advance was about to meet the Soviet advance by the Elbe River in 1945, Vlasov's troops were caught in-between. Some elements of his army, mostly the emigres, were allowed to cross over. Vlasov himself and the other generals accompanying him were handed over to the Soviets. There was no public trial in Moscow: they were summarily executed as traitors. Vlasov was hanged.

But our flight from Yugoslavia took place before these events had taken this final turn, and unlike Vlasov's fate, our trust in Max Sengewitz, our own Schindler, proved a winner in the long run. In the meantime, we were now on German territory, and our next stop was Vienna. Our convoy stopped in a side street, and we got off at last to stretch our legs. There was some commotion, however. I looked up. There was Dad, all alone against a wall, and I saw how people's faces change color; his face turned chalk-white, just like the wall behind him. Then there was more commotion. Then Dad took me by the hand, and the four of us walked, and kept walking. He told me later that as we walked, he looked up at a street sign, and it said *Marienhilferstrasse,* the street of Our Lady of Perpetual Help. He turned into it, and knew then that we would be safe.

What had happened, apparently, was that one of the women on his truck was missing a goose and had accused Dad of stealing it. A young punk of the Hitler Youth happened to pass by. Law and order in those days were in the hands of such youths for lack of other men folk, who were all at the front. No problem, the punk put Dad against the wall, and his revolver to his head. An elderly bystander intervened, distracted the punk's attention toward some other deed of valor, and thus saved Dad's life.

This was not the first time an Austrian had had Dad's life in his hands. When World War I broke out in 1914, Dad was still a student in a military academy in the Russian town then called Simbirsk. They let the school out and, at the ripe age of seventeen, Dad was deployed to the battlefront. At some engagement he suddenly found himself face to face with a seasoned Austrian soldier, who disarmed him. The man looked at him, and after a moment's hesitation, told him to "scram." Dad started to walk away, waiting for the bullet to hit him in the back. The bullet never came.

After wandering through the streets of Vienna for some hours we ventured back to where our convoy had been parked. Things had gone back to neutral. I don't know whether the missing goose had ever been restored to its rightful owner or had become someone else's unrightful dinner. At any rate, our *Volksdeutsche* charges had been handed over to proper authorities, and the drivers and their families were bedded down in a school's gym. It was a fun place. We were given folding beds to set up among a mess of parallel bars, trampolines, rings, and balance beams. The physical perfecting of an already perfect race had been completed here and its warrior products sent forth to conquer the world.

I was fascinated by the rings. They hung from the ceiling and swung tantalizingly over our heads. At night when the lights went out, especially on those days when the meals had been meager and the hollow gurgling in my gut was like the strumming of chords looking for a tune, *the hall began to fill with soft crackles and murmurs, and the designs on the ceilings circled and spread like leafy canopies, and the breeze moved the ropes to and fro like jungle lianas... and then the monkeys appeared one by one, and started their show... how they could drop from above or sweep across the whole breadth of the hall... how they let go of their hold, tumbled in mid-air, caught the another ring and disappeared away, taking me with them...*

Before we left Vienna, my parents took me to the famous Prater and a real circus, but I was sorely disappointed. I liked it at first, as a family of bears ambled into the ring. They were running around and acting silly. But then something terrible happened. There were a couple of yapping puppies which kept bothering them, and one of the bears picked them up and threw them into a giant meat grinder, while another bear began to turn the handle. A roar of laughter filled the place when a string of blood-red sausages tumbled out of the other end of the grinder. My screams of horror were so jarring among the general hilarity that my parents hastened to take me out.

But I can't leave Austria without retelling one last related episode. Actually, we need to revisit the time when Mom and Dad and I, this time without Babushka, whose body had been put to its final rest under some French tombstone, boarded a British liner at Gibraltar in 1958 on our way to Australia.

Austria comes into play on this occasion in the person of a young man. I was all of twenty at that point, and deeply immersed in the newly found revelations afforded by the Holy Book. I wore no makeup, affected demure clothing, and a severe hairstyle. I never went on deck without my Bible. When I first glimpsed Hans, however, the Good Book literally slipped out of my hands. His tall, well-proportioned body bore no traces of strenuous molding: it was naturally perfect. So were the regular features of his face, dense mop of pale blond hair, and blue eyes the color of the very depth of the sea. One look into those eyes and I was a body drowning.

I had initially feared that he might be British. Upon finding out that he was Austrian I thanked my lucky stars for having had the foresight to postpone the study of English in school in favor of holding on to my fund of German. Now Mom was urging me to make up for lost time by cultivating English-speaking fellow travelers, but her advice fell on deaf ears. I had a different kind of education in mind, if "mind" is the right word for it. Any distinction between mind and body was purely scholastic.

Unfortunately, handsome Hans paid me absolutely none of *his* mind. But is not all fair in love and war? Still, those were the fifties, and the register of what used to be called our feminine wiles was rather limited. I crossed Hans' path casually, but of course I couldn't actually accost him. I displayed my wit and charm within earshot, but ostensibly for someone else's benefit. I danced and played the silly games people play on board ship, keeping Hans on my radar screen all the while. But the sum total of these efforts came to naught. Hans seemed not just indifferent; he actually appeared to avoid me. Now that was something: indifference is one thing, avoidance another.

I had picked up on the right clue. A ship, after all, is not a large place. We kept bumping into each other, and the sheer flood of pheromones I was sending his way must have finally broken him down. He asked to be introduced. After the *Sturm und Drang* of my pursuit I prepared to yield to romance. NOT SO FAST. Soon enough Hans told me that yes, he had been avoiding me: it was because I was Russian. REALLY?

It was like this. His father had been a manual worker, and, touched by the great hope of proletarian deliverance, had become a member of the Austrian Communist Party. He had gone on marches and clashed with Nazi counter-marchers. Eventually there was a knock on the door of their apartment in the middle of the night, and little Hans watched men in uniform take his dad away. Hans never saw him again. But the memory of him and of what he had believed in, remained. That's why Hans and his mother and sister couldn't wait for the Red Army to liberate Vienna. They came at last, knocked on the door of his apartment in broad daylight, and young Hans watched them rape his sister.

So, all's fair in love and war... A wave of shame swept over me, as if my own longing, this blood's rush toward contact with Hans' body had been of a piece with the soldiers' forced penetration of that other young body, Hans' sister.

Hans took my hand. I had been waiting for this for so long, but now this simple gesture had too much to bridge. Can the story of Romeo and Juliet have a happy end? Say, Juliet wakes from her deathlike sleep, and Romeo's wound is not fatal, and the dead body of Mercutio between them is no object, and the Montagues and the Capulets kiss and make up, and no one on the United Nations Security Council vetoes the deal...

But now we were both on our way to Australia, the *terra incognita* of new beginnings - surely there was a chance? Hans, as it turned out, wasn't much of a Romeo to begin with. He was rather used to having his way with the "weaker" sex, and he had had neither practice nor much need of poetic balcony scenes. But then neither was I much of a Juliet - more a budding shrew. In a weird reversal of earlier behavior, I began to avoid Hans and he began to pursue me. It was his turn to make a spectacle of himself. He dove into the pool not from the diving board but from the upper deck of the ship, and was called in to the captain for reprimand. I was flattered, naturally, but his response was now so driven that it set off all my alarm bells.

His proposing marriage, this apparent token of male self-sacrifice, failed to disarm me. It looked like war by other means. Our war of the sexes seemed to mirror the sad history of our warring countries. We could not replicate the gesture of the Austrian soldier who had let my father live. I did not know how to heal Hans, and he had no clue that I might have wounds of my own. Life's Shakespearean plot could simply not be recast into an episode of "Dreamboat." When we landed in Sydney, we called a truce and, sadly, went our separate ways.

And here I was, on my train to Brussels in 1968, confronted by the German language again after so many years, on my way to meeting my life's mate who was not, fortunately, a Shakespearean hero. There he was on the station's platform, surrounded by all his relatives: Frank and Francine of course, and *oncle* Pierre and *tante* Berthe, and cousins and cousins' kids. They grabbed Peter and passed him from hand to hand, and there was much tribal affirmation.

I was surprised by the jollity and business-as-usual mood of the Belgians. Sure, there had been some student unrest earlier on, the usual stuff between Catholics and Liberals, but nothing had come of it. Sure, they discussed the doings of their volatile neighbors to the south, but felt that the turmoil would sensibly stop at the border. Besides, it looked like the General had things well in hand there again, so why not eat, drink, and be merry? And, of course, host a review of Brussels' treasures.

I must confess I was disappointed by the famous *Grande Place*. Its architecture looked like a marriage between Versailles and a sober row of Dutch houses with stepped roofs. Their progeny looked like neither of the parents and too much of both. The fact that the "grand" square was one big parking lot at the time didn't help either. But who was I to comment on the stylistic issue of two cultures? I followed everyone on a pilgrimage to the *Manneken Pis* and tried to "get" Rubens, with his fleshy nymphs lounging on fleshy clouds and his monumental Christs monumentally crucified.

A trip to the blurred Belgian shore gave me an insight into Rick's passion for southern seas and cloudless skies. It was on such a murky day that we indulged Peter's passion for climbing steps. He had already mastered the steps to the Capitol in Washington, D.C., and those to both the Lincoln and Jefferson Memorials. They were but a training ground for the Olympic performance of the 226-step climb up the memorial to Napoleon's defeat at Waterloo. Like Sylvester Stallone's "Rocky" on the steps of the Philadelphia Art Museum raising his arms in victory, Peter expressed his exultation by saying his very first words. He pointed at the stately Lion of Flanders who crowns the monument, and said: *"c'est le mouton!"* (it's the sheep).

His Biblical equalization of the lion and the lamb seemed quite fitting for the occasion. As I gazed down upon the drizzle-soaked plain, I recalled the French General Cambronne's famous retort at the battle of Waterloo. When called upon to surrender, the General's last word, perhaps also summarizing Napoleon's great adventure from the sands of Egypt to the snows of Russia, was *"MERDE!"* - "SHIT!"

Our Belgian visit was coming to an end. I would get other chances to revise these first impressions. We were anxious to move on to the next and final leg of our trip, a week in Paris for Rick and me alone. The family had offered to keep a collective watch over Peter and we were free to go. Many among the tribe, however, shook their heads in disapproval, trying to warn us of the dangers lurking south of the border. Nothing doing; it was Paris or bust.

The trains were running again, more or less, and Rick knew the city well. We had booked a room on the Left Bank at the *Hotel du Danube*. We arrived there full of *joie de vivre*, newlyweds all over again. As we were putting our things away and getting ready to see Paris, Paris, instead, came to us. I opened the window and there on the street below I watched as if from an opera balcony, a version of *Les Miserables*. People were running around, tossing what looked like lab tables and auditorium chairs onto a mounting pile. I called to Rick that the Parisians were building us a barricade, but he thought I was pulling his leg, and exercised his Flemish cool by staying put. By the time he took my jumping up and down at the window seriously and stepped up, the barricade was being stormed, and two white-clad men were running by, carrying somebody on a stretcher.

Evidently things had not been as settled as they had looked from the Belgian border. Daniel Cohn Bendit was back in Paris, and De Gaulle's decree to ban protests had provoked renewed actions, one of which we were witnessing just then. Now that Rick realized what was going on, he grabbed his camera, and we rushed outside to see for ourselves. When, however, we encountered an advancing black wall of fiberglass shields surmounted by dark helmets, we decided on a tactical retreat to our hotel room and joined those who, that night, made love, not war.

Our stay in Paris was something of a letdown after that fireworks beginning, if it could ever be said that Paris could let you down. At any rate, we walked about without further hindrance and did the usual things available for young impecunious tourists: lingering in cafes on one cup of coffee, rifling through the offerings of bouquinistes (used book sellers) on the banks of the Seine, strolling on bridges, and resting in cathedrals. Two doors away from our own hotel, a plaque caught our attention. It stated that on September 3, 1782 Benjamin Franklin, John Adams and John Jay had signed there the Treaty of Paris, which had concluded the Revolutionary War and recognized American independence.

I recalled Mt. Rushmore. Somehow this modest plaque on an ordinary house challenged all the majesty of Mt. Rushmore because it exemplified the human scale which makes democracy possible. It occurred to me that Mt. Rushmore said more about Gutzon Borglum, the sculptor and promoter of the project, than about the presidents it memorializes. A card-carrying member of the Ku Klux Klan, he had hit on the ultimate manifestation of the monumental, a model the twentieth century would emulate. Hitler and Mussolini would proclaim the glories of the master race in their public extravaganzas, while the giant statues of Lenin and Stalin competed with them, manifesting proletarian victory. Had Washington and Jefferson not objected to statues made in their likeness because they saw them as symbols of tyranny?

That resisting tyranny is a never-ending task was well illustrated by our visit of the Pantheon. Louis XV, King of France by the grace of God, wished to make a final statement against the trouble-making philosophes. He commissioned the church of St. Genevieve, the patron saint of Paris, to be rebuilt to emulate the grandeur of St. Peter's in Rome and the elegance of St. Paul's in London. But no sooner was the modern church to end all modern churches finished than the French Revolution of 1789 broke out. The new regime commandeered the church into secular service. Voltaire's remains, which had had to be smuggled into an ordinary cemetery under cover of darkness before the Revolution, were now moved with great pomp into what became known as "The Pantheon."

Then Napoleon, upon having himself crowned emperor, returned the building to St. Genevieve, reserving the crypt for the remains of great dead Frenchmen. The restoration of the monarchy which followed in 1815, however, would have none of it. But no sooner was Napoleon's head in the dome's fresco painted over into the features of Louis XVIII than the Revolution of 1830 broke out, ushering in a time when king Louis Philippe and the bourgeoisie cooperated under the slogan *enrichissez-vous* (enrich yourselves). But this left most of the people out of the game, and following Marx's *Communist Manifesto*, the popular revolution of 1848 broke out, and the contested building became "The Temple of Humanity."

Not for long. Napoleon III was crowned emperor and restored the temple to religious service yet again. But he was defeated by the newly united Germans in the war of 1870, and the people tried yet again to turn the march of history by declaring The Commune. The rebels deployed a red flag on the church's dome, but the regular French troops spattered its steps with their blood. The building was re-dedicated once more to a secular function in 1885 on the occasion of Victor Hugo's death. In a spirit of conciliation, the frescoes depicting the life of St. Genevieve remain in place in what is, once again, the Pantheon.

These musical chairs of political self-definition were hardly what Louis XV had intended upon planning his grand monument to the glory of king and faith. I wondered whether the towering mass of Mt. Rushmore, the immovable marker at the heart of the Western frontier, could be budged as well. The Native American Movement had indeed attempted to recover what was, to them, ancestral sacred ground. Like the French Pantheon, can Mt. Rushmore be reclaimed for change, and its presidents, no longer Sphinx-like tombstones, re-engaged in democratic dialogue?

And so, my first return trip to Europe had proved quite eventful. I had reconnected with old friends, and unwittingly found myself witnessing the aftereffects of a social earthquake whose early tremors I had caught back in Berkeley. The French student rebellion, as it turned out, was mostly an assertion of cultural liberation. The French, as they are wont to do, turn to their intellectuals for inspiration: and now Sartre and Camus were being crowded out by new, "post-modern," philosophers. Like the American New Left, they too sponsored a new priority: identity politics and international human rights.

In Germany and Italy, the '60s rebellions were also tamed. The Italian Red Brigades had nowhere to go. They were hemmed in by the American-sponsored conservative Christian party on one side, and the sizable Communist party, which was focusing on salvaging diminishing workers' rights, on the other.

The German Bader-Meinhof Group lasted longer, but was eventually dissolved as well. The Green Party absorbed the energies of the protesters, and Daniel Cohn-Bendit's leadership talents were redirected at castigating the human rights violations across the Iron Wall. But then Leonid Brezhnev had obliged by invading Czechoslovakia in 1968.

Our vacation was over. We met Frank, Francine, and Peter at the Paris airport, and proceeded to board a plane due home.

***

CHAPTER 9

GHOSTS

At home we picked up where we had left off. The playgrounds and pediatricians and Laundromats of Queens were still there, and my crying spells, faithful storms over the familiar landscape, returned. Something had to give. If there was no way to change the external landscape, maybe my internal landscape could do with some restructuring?

It was suggested that I try psychotherapy. I had heard something of Freudian slips and Freudian jokes, and I was willing. I showed up for preliminary evaluation. Those were the days of the Rorschach test. I don't know what possessed me, but I decided to give Freud a run for his money (actually, it was my money). I described in great detail how the symmetrical designs they gave me made me think of vaginas.

If truth be told, I didn't actually know what a vagina looked like. I had been put in a nun school at the appropriate age, and no one had even warned me about menstruation. When the first flow happened, I thought I suffered from some mysterious plague and would bleed to death. When the time came to put away childish things, it was penises large and small that were shown off to me, while vaginas still remained unvisualized. Except when I watched in a mirror Peter's head pushing out through a distended, tearing opening.

In any event, that's how I engaged Messrs. Freud and Rorschach and the man who opened the door and invited me to lie down on his therapeutic couch. When he asked me, what was going through my head, I told him I felt uncomfortable in the obligatory horizontal position he had assigned me. Considering the "evidence" I had volunteered in my test, I don't know why I was so surprised when his next question was whether I expected him to jump my bones. I sat up and looked at him. I would NEVER want YOU to jump my bones, I thought. Politely, I offered the opinion that I had had power relations in mind, not sex. Neither one of us was equipped to read my virtuoso Rorschach performance as a "vagina monologue."

But we tried, both of us. The therapist beat a quick retreat from our false start, the couch was pushed aside in favor of a chair, and we focused on the usual suspect, namely Mom. Of course, I did have issues with Mother; who doesn't? After all, she is the one who pushes you out screaming into the world, and she is the one who does too little or too much ever after. Mom, as it happened, was just then claiming center stage not only in my repressed self, but in the actual here-and-now. We hadn't seen each other in three years and the birth of her first grandchild so far away had stirred up a whirlwind of longing in her. Was the course of our lives permanently set oceans apart? It was not in Mom's character to accept fate lying down. She convinced Maurice that they too should emigrate to the U.S., and so we signed the sponsorship papers.

While we worked on their immigration application, we had another decision to make. It had been over five years since we came to the United States, and it was time to address the question of U.S. citizenship. I recalled Dad's faithful allegiance to Tsar and Russia long after there was neither Tsar nor Russia to be faithful to. Surely it was admirable to be a man of his word, but now I had my doubts. Even at the dawn of the twentieth century the Russian tsar had still been the "anointed of God" who was expected to run a vast and troubled empire single-handed. And he was making an unholy mess of the job. Yet Dad, prompted by family tradition and military training, had been prepared to die for him anyway.

But did Dad's loyalties have to be my loyalties? The map of my own national allegiances had been perfectly scrambled. If I had absorbed a certain family culture oriented toward nostalgia and idealization of pre-revolutionary Russia, this made me Russian mostly by proxy. If I happened to be born in Yugoslavia, was this not accidental? If I was schooled in German and French, who would want to be German during World War II or French in its disintegrating colonies? And it was only in Australia that anybody could have thought of me as Moroccan. Finally, how Belgian did it make me to be married to a Belgian?

Yet I had acquired these provisional identities, felt linked to them through shared experiences and cultural ties and entitled to every one of my hyphens.

Now it was a question of entering a brand-new national identity, only this time in the full consciousness of adulthood. That, at any rate, is the theory, like the argument for adult baptism. I recalled the mammoth Billy Graham rally I had attended back in my Baptist days in Sydney. People of all ages had streamed down the aisles of a huge stadium, and gathered on the field below: they had "made a decision for Christ." The choir had rocked the whole place with hallelujahs and Billy Graham's magnified voice lead on from above. For a moment I too had wanted to descend into that Roman arena to brave the lions of iniquity, wearing a white gown like Jean Simmons in The Robe. I had wanted to be made new.

But I had already crossed that line back in Morocco, and as we struggled on in Australia, my makeover proved disappointing. I was still the sensible young woman with limited options I had always been.

To help me in my decision about American citizenship, I thought back to Mt. Rushmore and its giant presidents. But my understanding of what they represented was still sketchy. Actually George Washington, the most remote of the mythical presidents now appeared the most accessible. Something about this father figure who had presided over the birth of the nation made me think of my own father. Not physically, to be sure. Dad had nothing of the stolid statesman in powdered wig. Yet what we know of Washington's dogged soldiering, his steadfast course amidst the political passions swirling around him, his timely withdrawal from the temptations of power, his freeing of his own slaves...

Of course, Dad's life had none of Washington's opportunities for greatness and he was the opposite of a revolutionary hero... and yet, there was something about them both of the country gentleman, of faithful service, of detachment and self-effacement, of kindness. Dad had been confined to a mostly private expression of these old-fashioned virtues. And who knows if Washington could have run on such qualities for public office today? It seemed that my "decision for America" had to be something of another leap of faith after all.

Ready or not, I decided to go ahead. I decided to bet on Jefferson. In his fiery Declaration of Independence, he had put the future of America in the hands of ordinary people – and this spelled the promise of America to me, this was what I was willing to pledge allegiance to. So, we stood before some official in some non-descript place in Queens, but this didn't matter. What mattered was that we stepped forward, raised our hand, and pledged.

Soon thereafter we found out that Mom's immigration visa had been denied: she had failed the interview at the American consulate. As far as we could make out, she had been cross-examined about her bout with mental illness, had acted fearful and evasive, and had been disqualified.

I had always identified with the Statue of Liberty. I liked her because she was a woman, and because she came from France, and because she lights the way to New York Harbor. Now I was having second thoughts. I began to understand why James Baldwin had felt betrayed by her. In raising her torch to welcome boatloads of white immigrants she had quite forgotten that her maker Bartholdi had intended her to celebrate the liberation of black slaves. Location, as they say in real estate, is everything. The Lady of Liberty was reclaimed by New York Harbor the way Mt. Rushmore had reclaimed Paha Sapa, the sacred Black Hills of South Dakota. Now it was my turn to feel betrayed by Emma Lazarus' "Lady of Exile." We had all been prepared to do what we felt to be right for Mom, but our newly chosen government, in its wisdom, had saved us from ourselves.

All this happened shortly before the elections of 1968, and remembering the big cruciform sculptures I had seen back on an empty beach in the Bay Area, I proclaimed my brand-new American identity by putting my name down for write-in candidate Dick Gregory, the black comedian, author, health advocate and Civil Rights activist.

But I couldn't dwell on Mom's troubles any more than I had been able to dwell on Babushka's troubles in the days of her decline. Peter claimed my attention and filled my days. We were stepping out of the local library one day. While I watched him practice counting the library's steps, a conversation developed with an elderly man. As often happens, he tried to place my accent. When he found out that Russian was one of the elements in it, he volunteered that his folks had come from Russia as well. He wanted to know my maiden name. When I gave him the name Litvinov/a, he approved it as "a good Jewish name." I told him that we were not Jewish, and asked him whether he was thinking of Maxim Litvinov, Stalin's Commissar for Foreign Affairs, but the reference was not familiar to him.

What's in a name? Once again, I recalled the particular intonation of Dad's voice when the matter of Maxim Litvinov came up. It was tense with bitterness. That *that* man, whose real name was Vallakh-Finkelstein, had appropriated the honorable name of Litvinov (whose family crest went back to the 15th century, no less) in order to besmirch it by association to Lenin and Stalin, was an unbearable insult.

Maxim Litvinov had indeed been born into a Jewish family in Bialystok in 1876. I found no reference as to why he settled on the name of Litvinov at some point, but the reason for the name change is hardly mysterious. As a capable and ambitious young man, he was looking for ways to circumvent the limits placed on Jews in the Russian Empire of his day. Like others of his generation, he was exposed to the writings of Karl Marx and the Russian radicals, and joined the Social Democratic Party.

Arrested in Kiev in 1901 for operating an illegal press, he managed to escape from prison, and joined Lenin in exile. From Switzerland he carried out the assignment of smuggling the revolutionary journal *Iskra* (the Spark) into Russia. When the October Revolution erupted in 1917, Maxim Litvinov returned to Russia and was soon nominated commissar (or minister) for foreign affairs, a post he retained through the 1920s and '30s.

The West had been opposed to the political changes in the Russian Empire, and had fielded interventionist armies during the Civil War, followed by economic sanctions and trade boycotts. In the face of a resurgent Germany, however, Maxim Litvinov had attempted to create collective security initiatives at the League of Nations. But his efforts proved unsuccessful. Ultimately, the West felt more comfortable dealing with Hitler.

All this kept the Soviet Union isolated and finally exhausted Maxim Litvinov's credit with Stalin. He was replaced by Molotov, and the Soviet-German Pact was signed in 1939. Stalin was counting on the German Reich and the West to exhaust each other in battle as they had done in World War I. No one expected the lightening successes of the Nazis in Western Europe.

Maxim Litvinov had started out with the idealistic dream of "a Russia without prisons." That he survived Stalin's purges is apparently due to his indispensable international experience and to a turn of mind which shunned ideological fervor and factional power struggles. We know little about the evolution of his convictions, except that his grandson, Pavel Litvinov, was a Soviet dissident in 1968. As to the name of Finkelstein, whether Norman Finkelstein is related to Litvinov's ancestors or not, the tradition of dissidence is carried on in his challenge to the Israel/Palestine situation.

During that discussion on the steps of the Rego Park library I could have given the Jewish man the foolproof argument of my non-Jewishness. I had been in a forced labor camp in Germany toward the end of World War II, and still lived to tell. Of course, there are Jewish survivors of such camps, and millions of non-Jews perished as well (the numbers, in the latest research, approximate 11 million). Still, while some Jewish men and women survived by virtue of some practical use, their children were automatically disposed of.

These pragmatic classifications went as follows: "unusable" Jews, gypsies, homosexuals and the disabled were pretty much slated for extermination, while others were saved for the privilege of slave labor. This process owed its efficiency to IBM's new technology of punch-card indexes. Hitler's government had been an eager client, and thus the numbers burned into people's forearms had their counterparts in these early versions of the IBM card.

There were all kinds of gradations within gradations. Mother had found out through the grapevine that it was safer to be Yugoslav than Russian, so before leaving Belgrade we acquired Yugoslav passports. My name, I was told, was no longer Galina Litvinov(a) but Mira Mirković. To make this stick Mom would wake me in the middle of the night and ask my name, and I was expected to rattle out: "I am Mira Mirković!" After this test, I could go back to sleep again.

Thanks to this (or because of our connection to Max Sengevitz), after leaving Vienna we had ended up in a work camp that was not one of the more notorious *Ostarbeiter* work camps for the *Untermenschen* (the "subhumans" from the East, i.e., Russians, Ukrainians, Byelorussians and Poles). The POWs we came across in our camp were French, Belgian and Dutch, and we were not even fenced in by barbed wire. The place was located on the edge of the little town of Blankenburg, on the northern rim of the Harz Mountains.

This compact mountain range was then smack in the middle of the pre-war map of Germany, which still included a sizable chunk of what has since become Poland. It was in the Harz Mountains, on its highest peak, the Brocken, that Goethe's Faust was taken to cavort with hoofed devils and alluring witches on *Walpurgisnacht*, the pagan celebration of spring. But the witches' sabbath the war was to bring to the region was not yet in full swing. A big chunk of Germany's war industry was being transferred into a vast system of tunnels under the Harz Mountains, and Wernher von Braun, the rocket genius, was pursuing his scientific ventures in a neighboring town.

Once we got to Blankenburg, Max Sengevitz' trucks were no longer in evidence. Mom and Dad disappeared into factory work from daybreak to late at night, while Babushka and I stayed in the barracks. Winter had come by then. When someone opened the door and let in a gust of prickly frost, I watched their footprints slowly lose their crisp white imprint of snow, melt into slush, and finally fade into the ever-present liquid mire on the concrete floor.

One day I stepped outside through that door, and some men in white pajamas with blue stripes, a long parade of them walking five abreast, came marching along, accompanied by armed soldiers. Just as they were going to pass me, they broke rank and threw themselves on a dark mound. And at the eye-level of the six-year-old I was then, as in a movie close-up, the only other thing I remember is a huge boot landing with a thud on the heap of bodies crawling, heedless, over what turned out to be a pile of raw potatoes, black with frost rot.

We too were hungry. One day Mom took me and Helena Ricin, the daughter of one of the other truck drivers in our original convoy, into the forest behind our camp. It was cold, our feet crunched in the snow. Eventually we came to a cheerful-looking house. Mom said it was a school. She had approached the director, a Frau Döppner, with a request to admit us. Mom, having been raised by a German governess, was fluent in the language, and Frau Döppner listened. She turned out not to be a witch and like Hansel and Gretel, we were spared the fate of baking in Nazi ovens.

The smell of steaming potatoes at lunch time became the smell of life itself. And when on occasion there were also ersatz sausages, the solemn ritual of their distribution became something miraculous, something akin to the Biblical multiplication of loaves and fishes. Everyone else received one sausage, while the girls from the camp were each given two.

One day Frau Döppner came in wearing black. She said her brother had been killed on the Russian front. Her husband was in Russia as well, still alive she hoped. It felt like a thin thread was connecting his survival there and mine here.

Survival was not to be taken for granted, however. Some had been granted that random miracle, or so it seemed. We got word, probably through a letter passed on by the Red Cross, that a sister of Babushka's was now somewhere in Germany with her daughter's family. That letter had brought news of the utter decimation of Babushka's family back in Russia. They had been doctors and engineers and professors, and the men folk had pretty much disappeared into the Gulag. A tiny remnant had opted not to escape when Kharkov was occupied by the Germans. They ended up in Germany, a camp near Magdeburg, not very far from our own Blankenburg.

Survival was not to be taken for granted. At some point toward the end of that winter of 1944, heavy Allied bombing came to our region as well. One day I was standing outside with Dad and some other men. They were pointing toward Halberstadt. The ground was flat in that direction, but I couldn't see anything. After a while, something like low clouds gathered on the horizon, though the day was sunny and the sky blue. "They are having a field day," the men said. Slowly, those clouds thickened, rose and blotted out the sun. The men spoke of a good day for "the Brocken Ghost." Later they said there was nothing left of Halberstadt: it must have been a hungry ghost. We heard that Magdeburg, a much larger town, was also hard hit around that time, and after those heavy bomb raids, we never heard from Babushka's sister again. We tried and tried after the war was over, but to no avail.

The Nazis had bombed London in the early phase of the war. Air Vice-Marshal Sir Arthur Harris, who had been testing the fledgling Royal Air Force by bombing Iraqi villages in the '20s, now organized the blanket bombing of German cities. But the policy of targeting civilian populations to achieve enemy demoralization failed on all these occasions - if the killing of hundreds of thousands of people can be called a failure.

Soon enough it was our turn to dance to the tune of the Grim Reaper. The German field commanders had assumed that the American advance would bypass the Harz and speed on toward Berlin. They had gathered a sizable force and were prepared to hold out in the wood-covered mountains. Blankenburg was chosen as their headquarters. But the Americans were not prepared to be outflanked, and started storming the Harz "fortress." There was heavy fighting, but one town after another was taken.

The German population was still called upon to stand and fight. Youngsters fifteen and younger were armed with hunting rifles and sent into the woods to resist. They were called the Werewolves. There was a rumor that some Russian POWs had broken out of one of the camps and were now hiding out in the nearby woods. The Werewolves were given the job to hunt them down.

The Americans advanced and the historic town of Goslar was given the ultimatum to surrender or be destroyed. When the German troops were given orders to resist, Colonel Poppe took it upon himself to disobey and his action saved Goslar. A similar decision by Colonel Petri in the town of Wernigerode resulted in his summary execution and the subsequent destruction of the town by the Americans.

Soon enough Blankenburg was in the same situation of confusion and contradicting orders. Gallows were set up on the *Adolf Hitler Platz* (Adolph Hitler Square) as a warning. When it was discovered that the Nazi leaders had vanished from town, the civilian population was emboldened to accept surrender. But the German troops holed up in favorable high ground positions above the town were determined to fight on. So, we became eligible for some days of softening up. This meant bombing and strafing by Allied planes and shelling from the German positions.

The town fathers decided to shelter the population of Blankenburg in the system of tunnels dug deep into the mountainside. The job of digging had been done by those men in "striped pajamas" I had seen. (Some 25,000 corpses were subsequently discovered by the Americans in a nearby camp sporting the pretty name of Dora). Mom found out about the shelter project, and decided to smuggle Babushka and me into the safety of those tunnels. Mom and Dad took us to the entrance of the tunnels, and instructed us to keep mum. Babushka took me firmly by the hand, and together with a huge crowd of other safety seekers, we soon found ourselves in a vast hollowed out cave. Happily, we were uncovered and promptly ejected before Mom and Dad had even left their vigil by the entrance.

From then on when the sirens screeched, we ran into the nearby forest and hid behind rocks. On one of those occasions, I was lying close to the moist earth. Patches of snow lingered between the roots of big trees. The ground ahead sloped toward a gurgling brook, and on its banks, I discovered an endless sea of violets. It was springtime.

And spring brought Liberation. On April 20, 1945, American troops entered Blankenburg. The Germans were now holed up in the houses that were still standing, and all the various camps erupted into wild celebration. Russians came from a nearby POW camp. The fact that they were Soviet men and Dad was, as they had been taught, "a bloodthirsty White guardsman," did not seem to matter. They fraternized as Russians. They invited him to join them on some forays into neighboring German villages. They suspected that there was food to be had, stashed away by German farmers. Perhaps they remembered their parents doing the same when the city commissars had come requisitioning in the villages back in the Motherland. But my "bloodthirsty guardsman" of a father called it looting and refused to go. Mother was less particular, and over his objections the boys hauled in a sack of flour, sugar, and fresh eggs. They were invited to a real Russian Easter with "*kulich*" (the Russian *brioche*) and hard-boiled eggs. Babushka had managed to color them, though the only color available, made from boiled onion skins, was yellow.

Everybody was urging me to eat. I remember the *gogol'- mogol'* Mom was trying to spoon into me, a concoction of raw eggs and sugar beaten into a creamy goo and much derided in Nabokov's *Memoir*. I just couldn't swallow the thing. Food, which had been at the center of all our preoccupations for so long, had lost its appeal to me.

There was someone else who was not celebrating either: Frau Döppner. She came to visit us in our camp, and we sat outside. There was music and dancing on some sort of makeshift platform. Frau Döppner watched the local German girls carrying on with foreign soldiers and former prisoners, and tears streamed down her cheeks. It was Frau Döppner, however, who identified my problem. She took me to a German doctor, who diagnosed me with TB. She then arranged for me to be placed in the local hospital, and it wasn't a day too soon. I am told my life hung by a thread. I don't know whether Frau Doppner's husband, at the other end of that thread, survived. His odds were slim.

I was seven by then, and Mom and Babushka took turns visiting and reading to me in the hospital. Somebody had given us a book, *Katya i Sharik,* ("Katya and Puff"). It was a story about a girl named Katia and her beloved dog Sharik. Their adventures of loss and recovery mingled with the course of my illness and the highs and lows of my fever. Sensing that I had my loved ones over a barrel, I had them read the book over and over again. At long last I must have passed the critical point of my illness and Mom rebelled. She had Babushka explain the letters to me, and during the long days of recovery at the hospital, I taught myself to read from *Katya i Sharik.*

One night something happened that was just as exciting as what I had read in my book. I was awakened in the middle of the night. Mom was leaning over me, a finger to her lips. While all the other people in the hospital ward sat up to watch, Dad snatched me out of bed, wrapped me up in my blanket and carried me out. His old truck stood by the curb and they handed me up to Babushka who was already inside the cab. Mom and Dad jumped in as well, and we took off. The road was winding and narrow and it looked like the pine trees were leaning over to hold us back. I knew I wasn't supposed to cry, but I couldn't help it. I was positive Werewolves were lurking in that forest, and the "Brocken Ghost" was after us. "There is no such thing as Werewolves… and the Brocken Ghost is a natural phenomenon due to colliding mists" Mom kept whispering.

BUT WHY WAS SHE WHISPERING? She was whispering because they were all cocking their ears for gun shots. Max Sengevitz had it on good authority that in accordance with the agreements reached at the Yalta Conference in February of 1945, Blankenburg was going to be handed over to the Red Army. The British, who had taken over from the Americans, registered everybody and gave strict orders to stay put. We were defying that order, and taking some back road out. But we made it to Goslar that night, where we joined Max Sengevitz' reconstituted convoy. The very next morning Soviet troops did enter Blankenburg.

Many years later, after the fall of the Berlin Wall, I did get a chance to revisit Blankenburg. Rick and I traveled there in the summer of 2002. What struck me then was that Blankenburg was in fact a town, even an attractive resort town, and not just a set of barracks on the edge of the forest. I had known nothing of the picturesque houses of the upper town, or the castle on the hill. The local nobleman, it turns out, was allied not only to the royal house of Prussia, but also to the royal houses of England and Greece and Spain. The castle, however, was now abandoned. The lord of the manor had made a timely escape west with trucks full of the castle's contents, which apparently included an invaluable art collection given into his safe-keeping.

Another escapee from that region was none other than Wernher von Braun. Together with some 500 of his engineers he had managed to steal a train, cross Germany, and take refuge in the American Zone. He was to become the director of NASA. Since then, the starry-eyed exploration of space has been redefined. *The Strategic Master Plan of 2004* of the Air Force Space

Command states: "Our vision calls for prompt global strike space systems with the capability to directly apply force from or through space against terrestrial targets." Von Braun's transition from German "master race" to American "Master of Space," the current logo of the American space program, was not too strenuous, like dropping the "h" from his first name or becoming a born-again Christian in Texas. There is definitely something about Texas that seems to facilitate miraculous transitions from sinner to saved.

During that visit to Blankenburg in 2002, I did try to find what happened to Frau Döppner. Phone books had been discontinued under Soviet occupation, however, as a standard security practice, and I was unable to find her. We also failed to find our old labor camp. It had been razed by the Soviet-German authorities, and a workers' housing project had been built in its place. We drove through neat streets named Karl Marx and Friedrich Engels and Rosa Luxemburg and Karl Liebknecht, and others less familiar.

I also looked for the hospital associated with the adventures of *Katya i Sharik*. It was pointed out to me, a set of small, inter-connected buildings called the *Thiehospital*. I approached two elderly women who were sunning themselves on a bench, and we struck up a conversation. One of them was a local inhabitant, and we shared childhood memories. Just as I had been unaware of the town of Blankenburg, she had been unaware of the concentration camps which had surrounded it. Soviet occupation, however, was something else, for by then she had been old enough to observe. Some people did O.K., while others did not. People became suspicious of each other again, the way it had been in Hitler's time.

At that point the other woman took her turn. She was a refugee from Danzig, now Gdansk in Poland. All ethnic Germans were expelled out of newly reconstituted Poland and Czechoslovakia. But then Poles had also been ejected from what used to be Eastern Poland, now ceded to the Soviet Union. All of these people, (the Germans called "repatriates," the Poles called "expellees") added up, together with the likes of us (called "displaced") to some forty to fifty million. The woman who was sunning herself on a bench in Blankenburg had lost all of her family during the turmoil, and was now ending her days alone.

It was getting late, and we left the two women to their memories. Our drive to Goslar was sunny, the road well-traveled, and the town itself a miraculously preserved page out of a book of German fairy tales. None of it helped me shake my belief in werewolves and ghosts.

After a brief stay in Goslar, Rick and I drove on to Dresden. I had not known the town before, only the pictures of its desolation in black and white after the firebombing of April 1945, and Kurt Vonnegut's evocation in *Slaughterhouse-Five*. Dresden's baroque heart was now beating again, bravely reproduced with exacting accuracy into a likeness of centuries past. Together with swarms of other tourists we feasted upon its art works. But our stay was curtailed because of the floods. It kept raining and the river Elbe kept rising. Rick had wanted to include an excursion to Prague, but the mountain road between Dresden and Prague was now cut off.

We decided to replace Prague with Weimar. Traffic was heavy because of the flood, but we arrived in Weimar at last, and with this unpremeditated visit, stumbled into the very heart of German myth. The first impression is quite innocuous. It's nothing like the sky scrapers of New York, or Mt. Rushmore, or the French Pantheon. The small-town aura was exactly the point, a throwback to a Germany that had pursued its existence in the breathing spaces left by Austria and Prussia.

We visited the Church of St. Peter and Paul. There, on the right panel of Lucas Cranach's triptych, I recognized Martin Luther himself. We probably know his features thanks to that very painting. He had been a frequent preacher at the pulpit here, and as a result, Weimar had become a vital center of the Protestant Movement. The local barons, seeing their chance to evade the control of the Holy Roman Emperor, had championed the cause. But when men of all social stations tried to claim the same privilege, and the *Bauernkrieg* or the Peasant War broke out, Luther sided with the princes and preached law and order. The result was a theology of *Innerlichkeit* or inwardness, a separation of inner spiritual freedom from outer secular or political freedom - and ultimately a tradition of obediently rendering unto Cesar that which he claimed to be his.

But the energy thus directed toward subjective and speculative pursuits also brought about the extraordinary German accomplishments in music and philosophy. As we stood in the little church of St. Peter and Paul it felt as if Bach was there at the organ again, his cantatas reverberating in its walls again, and that we were swept up into an unmediated dialogue with some elusive order of the divine.

Later the pulpit of that church was filled by Johann Gottfried Herder. Contrary to Kant's view that human progress entailed the orderly development of states, Herder had looked to the past and developed a theory of national identity grounded in ethnicity, location and language. These views were enthusiastically received by a new generation of Germans who looked to escape the dominance of French literary models. The *Sturm und Drang* movement, and later the Romantics, turned to their German roots for inspiration, and gloried in the newly found wealth of their folk traditions. After all, the French Revolution, which many Germans had welcomed as a harbinger of liberation from old feudal systems, had degenerated under Napoleon into a foreign occupying power.

We visited the houses of the most celebrated practitioners of *Sturm und Drang*, Goethe and Schiller, who had produced some of the greatest poetry and drama of their day. In time they shed their youthful indiscretions but not their literary genius, to make Weimar a byword for what is known as German Classicism.

But there was more. I was surprised to discover a miniature Russian church complete with golden onion domes. Maria Pavlovna, a Russian Grand Duchess, had married the local nobleman and continued the tradition of fostering the arts. She had invited Franz Liszt to become the new choir master of Weimar, and thanks to him Goethe's National Theater saw the first performances of Wagner's *Lohengrin*. Thus, after the classical Golden Age there had been a Silver Age. But Maria Pavlovna favored music and charity, not an open mind. After all, she was the sister of Alexander I who, after chasing Napoleon out of Russia, had presided with Metternich over the restoration of the old order. And she was also the sister of Nicolas I, who took over from his brother in 1825 to become "the gendarme of Europe."

But once Prussia succeeded Austria to the leadership of the German states and began championing pan-German nationalism, Weimar was left on the sidelines. The now provincially minded town was shocked by Harry Graf Kessler, who tried to capitalize on its cultural past by organizing exhibits of Nolde, Renoir, Rodin, Monet, and Gauguin. The work of famous architects like Henri van der Velde and Walter Gropius, while finding responsive echoes all over the world, was ultimately rejected in Weimar. It is perhaps fitting that Friedrich Nietzsche came to Weimar only to die.

Death proved very much at home in Weimar. A few miles away on the hilltop of Ettelsberg, where Goethe had loved to hike, had stood the concentration camp of Buchenwald. By the time of our visit the hill top had been leveled and most of the barracks had been razed. The smokestack of the crematorium and a couple of buildings to house the exhibits were all that remained. There were cars and buses parked at the gate, but the place had seemed to have swallowed up the people; small groups of them wandered about as in a landscape by Chirico. I too felt lost. I knew that this vast empty place had nothing to do with the Buchenwald of teeming bodies who had suffered here. But I didn't know how to bridge the gap. I thought of Dante's alter ego, trembling with life, descending among the wailing shades into the pit, circle upon circle of fiery hell.

Counting on Dante to guide me as Virgil had guided Dante, we entered the building with the exhibits. But they did not show the well-known pictures of human skeletons still alive, staring out of their hollow eye sockets. The people here looked quite ordinary, and I recognized some of them: Elie Wiesel, the Nobel Peace Laureate, who had said that the opposite of love was not hate, but indifference... Bruno Bettelheim, whose books on child psychology and the use of fairy tales I had read... Leon Blum, a French prime minister in the inter-war years whose sins were that he was a Socialist patrician dedicated to justice... Dietrich Bonhoeffer, a Protestant theologian who had dared to speak out against the persecution of the Jews. He had spent some time in the United States, and while visiting the Abyssinian Baptist Church of Harlem, had been inspired by its active social engagement. There were many others I did not know. In a group picture where people stood in line, one tall, powerfully built man looked straight at me; he might have been Hans' Communist father.

In Dante's *Inferno* a medieval God had exacted medieval justice, and exotic devils *à la* Hieronymus Bosch were busy devising exotic torments. Dante dwells on them with lyric horror, but with some Schadenfreude as well when he comes upon political enemies. So, what has changed? We still love to dance a medieval *Totentanz* (death dance). We still love to see our own fantasies of power and transgression inscribed on the bodies of others. We still don't recognize ourselves in the devil who appeared to Ivan Karamazov in the shabby clothes of a traveling salesman. Dante was no help: I was faced with Hanna Arendt's "banality of evil." *Das alles begriff ich nun und begriff es auch nicht:* "All this I now understood and understood it not." (W.G. Sebald, Austerlitz),

After half a century, memorial temples and chapels dotted the periphery of Buchenwald. Give it another half a century, and Buchenwald will be a theme park. There will be benches scattered throughout for weary tourists and surely the management will see to it that they replant trees for restful shade and meditation. And why not vending machines? Arm bands with swastikas could be set aside in a gift store for royals or street gangs. Pilgrims from around the world will wander about with their head sets tuned to the appropriate language, look up at the crematorium, and hear with interest that yes, it had been used for human sacrifice to propitiate the gods of racial purity once worshiped here. The visit and eloquent speech by an American president, Barack Obama, was the crowning witness to the utter eradication of racism in the world.

After Buchenwald there was no way of getting back to the earlier Weimar. It seemed inconceivable that the spirit of Weimar could have delivered the still-birth of Buchenwald. But the Weimar Republic had never had a chance. If the National Assembly met to debate the German Constitution in Weimar, it was because Berlin, Munich and Frankfurt seethed with violent opposition from both Right and Left. But the population of Weimar was not thrilled with the association. Like the rest of the country, its residents felt that what came to be known as the "Weimar Republic" had been made at Versailles. It was forever branded with the German defeat in World War I and its overwhelming burden of war reparations.

After centuries of providing their land as a battleground for others, Germans tasted unity at last under Bismarck's iron rule, and the heady experience of marching into Paris in 1870. And now in the hour of defeat and the chaos of conflicting claims whom should the people believe? The voices which advocated strong measures, clothed them in seductive slogans of nostalgia and national pride - then pointed to well-chosen scapegoats - had a definite ring of plausibility.

Was it not "true" that the Jews continued to flaunt their international connections and financial deals in the midst of inflation and unemployment? Were they not offering liberal panaceas in Parliament and the press while people went hungry? Were they not forging subversive alliances with the hordes from the east, the Bolsheviks? Clearly the Jews personified in striking synthesis all the modern plagues that bedeviled the German people. It was a relief to identify the enemy within the gates.

Hitler loved Weimar and Weimar loved him back. The people of Weimar loved his grand vision and they appreciated that he had put Germany back to work again. That he had done so by allying himself with the Krupp war machine rang no alarm bells. They locked step willingly and marched singing into their communal *Götterdämmerung*.

When it all came to an end and General Patton led the good people of Weimar to see Buchenwald in its terminal stage of human degradation, they were shocked. IT CAN'T HAPPEN HERE. But the earlier, gradual, imperceptible degradation had been with them all along. "Transports" arrived and left ceaselessly. "Work parties" sallied forth daily from the camp and headed for the nearby quarries and munitions factories. Deliveries of food and other necessities to the camp were provided by the local merchants. Of course, the people of Weimar knew about Buchenwald, and of course they chose not to know, for this is what kept them on the Weimar side of the line. Upon returning home after the compulsory visit to Buchenwald, Weimar's mayor and his wife committed suicide.

After General Patton's division withdrew, the Soviet army entered Weimar. Relieved of their Nazi obligations, the twin statues of Goethe and Schiller on the main square were now pressed into the service of the good news of Communism. And Buchenwald too found its uses. People deemed unsuitable for the latest new order were incarcerated there. The authorities shied away from the crematorium, and dug mass graves for them among the beech trees. Again, Dante's precedent proved un-instructive. The leaves of those trees did not turn black, and when I reached up and broke off a twig, it did not bleed. Instead, Fritz Cremer's monumental tower and sculptural group now welcome the visitor to Buchenwald. It commemorates a Communist uprising which some say never happened. But then again, they also say Buchenwald never happened.

***

CHAPTER 10

LITERATURE

The sunken ship of my Stamford nightmare, the one I thought had kept the secret of Mother's madness, had more secret doors after all. But neither I nor my therapist could penetrate below the surface ripples. If I had been able to open those doors at that time, maybe by reactivating my suppressed dream of writing, the dream and the nightmare could have faced off on the page. Maybe then those ghosts of my German childhood could have been exorcised.

Instead, what came out of my therapy was the practical idea of going back to school. I had toyed with such an idea before, but had held out for the dream of writing my own words instead of mulling over the words of others. But I kept running into walls – language struggles, mother troubles, child priorities. The writing on the wall this time, like a giant billboard, said "school." School, in spite of the confusion of tongues, had proven manageable enough in the past, and I bought in – or sold out.

I applied to the Graduate Center of the City University of New York (CUNY) and was accepted. As a field of study, I picked Comparative Literature since I already had all those languages under my belt. If I had been really practical, this is the advice I would have given myself: Seek out some obscure corner of literary history, and attach yourself to the worn but still sturdy coattails of one of its titular guardians with humble service and diligent stoking of burnt offerings. In time, after prospering modestly in his shadow, you too may become the guardian of immemorial prerogatives.

If, however, there is calculated room for risk taking, sniff out the burning controversy of the day, nothing too far out but something that is gathering critical mass in the shadows of Academe, and attach yourself to the iconoclastic mantle of one of its rising stars with humble service and diligent stoking of burnt offerings. Sooner rather than later you too may stand in the crossfire of academic searchlights, and become the guardian of immemorial prerogatives.

But I was too green at the time, and likely too pig-headed anyway to take such sensible advice.

Unexpectedly, Dad offered to come up from Down Under to help take care of his grandson. As he stepped through the Customs doors, he was still slim and erect at 70. There had been a tremendous snowfall in April of 1969, and this Russian, long accustomed to African and Australian sunshine, entered on the latest of his adventures walking guardedly between mounds of accumulated snow.

Since Dad was no Babushka, the usual household chores remained my responsibility. But he did spend a lot of time with Peter and the two of them got along famously. He told him stories, made him all kinds of toys and doodads, and took him to the park and library. In the fall of 1969 Peter and I were ready for school.

The Comparative Studies program at CUNY was cobbled together from various departments over a foundation of literary criticism and theory. It also required the choice of one major literature, and I opted for French. That proved unchallenging, and when a young Ph.D. in Russian from Harvard was hired, I switched to Russian. Since I was already fluent in the language, this resulted in a very satisfying option of individual study under the young professor's guidance. It was not, however, smooth sailing every step of the way. When another professor, who must have been in his '60s, invited me into his red convertible one day, I had the sinking feeling that the days of our scholarly collaboration were numbered. And by mutual disappointment at the red convertible's lack of effect on me, they were.

Finally, a scholar both high-powered and female appeared on the horizon, and expectations rose. She actually instituted a weekly luncheon with the students. When I opened the door to the separate dining room she had reserved, what I beheld was indeed a vision of the Holy Grail. The professor, who was a medievalist, presided at this large, and wouldn't you know it, round table, surrounded by a knightly court of graduate students. I stepped into this sacred circle like the proverbial neophyte, but the incense of abject fawning was so thick that I felt hopelessly unfit for knighthood. I beat a prudent retreat, but fair is fair; Queen Guinevere gave me an A all the same.

But grades are incidental, as are students. I found that out when I unwittingly stepped into the minefield of some obscure departmental power struggle. My orals turned out to be the battleground of the warring parties and the questions addressed to me flew over my head like poisoned arrows. I made it out alive, but barely.

Thus, life on the surface was not without its own struggles. Literature, however, has its own rewards. German literature was also part of my program and there, among the secret tremors between the lines, I re-entered the shadowy world of my childhood: *"Wer reitet so spät durch Nacht und Wind? Es ist der Vater mit seinem Kind."* ("Who rides so late through night and wind? It is a father and his child.") In Goethe's poem the child is ill and feverish, and he imagines that the King of the Elves is after him. Sure enough, when the father reaches his destination, the child in his arms is dead.

I was still alive when we arrived in Goslar on the night of our escape from Blankenburg in 1945. From Goslar we drove to a little town called Watenstedt, which I have since failed to locate on a map. Still, we did spend the winter of 1945/46 in that non-place. And it was there that a little brother or sister had valiantly tried to push its way into the world. But after so many dead, the world had not been ready to receive the child.

This time our family of four had a room of our own. Two bunk beds left little room for much else, but there was a table between them and on it some sort of single-burner gas stove called a Primus, where Babushka did our cooking. I loved climbing to the top level of the bunk bed. Babushka occupied the lower level, and when I jumped around on top, the innards of my mattress would begin to seep and Babushka below would begin to sneeze. The experiment never failed.

Christmas that year was memorable. We made an expedition into the surrounding woods. The snow on the ground shone and sparkled while our footprints filled with shadow. Dad chopped down a young fir tree and we hauled it home. All along we made a big show of stealth and secrecy: it appeared that we were poaching. At home Dad drew bells and stars and birds on a piece of cardboard. Mom and I cut them out and wrapped them in tin foil. There never was a prettier Christmas tree. Before falling asleep on my bunk bed, I could reach to the top of the tree and touch the star of Bethlehem.

Mom worried about my lack of schooling, and for a while a man with a crew cut and a Hitler mustache visited regularly. His name was Herr Friedrich. He taught me the fancy German Gothic script still in use in those days, at least by Herr Friedrich. My convalescence was coming along, but now my hair kept falling out by the handful. Under the principle that causes people to maintain their lawns by mowing them, it was decided that my head must be shaved. It was also decided that I was ready for school – a German school, for which Her Friedrich had been preparing me. So, I entered my school experience as bald as an egg.

Fortunately, this trial did not last very long. We packed up once more and headed south, this time all the way to Munich. We now landed in a camp with the Wagnerian name of Lohengrin, which proved to be the first of several such D.P. (Displaced Persons) camps. Here my recollections turn from black-and-white to Technicolor. The camp had a Russian school and here at last I was a child among children, with games and girl giggles and mischief. Moreover, thanks to my earlier commerce with *Katya i Sharik*, I kept up nicely. Fate had collected an unlikely group of people in this particular camp. There were dancing lessons and piano lessons, and we put on a ballet version of Andersen's *The Snow Queen*. I fluttered as a butterfly in Act One and as a snowflake in Act Three.

But once again we had to move. Dad was now driving a truck for the Americans, and his workplace was located near Pasing, a little town just outside of Munich. We rented a room from a German farmer, and I had to go to a German school again.

There was an incident on the very first day. Classes began with prayer, and it was supervised by a priest. He was an ox of a man and I noticed that he kept thrusting his powerful jaw in my direction. I tried to mouth the recitation of "Hail Mary" in German (I knew the Russian version of the same prayer), and I didn't know what the trouble was.

When the prayer was over, sure enough, the man in black loomed over me, grabbed my hand and began to instruct me in the proper way of making the sign of the cross. I had crossed myself Russian-Orthodox style putting thumb, forefinger and middle finger together (to signify the holy trinity of course) and touching the right shoulder firs. The Catholics, it turned out, made the sign of the cross keeping their hand open and touching the left shoulder first. Evidently, they had theological reasons of their own. I did not know that people had been burned at the stake for less, spoke up, and the hulk backed off. Who says miracles don't happen?

But things didn't work out all that well in Pasing. Mom arranged for piano lessons, but upon finding out that prevailing teaching methods included hitting my fingers with a cane if I produced a false note, piano lessons were abandoned. When I try to recall that year, it's as if I am looking through a fogged glass pane. I keep wiping it clean, but all I see is a child looking back.

This too did pass, and we moved into a D.P. camp again. This was Schleissheim, next to the Baroque Castle and its forbidden grounds. Life looked up once more. My maternal grandfather, Babushka's ex-husband, was the director of this particular camp. The UNRRA (United Nations Relief and Rehabilitation Administration) was trying to cope with masses of people and, whenever possible, delegated internal administration to the refugees themselves.

I have no idea how Grandfather cropped up in Germany. He was accompanied by his second wife, and I could not understand how he could have preferred that woman to Babushka. She looked like a giant dumpling with pasty skin to match while Babushka's beauty shone even in old age. But they practiced old-fashioned hospitality, and their one-room apartment was always full of young and old. With vodka and herring on the table sooner or later somebody would strum a guitar, and the people would start singing. Those voices, which harmonized so effortlessly and flowed together into melodies of infinitely sweet longing, stayed with me forever.

The name of Vlasov came up again. A whole barracks of Russians due to be handed over to "Uncle Joe" (as the Americans called Stalin) had set themselves on fire, "and just stood there, burning, as straight as candles." In this story of human torches, what seemed to matter most to the adults was that those men had stood so straight.

The Americans taught us to play baseball. We tried to follow their incomprehensible instructions, but swinging a bat or reaching a base proved a universal language. And the Schleissheim Castle park grounds had a stiff competitor - the garbage dump. The day I lifted a coat hanger out of the muck was a day of triumph. Coat hangers were precious because the Americans were sending us clothes. We simply couldn't believe that people would discard such gorgeous garments, and sashayed about in them with the flair of film stars.

Then Mom got it into her head to send me to the German school outside of camp. Maybe she found the camp school unsatisfactory. Schleissheim was not just a Russian camp like the camp at Lohengrin. My friends were Poles and Ukrainians and Lithuanians and Latvians and Estonians, and we communicated perfectly across those subsets of some proto-Slavo-Baltic idiom. This was fine on the garbage dump, but could, I imagine, be a challenge in the class room.

In any event, I was marched off to the German school, and it did not prove as bad as I had feared. The stint at Pasing had gotten me over the hump, and I was pretty fluent by now. In due course I passed the dreaded exam to enter sixth grade. Going to school now meant taking the train to Munich. Soon it was cold and still dark in the early mornings as I ventured out to the train station. The trains were packed, with bundles of men hanging out the open doors like bunches of bananas. Some man usually scooped me up and pushed me through so I wouldn't fall off. These goings on seemed to wear me out, and I developed a persistent cough. Since there was serious talk of emigration to Canada, and sticking it out in a German school seemed pointless, Mom let me quit school. Instead, a friend of Grandfather's, a former professor, started giving me English lessons. We were making good progress (I was beginning to crack *The Three Little Pigs*) when plans changed abruptly. Canada required that Dad leave six months ahead of the family. We felt that the one thing that had gotten us through was sticking together like glue so we dropped the Canadian prospect.

I learned later that the United States were not taking immigrants at the time, barring exceptional cases. Here I was, getting the hang of *The Three Little Pigs* - was this not exceptional? To think that if only I had made it to the U.S. at the age of eleven as Madeleine Albright did - I could have been somebody... I could have been a contender... For one thing, I would not be stuck with an accent, though this did not stop Kissinger. It's hard to pick up certain things in later years. The simple gesture of the hand on the heart while reciting the pledge feels a tad contrived. Yet I still get goose bumps at the very thought of the old Russian anthem "God save the Tsar!" They did catch me early with that one, and the groove in my amygdala (or is it the hippocampus?) seems permanently cut.

That is why I think that if only I had come to the U.S. at the age of eleven like Madeleine Albright, I would have learned to do fund raisers for private schools and politicians, I would have had Zbigniew Brzezinski to impress, Jesse Helms to coddle up to, and cojones to display. President Clinton could as well have made the famous phone call to me.

Instead, the option before us now was Venezuela. No one knew Spanish among Grandfather's many contacts, and Mom gave up trying to prepare me for my future. I was left to weeks and then months of woolgathering. I experienced my first crush. He was a devastatingly handsome sixteen-year-old, and he came to my eleventh birthday party, gave me a bottle of perfume, and kissed my hand. Does it get any better?

Then the poker players up on Mt. Olympus cracked a new deck of cards and Morocco appeared as yet another option for emigration. It was a French Protectorate and therefore more desirable than Venezuela because of Dad's fluency in French. So now it was a matter of more waiting and more reading of the tea leaves of the eligibility process. Mom tried to talk Dad into teaching me French, but he took me fishing instead. After yet another stint in another D.P. camp, known as a "holding camp," we finally left for Morocco in the spring of 1949.

We had left Munich in ruins, but during my return visit in 2002 everything in Munich was new and nothing was in its place. When we arrived in Schleissheim, the barracks were gone; the place was now a soccer field. There was now a beer garden across from the castle grounds, and we sat down for a rest. The big lilac hedge, which once had masked the barbed wire behind which we lived, was still there. I remembered sneaking past my friends the Black Giants to steal an armful of lilacs to give Mom on Easter Day. The smell of fresh lilac came back in a gust of memory, and for a moment the hedge stood heavy with bloom again. So, the lilac hedge was still there and German poets' words were still there, locked into the rhythms of human seasons. And literature at the Graduate Center had been its own reward.But I also enjoyed the company of my fellow-students. Nancy Gray Diaz is still a dear and close friend some fifty years later. She hailed from Decatur, Illinois, a long-legged Midwesterner with green eyes and light-brown hair parted in the middle and worn straight down the back as the '60s required. She had defied the proprieties of her milieu and married a Colombian. We both lived in Queens and we both had three-year old sons.

In the midst of juggling my home duties and graduate studies, I found myself pregnant again. Rick and I considered what the optimal size of our family might be and settled on two kids. I discovered something called a tubal ligation, which can be easily done during delivery. I brought it up to my gynecologist, and what ensued was rather unexpected. This young, nice, competent doctor accused me of the prospective murder of unborn souls. He had raised his voice, and after the minute or so it took me to recover, I shouted back that the planet was sinking under the weight of hungry children, that my decision was the very acme of morally responsible behavior and that, besides, he was my doctor and not my father confessor! At which point he showed me the door and I waddled proudly out through a waiting room full of staring eyes.

Rick was supportive through all this, but in a sort of helpless, distracted way, and I sensed him far away, caught up in his own world of statistical analyzes and crucial reports to the Big Guys. I had not cried in a long while, and I didn't cry now. I was out of touch, had no time to listen to WBAI, and had never heard of Betty Friedan or Kate Millett. All the same, I like to think that, like Venus born of the sea, Muriel emerged to life on the crest of the big wave that rose up just then from the hidden depths of women's longing for their own voice.

Muriel Catherine Denise was born on May 20, 1971 at Booth Memorial Hospital, Queens, N.Y. Because of the tubal ligation natural birth was out of the question, so they put me out for the duration. Soon but not soon enough we were on our way home. Here again things proved different. Rick did not have the option of taking time off, and Dad stepped up to the plate. If anything, he bonded with Muriel as strongly as I did. He had asked that she be named Catherine in memory of his mother Yekaterina, but Rick felt that we already had a Peter the Great, and that Catherine the Great would be much too much greatness for one family. He liked the name of Muriel, and that's our daughter's name.

What's in a name, anyway? We never thought that "Muriel" would be associated with a brand of cigars, but that's what happened. I might have anticipated something, for I myself am routinely taken for a mineral: did I know about the town in Illinois called Galena? No one, but no one associates me with the wonderful ballerina Galina Ulanova or the diva of the Bolshoi Theater, Galina Vishnevskaya. Lucky for me people don't know Latin languages either, and miss the naughty implications of chicks as street walkers that I had suffered in my teens. "Galina," as it happens, is a very common Russian name. It was given to me in memory of my aunt.

When Babushka left Russia with her two daughters, Helen (Yelena) and Galina, they became boat people. Nabokov describes his evacuation from Crimea in 1920 in his Speak, Memory, and Dad told me the exact same story. The British navy had rescued their White allies, and taken them to Istanbul. From there people went elsewhere. Babushka had received word from her husband that the White cause for which he was fighting somewhere was lost and that she was to take the two girls and head south. But they failed to connect, and together with many other families, she too was evacuated by Allied ships. But then no country was prepared to receive them, and they became what we later called boat people.

We have all seen newsprint pictures of gaunt black bodies piled on top of each other on some wooden bark askew on a frozen white wave. They used to turn them back to Haiti to the gargantuan ogre called Papa Doc and machete wielding creatures called Tontons Macoute. There are also pictures of emaciated gray bodies piled up on shaky fishing trawlers that used to be sent back from Australia to a place called Cambodia, otherwise known as the Killing Fields. Now those boats carry Afghans and Iraqis and Sikhs, and they say these people are often set upon by pirates.

What do they have to do with the ordinary, respectable lives familiar to us? I have in my possession a snapshot of Babushka and her two daughters taken before they left Russia. It is one of those old-fashioned, posed pictures which epitomize the very definition of gentility. The trio wear *belle époque* dresses of light muslin with low waists and puffy sleeves gathered at the wrist. Babushka is young. She stands behind an ornately carved seat wearing her pearl drop earrings. Mother, who was always on the skinny, vivacious side, is hard to recognize in the serious little girl with puffed out cheeks and a big bow in her hair. Her younger sister Galochka (the diminutive for Galina), her hair evidently curled for the occasion, stands snuggling up against her sister, a finger stuck in her mouth, looking straight at the viewer. The composition they present is the classical one of the sacred triangle favored by Renaissance painters, whose exemplar is Da Vinci's *Virgin and Child with St. Anne.*

Yet those delicate angelic creatures became boat people just like all the other bodies piled up in their wooden barks. Haitians have since been returned to a man called La Tortue, which my spelling program keeps correcting to "torture." His supporters' acronym FRAPH means "hit" or "beat" in French, but hardly the musical kind. And our mighty navy circled their earthquake and cholera-ravaged island to make sure they stay there. There are also plenty of little islands scattered in the Pacific on Australia's northern periphery. There the Australian government sorts them out into "independent or concessional categories" as "unprocessed," "designated," or "illegal."

Babushka and her two girls were also dumped on an island - the Greek Island of Lemnos. There they lived in army tents and suffered various epidemics. Babushka's youngest daughter Galina, by then six-years old, came down with scarlet fever and died. A picture of her grave also came down to me among old family photos.

So that's how I came by my name. However much I like it to resonate with great ballerinas and opera singers, and however much people see in it chickens and minerals, "Galina" puts me right into the boats with all those Haitians who venture into the Caribbean, and Afghans and Sikhs who venture into the Indian Ocean, and Africans who attempt to cross the straits of Gibraltar, known of old as Scylla and Charybdis. Boat people get stuck there, forever tossed between the rock and the hard place. And after regime change in Iraq, our attempts to liberate the Syrians from their sinister "strong man," caused a new wave of refugees to be loosed on Europe's shores.

In the summer of 2004 Rick and I flew to Lemnos to look for my aunt's grave. It is a pretty island washed by the Ionian Sea. Like all Greek islands, Lemnos has its old myths: Jason is said to have lingered there on his way to capturing the Golden Fleece, and Hephaestus, Aphrodite's luckless husband, fell to it and became lame, having been thrown out of Olympus by Zeus himself.

Unexpectedly, we came across large cemeteries of British, French, and ANZAC (Australian and New Zealand Army Corps) soldiers, fallen in World War I. Something about all those cemeteries, still kept in a pristine condition so far from home and a hundred years after the event, spoke of war as an institution. It's as if ancient Troy, located right across from Lemnos on the Anatolian mainland, was condemned to fall again and again as it once had in Homer's *Iliad*. And it still does so on the silver screen.

As for, Wolfgang Peterson's *Troy*, although he recreates in archeological detail the paraphernalia of ancient warfare, the whole masquerade seems transparent. What will it take to be "shocked" rather than "awed" when they come bearing Greek gifts? Surely Agamemnon is a neo-con, the overblown stage set of Troy signifies the black gold of the oil fields, beauteous Helen is our soiled democracy, Achilles and his Myrmidons are the brave soldiers fated to be cheated of their veterans' benefits (though they do get their jollies while they can on the night shift at Abu Ghraib) and finally the Trojan horse, chock-full of weapons of mass destruction, leads us within the gates.

Thus, the inconspicuous island of Lemnos turned out to be, like Weimar, unexpectedly prodigal of historical quicksand. As we pursued our search, we met a woman whose mother had known something of a Russian refugee camp. She drove us to a barren stretch of sand, close to the seashore, and the windswept landscape matched the background of the grave on my photograph. I had found Galochka after all, only instead of resting under a mound of sand and a wooden cross, her fragile bones were now so many grains of sand under our feet.

As to all the other boat people plying the seven seas since then, parked on islands and in detention camps, they too, I imagine, will find enough earth to bury their dead. Whether there is earth enough left for them to live remains an open question.

***

CHAPTER 11

VILLAGE GREENS

Muriel's arrival into the world had brought to a head the need for us to look for larger living quarters, and we began to dream of a house of our own. We looked around and finally settled for something called a "Planned Unit Development" on Staten Island. It was a modest enough development of row houses, but it was well designed and the main attraction was the promise of a large common area and a new neighborhood school. An additional lure was that the development was to be explicitly integrated. Our world had considerably narrowed since our days in Berkeley, but this much we could do: raise our children in an integrated environment.

We chose one of the models, picked a location on the map, Frank and Francine advanced us the sum of $10,000 and with much trepidation and excitement, we signed on the dotted line. The builders took their sweet time, and in the meantime, we explored Staten Island. The place enchanted us: we discovered quaintness and charm everywhere. We drove down winding Arthur Kill Road past an old boat graveyard to visit PS 4, the tiny school Peter would soon be entering. It had been built, if memory serves, in 1896! Just a few miles further south on the tip of Staten Island stood Conference House. We were duly impressed that General Howe on the British side, and Ben Franklin, John Adams, and Edward Rutledge on the American side, had conferred under its roof.

The one thing we had altogether missed was the garbage dump. It was only weeks later after our move, when I happened to take the express bus to Manhattan, that the elevated highway gave me a full panorama of the wasteland which collected the refuse of all of New York City. Its name, "Fresh Kills Disposal Site," was a rather unpromising mixed metaphor. But for now, we had to focus on our more immediate environment. Our own future park, which was still a mud field, would one day justify the name of our new neighborhood, "Village Greens."

Nancy and Luis and Luco had also moved out of Queens around that same time and settled in Piscataway, N.J. We had worried that our respective moves would undermine our families' friendship bonds, but Piscataway turned out to be quite accessible over the Outerbridge Crossing, and our friendship was saved from the perils of long-distance attrition. In Village Greens, in the meantime, I met Jane de Jesus, born Jane Lahey, and that proved the beginning of another lasting friendship.

It was high time for me to resume my studies after my leave of absence to take care of Muriel, and like Rick, I too began to take an express bus to Manhattan. After watching barges along the Amboy River deliver their goods to the garbage dump in a swirl of sea gulls' wings, I sped along the New Jersey Pike to emerge at the Port Authority Terminal in Manhattan. CUNY was still located on 42nd Street across from the Public Library. Porn shops and movie marquees on "naughty, bawdy, gaudy, fraudy Forty Second Street," as the popular Broadway show has it, accompanied me from bus to school.

I tried to leave Manhattan before dark, and the sunsets on the New Jersey Turnpike were spectacular. The sky, lit up into apocalyptic reds to the right, outlined the mammoth erector sets of oil refineries, then paled into ghostly gray through which the Manhattan Skyline, to the left, slid out of sight. And soon enough we would be moving full speed against the rivers of light of on-coming traffic.

Most days, however, I stayed home and wrestled with Arundhati Roy's "god of small things." Our new house was full of problems. The heating stalled, the bedroom toilet didn't flush, and a pipe burst and flooded the laundry room in the basement. Upon opening a wall, the workers found that one of the pipe connections had been secured by means of a beer can. Dad grumbled, but was too busy keeping up with Muriel as it was her turn now to become passionate about steps. We had plenty of those in our three-level town house.

Peter was happy. He joined the whirlwind of boy activities, trying to keep up with his new friends who roamed the woods across Arden Avenue, explored the construction sites, and disappeared into sewer pipes. I recalled my untutored days in D.P. camps, and saw no harm in what he was doing.

Dad, meanwhile, grew despondent. He squinted in the direction of the garbage dump and muttered that I would not have far to go to dispose of him. In Queens he had been able to hop on the subway and visit his Russian friends. Some turned out to be fellow veterans of the Russian Civil War; he had crossed paths with others in Istanbul or Belgrade or some D.P. camp in Germany; others were even vaguely related. I recalled Tolstoy's novels, where everyone knew or was related to everyone else, and Moscow seemed one big village. Now Russian émigrés had turned even New York into such a reconstituted network of relationships.

But on Staten Island there was no subway, and the local buses were utterly unreliable. On one of his expeditions Dad had missed a connection, frozen his bones taking the Staten Island Ferry back, and arrived home at 2 a.m. He had also experienced a quintessential New York incident. He had attempted to yield his seat to a lady on the subway, but the lady in question, misunderstanding his old-world flourish in doing so, had attacked him with her sharp-edged purse. Such adventures were no longer age appropriate for him.

I might have taken his dark hints more seriously, but I was absorbed in my own affairs. He simply announced one day that he was going back to Australia. I was in shock. Muriel was still under two, and I had just resumed my studies. But he was firm, and there was little, in good conscience, that I could say to dissuade him.

The day of his departure came. We stood waiting at the airport, and then said our farewells. I didn't want to alarm the kids with a show of tears, but my chest ached with the question of whether I would ever see him again. Peter didn't say much: his life as well was beginning to take an independent turn. Muriel, however, watched Dad step out of sight and only began to cry once we ourselves started to walk away. She must have believed that the passageway through which he had disappeared was a temporary hiding place, and that the game would soon be over: her beloved "Dieda" would reappear, pick her up, and sing her one of his soothing ditties.

In the days that followed she cried and cried. My efforts to console or distract her worked for a while, but then she would start crying all over again. All along, Muriel had been pretty different from Peter. She seemed more sensitive to touch and noise, a lighter sleeper, a fussier eater. She loved to be held, and Dad had been only too happy to oblige. The two of them had been joined at the hip.

We had agreed to stay focused on French as the family language. This had worked well for Peter, who was already perfectly bilingual. With Muriel, however, Dad exercised his own favorite option, and whenever I was out of sight, I could hear him coaching her in Russian. Poor Muriel was now expected to respond to him in Russian, to her parents in French, and to everyone else in English. In the face of these multiple linguistic assaults, she stopped talking altogether. Eventually English took the upper hand, and she became a typical American monolingual.

Dad's departure put my studies on hold again. It now looked like our developer was about to renege on our promised common grounds, and a homeowner's association was formed to safeguard the terms of the contract. The whole point of attached houses had been for the benefit of saving land for a common use area and a neighborhood school. This too was in question now.

Peter had entered Kindergarten at P.S. 4, and we had every reason to appreciate the benefits of a small local school. We mothers used to sit on the stoops in front of our houses, and endlessly discuss the teachers and programs of P.S. 4. Mr. De Palma, the principal, was a sweet man who put up with our anxieties and nosy ways as well as with our bake sales.

My new friend Jane was a firebrand. Something about her looks and manner was akin to the irrepressible drive and down-to-earth grit projected on screen by Barbara Stanwyck. I now recalled my days at Berkeley, and vowed to "think globally and act locally." The two of us became the dynamic duo to rally the troops in the cause of defending the original plan of a neighborhood school on the grounds of Village Greens.

At some point in our public travails, we filled a whole bus with mothers and kids and took the lot to City Hall in Manhattan. I was delegated to present our case at the Board of Estimate Hearing. Muriel, in the meantime, had fallen asleep during the interminable wait to which our delegation had been subjected, and she had done so right over the pocket with my maiden speech in it. Fearful of waking her by shifting her from my hip, I made my public debut ex-tempore, my sleeping child in my arms.

This gave us a touching picture in the papers, but it didn't give us our school. A school was eventually built, but it was not the small school of our dreams to which our kids could actually walk. At least we had wrested a sizable open space with all the amenities from the original builder. In the summer the Village Greens Association hired a team of young life guards for the pools. There were tennis tournaments, baseball meets, and fests with three-legged races and pie eating contests.

As we had hoped, this happy togetherness was not based on exclusiveness. Our own next-door neighbors were African-American. Rosalie Barret, whose family hailed from Jamaica, was a reserved woman and church-going Episcopalian. We became good friends over the years, and see each other still when we make it to the Big Apple. The experiment of integration in Village Greens seemed to have worked out. The presence of African-Americans among us, however, was not as readily accepted by the larger community of Staten Island. We discovered that our neighborhood was informally listed as "Village Black" among the local real-estate agents, and the value appreciation of our houses suffered accordingly.

This being New York, however, Jewish influence was predominant in Village Greens. A Jewish Center was eventually constructed off Arthur Kill Road and opened with a bang with an amateur performance of *Fiddler on the Roof.* I could have sworn I was back in the halcyon days of my D.P. experience, with its bustle and show of unsuspected talent. It was fun to watch a neighbor break into fine voice and strut as Tevye the Milk Man. We were also invited to Bar Mitzvahs and weddings, and I felt at home.

All in all, the early days in Village Greens were busy and satisfying. But then somewhere in second grade something went wrong for Peter. He began to refuse to go to school. He would cry disconsolately, but remained tongue-tied. I looked into his eyes and tried to read whatever it was that he couldn't put into words. There was much talk and writing about alternative schools in the '70s, all about Summerhill and "open classroom." After some six weeks of daily turmoil trying to figure out what ailed him, I found another school for him called the "Free School." It was run by hippie types much given to guitar playing and clay work, and I had my doubts. Peter seemed to take to the change, however, so I committed myself to the daily drive.

Some of my doubts had to do with a boy I sometimes drove to the same school. His name was Charlie, he was Peter's age, and he had set his mother's house on fire a couple of times. Charlie didn't have a father; or rather he seemed to have several, as different men came to the door when I picked him up. It was hard not to jump to conclusions.

One conclusion I had avoided thus far was the role of my own children's father in their lives. He was working hard, and was tired when he came home or returned from his business trips. Was he not entitled to some temper when the kids squabbled at the dinner table or neighborhood kids swarmed in? The trouble was, we never talked anymore. I couldn't claim to understand macroeconomics on the global scale, but who's to say what's macro and what's micro? Were our personal and family priorities too insignificant for Rick to take an interest? His answer, apparently, was express sex in time for the express bus in the morning, and post cards from around the world. But I was loath to jump to conclusions. Maybe this development was in the natural order of things? Nancy had her issues with Luis, and Jane had her issues with Foster. Rosalie's husband was no longer around. She had been an "at home mom," but now she left for work every day.

One thing Rick was a good sport about was taking the family on camping trips. Plymouth Rock and our visit to the Mayflower replica was a general favorite. Salem and the playlet about the witches we attended there was a special hit with Muriel. The Smokies were especially memorable. We played a tape about Davy Crockett in the car, Peter wore a coonskin cap, and our hikes in the woods satisfied our spirit of exploration. Chincoteague in Virginia, the place where wild ponies have roamed from the time their ancestors swam ashore from a sinking Spanish galleon, was just as magical. Both Peter and Muriel grew up to love the outdoors.

On one of these trips Peter turned to me and declared, "Mom, I don't want to grow up to be a dummy. Let me go back to P.S.4." Thus, the mysterious episode of Peter's school phobia was put to rest.

❧

With Muriel joining a Montessori pre-school and Peter back at P.S. 4, I could reconnect with my own schooling. One missing element in my professional preparation was teaching experience. I found an appointment to teach French at St. Peter's College, a Jesuit institution located in Jersey City. Back in the antediluvian '70s the study of French was still pretty hip. Every word of the "oo la, la" language still had a full charge of sex appeal. Since I had taken over from an elderly priest who had to take time off for health reasons, my age and gender revitalized prevailing expectations, and the students and I had a love fest.

My teaching at St. Peter's, while I finished my course work and passed my finals at CUNY, lasted three full years. But the elderly priest reclaimed his turf in 1977, and I was let go. It was high time to buckle down to my dissertation.

As the saying came and went in the feminist '70s, however, I did not have a "wife." Her job would have been to attend to the hungry mouths and thirsty souls of my sweet family while I charted new pathways on the oceans of literary theory. Instead, it was driving Rick to the airport and picking Rick up from the airport; and then driving one or the other kid to karate practice, trumpet lessons, ballet, baseball meets, scouts, piano lessons, choir practice, birthday parties, graduations, and doctor check-ups.

And with Peter and Muriel being almost five years apart in age, there was an unending parade of two sets of friends. The boys hanging out in the family room or building go carts in the garage, and the girls playing dress-up upstairs. Or, as was Muriel's wont, sneaking in stray dogs. That's how I found a litter of nine puppies in my garage one day.

Then there was the food problem. There was plenty of food to be had, but was it nutrition? Even the most casual mother would be put off by the food served in school cafeterias. Once you opened that can of worms, Wonder bread lost its wonder, soda its pop, and the Golden Arches their gilt luster. Life became a daily struggle over snacks and drinks and food shopping.

And there was the Pied Piper's tune piped daily into our home by means of a rectangular object with a cord plugged into the wall. I tried to control the intruder by confining "IT" to set hours in the family room. When Francine, observing the kids fighting over favorite programs when we visited Stamford, unexpectedly sent each child his n' hers very own mini monster, I was NOT amused. I resorted to desperation, and attacked the THING oozing into my home by chopping off its tentacles. The kids still laugh about how their crazy mother actually took a pair of scissors and cut the cords of their TV sets.

In that year of 1978 Rick's dad Frank passed away. He had been struggling for some time with all the ailments bestowed by our advanced civilization: high blood pressure, emphysema, and diabetes. Finally, he completed the list by developing cancer of the pancreas. We had traveled regularly to Connecticut over the years. Now our trips took us to St. Joseph's Hospital in Stamford. We had a good visit with him on one of those Sundays, and it turned to be our last.

That same year my father decided to return. He looked remarkably unchanged, but I did note some new stiffness in his gait. I figured he knew the limitations of his life with us, and that he must be resigned to them. Sadly, however, the old rapport with the children was now broken. Peter and even Muriel were too busy with their friends to give him the time of day.

It was at this general point of existential malaise that Muriel, our eight-year-old, intervened and redirected the course of events. Evidently, something was missing for her as well. She approached me and in her inimitably way wanted to know, "So Mom, are we Christmas or are we Chanukah?" We had always celebrated Christmas with all the trimmings and knew little of Chanukah, but that was not the point. The child wanted to know the substance behind the show.

Confronted by my little girl now, I remembered the little girl I had been, standing during the long Russian-Orthodox services next to my beloved

Babushka, and trying to make out the voices of Mom and Dad among the voices in the choir. It occurred to me that we were not giving our children something to believe in - or to rebel against. Teaching through the example of an orderly and decent life was not enough. Muriel wanted something more formal to define her place among her peers. As to Peter, our orderly and decent ways must have appeared terminally uncool to ever stand a chance against the prevailing religion of "Sex, Drugs, and Rock n' Roll."

Somebody suggested that a Unitarian Universalist Congregation might be a place for us. Rick balked at any institutional setting, but I recalled our days in Manhattan when our connection with the world had depended on Pacifica's WBAI. Among the voices coming over the airwaves, one voice had been associated with that denomination. I recalled how sensibly it had cut through the accumulated denials and hypocrisies of the race issue. I was willing to give such a voice a try.

***

CHAPTER 12

TROUBLE IN PARADISE

The Unitarian Church of Staten Island is an attractive old building, and looking very much like a church, complete with wooden pews polished by time and stained-glass windows. I was reassured by Reverend Horace Colpitts' sermon on our first visit; he did not sound like Billy Graham. I was also impressed that a woman, the church president, stepped up to the pulpit and also addressed the congregation. Rick, for his part, was impressed by the music. The music director taught at Juilliard and his students regaled us with a superb performance of a Schubert trio.

During subsequent visits our observations were confirmed. No one expected us to believe the Virgin birth of Christ or the Bible as the word of God or the infallibility of the Pope. And it was fine to think of Jesus as a Jewish rabbi; it was the value of his message, not the presumed divinity of the man, which deserved reverence. The Bible had been written by inspired people, but that inspiration was human, all too human. In short, the message seemed to be to trust the divine light within you and not to worry about those who claim that you can't tell right from wrong without their say-so.

And then the big question, at least to me, was: what do you do with your inner freedom? This reconnected me to Tolstoy and Dostoyevsky and to the French Existentialists I had read back in Morocco, and I was truly home. I also found that Unitarian Universalism had a respectable historical tradition. In the United States, that tradition was Congregational and Jeffersonian and Transcendentalist and Abolitionist and Feminist and Humanist. If I had lost my connection to a personal anthropomorphic God, particularly a patriarchal God, I still wanted to believe in godliness – or at least some mental and social space where my incorrigible longing for a better world could find an echo.

But the welcome mat offered by the Unitarian Universalist Church of Staten Island was not strewn with rose petals every step of the way. Rick and I still led parallel lives. Dad was his usual tactful self, but evidently alerted Mom on the other side of the world: during a lengthy and intense cross-examination over the phone, she wanted to know whether from now on she was to think of me peddling long-stemmed roses at airports. Peter and Muriel did not start coming home with straight As. Mimi the cat still refused to use her scratching pole.

Still, I was offered the opportunity to explore different religious traditions. Buddhism was making inroads in those days, and we were invited to learn to meditate. But sitting cross-legged under the mythical Bodhi Tree awaiting enlightenment was something of a strain for me. The monkey thoughts, which our practice of breathing was to neutralize, kept intruding. During one such session of guided visualization our facilitator asked us to focus on our foreheads where our hidden Third Eye is said to be located, and to imagine its opening. Sure enough, two tiny shutters opened up in my forehead like in a Swiss clock, and a tiny bird popped out singing "cuckoo, cuckoo."

All the same, it was perhaps as the result of my efforts at meditation that early childhood memories came up again. Someone was still crying in the house with the big porch in Belgrade: was it me because my dolly Natasha was hurt, or was it Babushka, crying out there on the porch?

It seemed to me now that those two episodes had happened on different occasions, and that what brought them together in my dream was the crying. Maybe the broken doll in my arms was saying something about my own tenuous position in life. And Babushka's tears in the dark, they too stood for some unfathomable mystery of pain in the world.

And now, so many years later, the world was still full of pain and darkness. It was the early '80s and we were on the brink of nuclear extermination. No wonder then that it was only a matter of time before the peace and justice work of the church found me.

The Social Concerns Committee had decided to organize a program on nuclear weapons. We turned to a peace group and they sent us a speaker. He was a mathematics professor. He held forth on ICBMs and MIRVs and MXs and nuclear-tipped cruise missiles. He spared us none of the cheerful statistics. The world's scientific geniuses were working day and night so that millions of people could be snuffed out in an instant.

If that wasn't enough, the man stuttered. The "p" in stockpile exploded into stock--p-p-pile, and the mangled "m" in m-m-m-million multiplied the dead bodies over the face of the earth like a metastasizing malignancy. That stutter really got to me. I was upset at the organizers for sending us this bumbling do-gooder who was trying to stutter and sputter us into stepping between the two world powers and invite them to trade in their intercontinental swords for food stamps. That's the way the message struck me, and I, for one, was quite prepared to kill the messenger.

But that stutter, upon which I had so diligently built my defenses, was also the arrow that searched out and found the chink in my armor. Deep inside, I harbored a hidden stutter, hiatus, and inner split of my own, which mirrored the apocalyptic confrontation between the Soviet Union and the United States. Was not Russia the mythic cradle of my foundational identity? Was not America now my "home of the brave and land of the free"? What hyphen could possibly bridge such a gap?

Was being a Russian-American an oxymoron? What made the hyphen so powerless in this instance? The McCarthy era is still remembered for its grand attempt to fix the gold standard of essential Americanism. Spreading across continents, the corrosive power of Communism threatened to penetrate the stainless shield of Americanism itself. Its blight assumed the proportions of an epidemic and this called for strong medicine: the litmus test of un-American activities. The "red" of rebellion in the red-white-and blue of the American flag was bleached out. The choice of Communist-American was simply not an option.

So, it was the Russian-Communist connection that was the problem – but what did this have to do with me? I remembered the red-faced soldiers chasing me in my sleep in Hungary during our flight from Yugoslavia in 1944. Was I also trapped in my childish nightmare of primary colors, and the dead-end choices of BETTER DEAD THAN RED? BETTER RED THAN DEAD?

As I kept listening to our stuttering messenger of doom, something began to shift. I began to relate to the man's stutter from yet another place in myself. Why had I come to identify with the colonized and the occupied while Dad had remained as faithful to his soldier's pledge as ever? My gender, with all its drawbacks, afforded the advantages of weakness. It did not require me to kill or die fighting. What it did require of me was that I see to it that the children I bore had a chance at life. The man's stutter, the stock-p-p-piles and m-m-m-millions snowballed, and just as if this were a religious revival, I stood up and pledged to work for peace.

Surely the good professor was right: we were not children, we could learn. The unbridgeable gap of my double identity HAD to be bridged. When Senator McCarthy had sounded the trumpets of last judgment and ordered the citizenry to either the Right or the Left of the American flag, this did eventually call forth its own counter-reaction. The Civil Rights movement offered another acid test of what it means to be an American. Race had been a troublesome shard in the loins of America's self-conception. For a long time, skin color had been a godsend marker for unnatural selection. But the sweat of Blacks in the cotton fields, and the blood of Blacks in the battlefields cried out and, at long last, Blacks ceased being non-Americans, and became African-Americans. So now I too found my voice; I became a Russian-American peace activist.

As I was entering this new phase of my political education, the rest of the family was not that thrilled with church activities. To be fair to the kids, the children's program was hardly worth the fuss and bother of getting there. There weren't enough young families with children to make it work.

Muriel, at least, found her own solution. Just around the corner from church lived an elderly woman who had turned her house into an animal shelter. We usually parked our car across the street from her run-down place and I tended to give it a wide berth. Not Muriel. One day she just walked into the swirl of snarling dogs the way Daniel was said to have walked into the lions' den, and the beasts licked her hands and face instead of tearing her apart. From then on, she and Mrs. Green, "the dog lady," became fast friends, and she spent most Sunday mornings with her instead of at church.

For Peter, who was becoming a real teenager, there were only a couple of kids his age who showed up from time to time. Then they were all found smoking pot behind the church building. We had looked for a safe haven from the outside world, but its walls proved porous.

This also proved true at Tottenville High. I had to pick Peter up early one day, and drove up to the building, an enormous concrete structure. While I waited by the curb, a car drove up and slowed down just long enough for a man to jump out and throw a package over the school's fence. A man in uniform, presumably the school's security guard, showed up immediately on the other side, picked up the package, and walked away. I did not need to have seen many gangster movies to identify this as a "drop off."

Rick and I decided to ship Peter off for a time to Rick's cousins in Belgium. We hoped that drugs would not be as readily available in Brussels, and that a change of scene away from his peers might give Peter the break he needed to grow up.

There was another departure that year. Dad, neglected and unhappy, had once again decided to go back to Australia. Although he never uttered a word of complaint, I knew I had failed him. Our hectic and self-absorbed ways had not given him much of a part to play in our lives. He had a plan. He would buy an old van and just go bumming around Australia. His favorite writer was Jack London; surely Dad never knew that the man had been a Socialist. After a long life of scrupulous right living, Dad decided to live out the rest of it in free style, emulating one of Jack London's adventures.

The news from Brussels looked good. In the meantime, we researched private schools in the U.S. When Peter returned, we enrolled him in Darrow, a school located in northwestern Massachusetts. Darrow occupied a property once inhabited by a Shaker community. The sober, elegant lines of its buildings and interiors, surrounded by a spectacular New England landscape raised our hopes that such a place would find ways to mitigate whatever it was that seemed to trouble Peter.

But our hopes were to be shattered once again. On December 7, 1981, we experienced our own private Pearl Harbor Day. The phone rang, and the voice on the other end of the line was that of a policeman. Peter was in custody for "breaking and entering," and we needed to drive up to Massachusetts to deal with the incident. We drove up, and there he was, this stranger, our son. Peter had never been defiant, not even rude in the way of teenagers. He was unfathomable. He and his partner in crime, the son of a New York doctor, were both minors, they hadn't had time to steal anything, and the charges were dropped. They were, however, both dismissed from Darrow. After this episode, Peter went back to Tottenville High, and Rick "washed his hands off him."

I envied Nancy because her son Luco's main absorption at the time was "Dungeons and Dragons." Jane's problems were more severe. Her husband Foster took to visiting a woman a couple of doors down the street; it was the talk of Village Greens. I had no way of catching Rick in the act, but I just "knew" that he must be having affairs on his trips. I said nothing because plausible deniability was all in his favor but, drop by drop, this knowledge gathered in my throat into a hard, bitter lump. It was ironic, culturally speaking, that Nancy's husband, the "Latin lover" among our husbands, was the one who did not seem to stray.

We carried on. We decided to go on one of our summer family trips, which had been so successful in forging togetherness in the past. We had good memories of Disneyland, and were looking forward to seeing what Disney World in Florida had in store for us. Peter, however, must have been past the age of family adventure. He and Rick had words over everything: what music to play in the car, how to set up camp, where to stop, and what to see. The Kennedy Space Center left Peter unimpressed and we fled the Everglades, pursued by storms of mosquitoes.

Disney World took the cake. I did not expect that the Florida model would be the exact replica in every spitting detail of the California model. I guess I failed to appreciate the commercial genius of serial reproduction. Still, we gave it our best shot. It was hot, the crowds carried us forward, the music played the familiar tunes, and the bands marched smartly. Goofy goofed and Minnie waved and Mickey shook hands.

Muriel, at least, seemed to have a good time. Still, the smiles on the young women's faces as they tossed their batons and kicked up their shapely legs looked unnatural. What a poor imitation of those early smiles, when Peter, tucked away in my belly, had carried all our young hopes for the future in California, and Rick and I held hands, and the world and Disney were in their prime. Look at them, look at us now: our family was a failure.

Failed or not, the family carried on. Peter returned to Tottenville High. Rick returned to London, Paris, and Frankfurt. I returned to the Unitarian Church of Staten Island. My growing involvement in the peace movement now called for a bold new step. We heard that an International Peace Conference was to be held in Prague in 1983, and the people at church nominated me as their official delegate. I was hesitant. Could I actually travel to a Communist country? This felt like another major boundary crossing, the opening of yet another door into the dark unknown.

As if my internal conflict was not enough, the opposition on the home front was fierce. Rick pushed all my buttons. What was I thinking about, walking out on the kids and taking time off from working on my dissertation? Who did I think I was, traipsing off on some fool's errand, expecting to raise the Iron Curtain all by myself? My back stiffened and my whole body prepared to go into the "opt out" mode. But I talked to it the way Robert Redford talks to horses in *The Horse Whisperer*, and very slowly, packed my bags. A friend drove me to the airport, and I took off for Prague.

My cramped back was a clear indication of my cramped mind. I looked at the people on the plane, some two hundred of them in the American delegation, and wondered why we were not allowed to fly directly to Prague, but had to do it by way of Canada. Sitting on that plane, I felt I had been highjacked into the movie titled *The Invasion of the Body Snatchers*. There, monstrous pods, secreted in nurseries, are swelling to human form and producing aliens (Commies, don't you know) and preparing to take over the land. I too "knew" that all those people around me only looked like people: if you took their clothes off, their red diapers would give them away.

The woman next to me looked especially suspicious. Her story was that she was a council person in some city on Long Island. My story was that I was just a wife, mother, and student. The way she kept glancing at me was a little odd, and I finally recognized my own fear in her eyes. We ended up rooming together in Prague, and laughed heartily at how we had been afraid of each other. Her diapers had been made of American homespun and her trip to Prague was her enrollment in Peace 101 just the way mine was.

Old Prague is beautiful, and we had a few snatches of time to walk on the Charles Bridge and to enjoy Prague's boisterous welcome to us. The opening plenary session was held in a huge auditorium. I had expected to hear the *International*, but they started with Beethoven's *Ode to Joy*, which is, apparently, the official anthem of the United Nations. After that I braced myself for dull speeches but suddenly all the side doors of the auditorium opened up and children in Czech national costumes burst in singing, IN ENGLISH, "We Shall Overcome." I, for one, was truly overcome. I was still as leery as ever of being manipulated by Communist propaganda, but "we shall overcome" was not it, unless when WE sing it, it signifies Martin Luther King's dream of justice and peace, and when THEY do, it signifies "world domination."

It became clear pretty soon that the conference was a huge free-for-all. After some session hopping, I settled on the one entitled "Economic Aspects of the Arms Race." Still expecting the debates to be dominated by Soviets or their proxies, I found this one to be centered on Third-World issues. Most speakers were passionate and bitter non-Whites. They said that the cumulative debt of the developing nations was equal to world military expenditures for a single year. They blamed the military giants and wished a pox on both their houses.

In one of the workshops for delegates from religious organizations, I found myself sitting next to a man who turned out to be His Eminence Pimen, the Patriarch of all Russia. Overcoming my shyness, I finally introduced myself as a speaker of Russian. I asked him about the conditions of peace work in the Soviet Union. He replied that the Soviet state could not afford the arms race, and therefore not only did not persecute, but encouraged peace work. "If you," he pointed at me, "insist on putting your Pershing missiles in Europe, we will have to match your missiles with ours, and there will be fewer resources for the needs of ordinary people everywhere." I said O.K., I would see to it that we didn't, and we both laughed, as it was obvious how little power either one of us had to send or not to send missiles.

I decided to try to shed my fears and use the opportunity of this conference to speak to Soviets. When it came to lunch time, I found a table with Russian-looking people, and joined them. But I struck out. They ignored me, and I ended up talking the whole time with some delegates from New Zealand.

At the next lunch break I sat with a group of Danes. As I was leaving the dining hall, one of the Russians (the one with the Brezhnev-like eyebrows), approached me and said that his table had saved a seat for me – so why didn't I show up? Go figure. So, I joined them the next day, together with some people from Senegal, and once again ended up speaking the whole time with the latter. The only sign of acknowledgment was that one of the Russians, pointing to my signet ring with Dad's coat of arms on it, asked me if I was a princess. I replied that my father had been the son of a princess, but that I was the daughter of a proletarian (sorry, Dad). My remark was met with silence, but the man who had asked the question just pushed his dessert in my direction.

Clearly, I had thrown caution to the wind, but the Russians remained on their guard. On their guard against ME? I saw myself in a skintight black gown with a plunging neckline, languidly waving away the curling wisp of smoke rising from my amber cigarette holder, whispering sweet nothings, in Marlene Dietrich's husky voice, into the ear of the man with the bushy eyebrows. However off-the-wall my presumed spy persona appeared to me, this is just what I read in the Russians' eyes.

Another odd occasion soon followed. This time a fellow American from L.A. and I, both exhausted by the non-stop conferencing, decided to look for a quiet spot to rest up. We pushed open a door, and found ourselves at the top of the large auditorium of the initial plenary session. It looked empty, and we sat down on the back seats. After a while we noticed that the place was not altogether empty. A dozen people or so were gathered all the way down, just below the stage. We looked again: surrounded by a few hangers-on and holding a mike, probably broadcasting to his followers, was Yasser Arafat. Still, it looked like he was making a speech to the empty auditorium, and we giggled.

Perhaps the keynote of this Peace Conference was the random explosion of laughter. It felt good to laugh. It seemed to open a safety valve so that stores of compressed fear, as lethal as the atomic nuclei locked up in all those warheads, could be defused. When it was all over, and the time came to fly back to New York, I did so, filled with good will toward all living things.

Rick was waiting for me at the airport, and after the usual struggle on the Belt Parkway and over the Verrazano Bridge, we made it home. He showed me the only two articles he had found about the Prague Conference. One of them was headlined "Moscow stages a Peace Conference." In a few lines it explained how it had been organized by a Communist front organization. But the visual presiding over the other article, a picture of Yasser Arafat, was even more surprising. Arafat was holding a mike and addressing, by omission and implication, a FULL auditorium. My mouth dropped open. If I had not walked in on Arafat's actual performance to an empty auditorium, I would have filled in the audience myself just as the article intended me to do.

Contrary to my own paranoid expectations, the conference had been as harmless as a church picnic. People just talking to each other, hoping that peace across nations was possible. The real shocker turned out to be the reporting of events by our vaunted free press back home. And what about the millions of people who lived and died altogether off the map colored in by East and West? In the mirror the Third World was holding up to us, all our comforts, material and spiritual, looked terminally ill gotten.

***

CHAPTER 13

BACK TO THE FUTURE

Back home, my sleep was fitful that night. The mirror above the dresser was a dark pool, and I dove into it, looking for something. When I woke up again, the mirror was beginning to gather the first light of day. It touched our wedding picture below, and the picture of the kids kneeling in the grass with the dog Bibi between them.

Peter was keeping a low profile just then, and our attention was diverted to Muriel, who had begun to show "attitude." The thought of her entering Tottenville High and its academic pastures so generously laced with weed was not reassuring. The costly diversions of Belgium or boarding school in Massachusetts had been a spectacular failure with Peter, and we considered the less radical option of a local private school for Muriel. As she was to reassure us later, this was a step up, for the drugs available there were upgraded from pot to cocaine.

Nancy was now teaching Spanish at the Newark campus of Rutgers University. The Department of Foreign Languages which had hired her was in the process of consolidating their Russian and German programs, and they were looking for a candidate competent to teach in both those fields. I was comfortable with my competency in Russian, but German was somewhat of a stretch: I had had little occasion to speak it since my romance with Hans. But my interview went well, and they hired me.

It was great to be reunited with Nancy again as in the old days of our graduate studies together. The big issue for both of us now was to get our dissertations out of the way. The real challenge for me just then, however, proved to be on the home front. I had not been as imaginative in acting out as my kids were. Well yes, in my boarding school days in Marrakech we did puff on cigarettes in toilets, and some boys did try to sneak into the girls' dormitory once. But we still got up early, made our beds, brushed our teeth, attended classes, played sports, and went to the movies once in a while. No one ever "yoked" anyone in some dark alley - and street drugs were unknown.

Peter turned eighteen in 1984 and actually graduated from high school. Rick and I were planning to travel to Europe, and invited the kids to join us; Muriel agreed, Peter refused. He wanted to go to Jamaica. Our neighbor Rosalie had relatives in Jamaica who were gracious enough to invite him. He was eighteen, so we stood aside.

Peter took off for Jamaica and we took off for Europe. I had an additional plan. As a sequel to my trip to Prague I now arranged a trip to the Soviet Union. A Quaker peace group was organizing a cruise down the Volga River and I signed up. But first Rick and Muriel and I would spend some time in France and England.

We began by spending a week in a *pension de famille* in the coastal town of La Rochelle. Muriel enjoyed the food, the beach, and the style of sociability one sees in French movies. England was also pretty "cool," even though Muriel was terminally embarrassed when I actually became teary-eyed at Stratford-on-Avon. Of course, the place was a tourist trap, but I could feel the presence of the Bard all the same. Muriel got her turn in Birmingham wading through mounds of Duran Duran fan mail with local groupies. On the way back we stopped at Greenham Commons, where women were camping in protest by the gates of the nuclear arms facility.

Then it was back to France. While Rick and I marveled at the miraculous stained-glass windows of Chartres Cathedral, Muriel found her bliss contemplating the most adorable statues of poodles and dachshunds at the dog cemetery in the Parisian suburb of Asnières. Then it was time to go our separate ways. Rick took Muriel to reconnect with his family in Brussels and I took off for Moscow.

This time I felt somewhat more at ease finding myself among likely "fellow-travelers" on the plane. But my feelings about entering the Soviet Union at long last were as divided as ever. I was about to enter the birthplace of my Russian soul, but I was also about to cross the threshold to the Evil Empire. Both Mom and Dad had sent dire warnings from Down Under. Mother, whose madness provided direct access to secret Communist networks, "knew" that "they" already had an eye on me, and that I was treading on thin ice. Father, despite his otherwise ironic turn of mind, was just as adamant. He knew that "they never forget and never forgive," and that I was seriously flirting with the Gulag.

The initial leg of our trip took us through Moscow and Leningrad. At first, walking through the streets of Russia's alternate capitals was like walking through haunted places. Moscow's vast and empty Red Square was alive with phantoms dressed in the bright colors of Surikov's historical paintings. People were kneeling, cap in hand, waiting for the silence to produce the fall of the executioner's axe. Successive tableaus of disloyal boyars in long caftans and beards, proud rebellious Cossack chieftains, disheveled, wild-eyed heretics, followed each other on the scaffold. I barely noticed the real people standing four abreast in a line which seemed to have no end, silently awaiting their turn to peek at the mummies in the sacred mausoleum.

Leningrad was still called Leningrad in 1984, but it was the city of Peter to me. The famous equestrian statue of the great founder immediately became Pushkin's *Bronze Horseman*. He was about to fly from his pedestal again in nightmarish pursuit of the "little man" who had dared to raise his fist at the likeness of the mighty emperor. By playing God and building his new capital on a swamp, Peter the Great had exposed the city to disastrous floods. In Pushkin's story, the protagonist's fiancée loses her life in such a flood and the resulting madness of her lover is forever haunted by the pursuit of the galloping potentate.

But Leningrad was also the Petersburg of Gogol and Dostoyevsky. I held tight my raincoat just in case of coat-snatching ghosts, and at every bend of a canal in this "Venice of the North" I expected to meet the brooding figure of Raskolnikov.

As if to confirm the rule of the watery elements in Leningrad, it had rained hard during our tour of the city, and the Intourist guide decided to cancel the visit to the Smolny Museum. I begged to stop at least for some few minutes, and ran out into the rain to take a closer look. When I came back someone on our bus asked whether I had braved the rain to look at the place where the October Revolution had been born. He was referring to the fact that that building complex had housed the first Soviet Government, until the decision was made to move the capital back to Moscow.

I smiled and said nothing. The Smolny had been endowed by Catherine the Great to become a finishing school for girls of noble birth, and Dad's mother, the grandmother I had never known, had gone to school there.

The Smolny finishing school had caused my grandmother to become an accomplished pianist, as Dad tells it, as well as handy with charcoal and sketching pad. Apparently, she produced beautiful sketches of her beloved horses and greyhounds. But this did not seem to stand in the way of more practical skills. Having lost her husband in 1905 to the Russo-Japanese War, she took care of her four children and ran what we would now call a ranch, raising horses for the Imperial cavalry.

Just as the chance to know her had not been in the cards for me, the chance of getting a glance at a picture of her had been lost as well. Dad tells the story of how during the Civil War his White Guard unit was being pursued by a contingent of Red Guards, and how, fearing capture and likely repercussions for his family, he took the time, at full gallop, to tear up the photograph of his mother he had been carrying in his breast pocket. He did manage to elude his pursuers, however, and regretted all his life having destroyed the picture: a full-length shot of a young woman in a formal black gown, taken modishly from the back, her head tilted over her left shoulder showing her face in profile and the plunging "V" of her bare back. Very much a Smolny graduate.

Little by little, I was able to shoo away some of the ghosts and look around. The people and buildings did look shabby and drab, just as Western newspapers tended to describe them. And there were no skyscrapers. The place did have a 19th century look about it. But then so does newly scrubbed Paris, having relegated its skyscrapers to the periphery of *la Defense*. Then again, *la ville lumière* (the city of light) did not have to sustain a 900-day blockade in World War II, and the death toll from hunger, cold, disease, and bombing of about a million of its inhabitants.

But our schedule rushed us on to the segment of our trip that was to take us down the Volga. I was sorry that we were to bypass the city of Gorky. The town had been renamed to honor its famous native son whose writings about the ills of pre-revolutionary Russia I knew well. He had chosen to write under the name of "Gorky" because the word means "bitter" in Russian.

Before its Soviet renaming, the town's name of Nizhniy-Novgorod had been famous in its own right. The original Novgorod, one of the major seats of Russian medieval activity, had been oriented toward trade with the Baltic Sea and had belonged to the Hanseatic League. The city state, run by its patrician republican government, was subdued by the principality of Moscow in 1477. A large number of its citizens were banished to the middle Volga region, where they founded Nizhny (lower) Novgorod. True to their mercantile ways, they developed it into a thriving trading center, and its yearly fair became legendary.

Now under its new name, Gorky had become a closed city. We did not know that one of the great peace activists of the century, Andrei Sakharov, was living there in banishment. His early claim to fame had been that of father of the Soviet H bomb. At first entirely absorbed in the scientific challenges of his work, just like his American counterpart Robert Oppenheimer (the "father of the A bomb") he later experienced a change of heart.

This happened in 1955 at a reception in his honor. His statement, "May all our devices explode as successfully as today's but always over test sites and never over cities," was met with an awkward silence, and then the admonition that "Sakharov was expected to make devices, not to guide them." Oppenheimer's feelings after his interview with President Truman, who called him "that crybaby of a scientist," are also well documented. Both scientists came to realize the enormity of what they had done: foolishly delivered into fallible and potentially irresponsible hands ultimate power over humankind.

From then on Sakharov and his second wife Elena Bonner joined the dissident movement. The dissidents wrote position papers, copied and distributed the writings of forbidden authors, and chronicled the searches, arrests, and convictions conducted by the KGB. But Sakharov had an international following, and the KGB had to limit persecution to harassment.

During the '50s dominated by McCarty's rantings, Oppenheimer had also been subjected to censure. He had been called to humiliating hearings, attacked in the press, and stripped of his security clearance. This aborted his scientific career and silenced his eminently rational voice for a sane nuclear policy. Some twenty years later, on the other side of the Cold War, the Sakharov and Bonner team managed, against all odds, to win some of its battles. In 1972 the Treaty on the Limitation of Antiballistic Missile Systems was signed, and in 1975 Andrei Sakharov received the Nobel Peace Prize. George W. Bush was not looking for the Nobel Peace Prize when he scuttled the hard-won treaty in 2004. They could as well have awarded him one. They gave one to President Obama.

As for Sakharov, the Nobel Peace Prize only intensified the public vilification and private hounding. It was decided that he needed to be deprived of his contacts with the outside world, including his wife Elena. In 1980 he was banished to Gorky. Sakharov began another one of his hunger strikes, this time determined to hold out until reunion with his wife, or death. We missed the irony, my peacenik friends and I, of our floating down the Volga in 1984 while Andrei Sakharov was undergoing the painful indignity of forced feeding in Gorky.

The plan was to board our boat in Kazan, located about half way down the long course of the Volga, the mother of all Russian rivers, and we arrived there by plane. The city of Kazan used to be the capital of a khanate or Tatar principality which had been conquered by Ivan the Terrible. Our visit of the city was brief. There was no time to visit Kazan's university, founded in 1804 and made famous by two notorious former students. The first one, Leo Tolstoy, bored by the curriculum and faculty, had dropped out. The second one, Vladimir Ulyanov (better known as Lenin), had been ejected for political activism. As we walked down the main street of Kazan, with its decrepit buildings and empty stores, the general impression was one of glaring poverty.

When we settled down for our first meal on board the River Boat Pushkin, I looked up from my table and noticed that a large crowd had gathered on the dock. In the gathering dusk they were just one large mass of gray bodies and blank faces staring at us in silence while we sat there in our boat like in some lit-up bubble from outer space. I felt caught in a time warp. Floating in my pristine boat with caviar and champagne on the table, I might as well be my paternal grandmother, waltzing away in some crystal-lit ballroom. The people gathered on the dock in Kazan were the exact same people who had sullenly looked on for centuries, with hunger in their bellies, while my ancestors danced. Nothing had changed; they were now looking at me.

I recalled Dad's version of why he had joined the "Whites" in the civil war. He had walked away from the Austrian soldier who could have killed him but did not, and kept walking. By then the Russian army was falling apart.

In the general disarray Dad made it home, and discovered that it was no longer his. People's *soviets* or councils had been organized in the region, and a delegation of peasants came to the house one evening. Apparently an order had been issued by the local commissar to chop down the family orchard. His mother kept telling them that they all held the property in common now, and they nodded their heads - but orders were orders.

As Dad, who had just turned eighteen, listened to these democratic proceedings, the decision made itself. That very night he received his mother's blessing, chose a good horse, and rode out into the night. He was never to see either his mother or his younger siblings again.

The ensuing years of the Civil War remain a blank. Dad would simply not speak of them, and my only recourse was literature. In Isaac Babel's *Red Cavalry* the narrator is a young Jewish intellectual, a true believer in the October Revolution who, assigned to a detachment of young Cossacks, strives to become just like them: fearless and casually cruel. But what seems to come so naturally to those born warriors is an unnatural struggle to him. Just killing a goose provokes a Hamlet-like soul-searching: "to be or not to be."

Dad, born into the presumed security of the land-owning class, would not have been expected to wrestle with Hamlet-like dilemmas. In return for his privileged position, he was honor bound to dedicate his life to the defense of his country and its ruler. As a symbolic baptism into his soldierly calling, he had been placed on horseback even before his religious baptism.

In my recollection, however, Dad is anything but a bronze likeness of a hero on horseback. He replays, instead, the story of Isaac Babel's hero with the goose dilemma. Back in Morocco we had a rabbit pen. Dad had been given the fittingly male job of selecting a rabbit for the dinner table. As he failed to return and I was sent to investigate, I found him sitting on the ground among his presumed victims, allowing them to crawl all over him, which failed to produce a rabbit stew.

And yet he too had ridden furiously into battle during the Civil War. He had been an actor, in a script written by others to be sure, but acting his part all the same. As I write this, the unrecorded, untold scene takes vivid shape in my mind. A man sinks to the ground and the gaping hole in his eye has been made by the bullet of Dad's rifle. Dad's horse's hoof crushes another man's skull. Dad is thrown off his horse. He doesn't know if the slippery goo under his fingers is the other man's blood or his own. At long last the other man's body slackens and in one last effort against the pull of gravity, Dad heaves the dead weight off, and lives. Lives NOT to tell. Surely the unspoken, unspeakable truth was that my sweet, patient, kindest Dad, whom I had watched sitting still as rabbits came to nibble on his sleeve, HAD killed.

In 1924 Dad, now living in Yugoslavia, received a letter from his younger brother, Andrei, by way of the Red Cross. He and the youngest brother, Piotr, and their sister, Liuba, were fine. As a matter of fact, Liuba had crossed over and married what he referred to as a "new man," who had been sent as an ambassador to Czechoslovakia. Their grandmother, she of the famous rule of speaking only French at the dinner table, was still alive. She had been taken in by local peasants and passed off as one of their own. Perhaps they remembered that she had built a school and a clinic in their village.

Their mother, however, had died on her own separate property. Hunger had stalked the Volga region after the Civil War, and she had starved to death.

Why not, asked the younger brother, let bygones be bygones and return home to join in the glorious job of building a new Russia? But Dad was not prepared to let bygones be bygones. He did write back, however, and the reply came four years later, in 1928. His brother now wrote him not to return and not to write. The brothers did not wish to be found.

Unlike Dad, however, I had been prepared to let bygones be bygones. I had come all this way because I wanted to stop running from the red-faced soldiers of my childish nightmare in order to salvage a future for my own children. But looking at the crowd on the dock of Kazan in 1984, I couldn't keep the past from bleeding into the present. Staring at the chicken à la Kiev on my plate, I tried to imagine what it must have been like for my grandmother to starve.

Dad had told me that their house had been built by French prisoners going back to Napoleon's invasion of Russia in 1812. I tried to imagine that house now, something like a Southern ante-bellum mansion, where a woman waited. But it was unlikely that she would have been allowed to stay in the house. It must have been taken over by new masters.

Maybe they let her stay in one of the dependencies. I imagined her making herself at home in some old shed. I imagined that among the things she would be allowed to take would be her sketching pad and charcoal, and I imagined her sketching away. Lovely horses, maybe a cow and a goat (Dad had mentioned being chased by a goat as a young boy) and there must have been geese and ducks and chickens running about. And of course, she would sketch the greyhounds.

At first what she missed most was the tea. There was a whole ritual to Russian tea drinking. The maid brings in the samovar and places it at the head of the table. From time to time the hostess lifts the little tea pot placed on top of the samovar, where the tea leaves are steeping. She fans the glowing bits of coal in the central tube which heats the water, and checks the brew in the tea pot. When it has reached its proper point of concentration and the water in the body of the samovar is near boiling point, she begins to fill the tall glasses in their filigreed silver holders. First some of the fragrant dark liquid from the tea pot, then the hot water from the ornate samovar spigot. The guests watch the tea turn to the desired shade of transparent gold and receive their glasses.

But was it the tea she missed or the gathering of family and friends around the samovar? Everyone was gone now. There used to be twelve, fifteen, even twenty people around the table; all scattered far and wide now, many dead. Her husband fallen long ago somewhere in Manchuria. Her first-born fallen perhaps, or maybe in hiding, or maybe abroad. The two younger boys were gone as well. Gone to fight? Gone into hiding? Or just gone to scrounge up some food? Her daughter too was gone. They whispered about it behind her back; she has left with one of "them."

As for tea, she has managed to harvest a goodly supply of rose hips. She found an old barrel and filled it with the precious buds. The hot brew is a life saver. Of course, there used to be the sweet taste of cherry preserves melting in the mouth with the hot tea... But did they really chop down the orchard? The policy of War Communism had backfired badly. In an attempt to feed the hungry cities, forced food requisitions had resulted in peasant revolts and the burning of crops.

I imagined my grandmother sketching away: barns bursting into flames, horses led away... sketches of gaunt, misshapen, wasted animals piling up in a corner of the shed. The mythical goat was found in a ditch, recognizable by his horns, hoofs, and mangled hide. As to the geese and ducks and chickens, the vanishing act took a little longer; she locked them up in a shed at night. But the new masters of the house, who changed often, were also hungry. As she lay awake, she would hear a sudden cackle or muffled cry, a fluttering, a beating of wings, and the suppressed growl of a human voice. And then there were none.

The dogs too had wandered off. They scoured the countryside in bands. But her favorite, Kashtanka, had stayed with her. They might have gone hunting together, but "they" had taken away her rifle. So now she could feel Kashtanka's ribs and haunches as they snuggled together at night to keep each other warm. For the winds had begun to blow and the leaves had fallen.

She had been gathering mushrooms all along, talking herself into one more expedition into the woods. But the season was over. She had been trying to dry and save the mushrooms for another day, but they had melted in her mouth one by one. Yet her stomach remained so tight that it eased her to stay bent over. It was a good thing she had not brought a mirror into her new habitation: what would she see in it? The likeness of the young woman in formal black gown and the plunging V down her back?

What would her neighbors, those among the women from the village who dared to visit her, see in their former "mistress"? Her Smolny education had ill prepared her after all. They had to teach her to make nettle soup, or to set traps for squirrels and rats, or to collect acorns, grind them down, and boil them into gruel.

But the inevitable Russian winter was bound to bring all such last-ditch efforts to an end. If she had managed to gather wood before, she no longer has the strength. And if all she needs to do for water now is step out and scoop up some snow, the effort is beyond her. The day Kashtanka didn't wake up, she sketched her last sketch: one horizontal black line across the middle of the page. Whether it was intended to draw a boundary between the white of the sky and the white of the earth in the wintry Russian landscape, or square accounts between life and death on some last balance sheet, is for anyone to say. Still, I like to imagine that her very last thought was for her first-born and that she knew, somehow, that he was alive.

Did my grandmother, did all those people die in vain? Was the Revolution a failure? Karl Marx, the man with the unkempt beard and imperious eyes we see in familiar portraits, grand-son of rabbis, German philosopher and 19th century revolutionary, dedicated his life to redress the scandal of the exploitation of man by man. How did his theoretical wrestling with Hegel's idea of historic necessity, his joyless experience of the Prussian state, his observation of the Dickensian conditions of the industrial revolution in England lead to revolution among the peasants of Russia?

The encyclopedic historian and critic of Capitalism, fierce polemicist, old-time prophet, and utopian dreamer was astonished to discover that it was in Russia that he was most enthusiastically read. Surely Russia was not ripe for the revolution as he had defined it. The country had no technologically advanced, capital-driven industry, and it had no proletariat to speak of. Yet Marx's dream of a better world was also Russia's dream.

In the winter of 2007, Rick and I flew to New York to see Tom Stoppard's trilogy, *The Coast of Utopia*. I was thrilled to watch on stage at Lincoln Center the historical characters whose lives and legacies I too had struggled to grasp. Alexander Herzen, the principal hero of Stoppard's play, shared Marx's revulsion against a society organized legally, politically, and economically around the premise of self-interest. Born into the wealthy land-owning class, he was nevertheless against Russia's autocracy and religious establishment. Forced into exile, he published his oppositional journal, *Kolokol* (the Bell), from London.

He felt that Russia had much to learn from the West, and represented the liberal Westernizers. His antagonists were the "Slavophiles," who insisted that Russia had made and should continue to follow its own path. This dilemma of where Russia belongs on this earth is still in question. Boris Yeltsyn turned his back on his country's Socialist experiment, and accepted the "liberal" advice of his American well-wishers. His successor, Vladimir Putin, has called the foreign intrusion as disastrous to the country as World War II. He too is charged with the problem of balancing Russia's position between East and West.

Back in Herzen's day, the disappointment caused by the failure of the 1848 revolutions questioned Hegel's idea of a universal march toward progress. Herzen now also turned expectantly to the institution of the Russian "mir" - a tradition of self-government vested in the common ownership of land and a council of village elders. Once liberated from the class of land-owners, the peasantry would regenerate Russian society.

Mikhail Bakunin, Herzen's antagonist in Stoppard's play, was also an aristocrat. Unlike Herzen, however, he was an apostle of anarchy, and fought autocracy on the barricades of Europe, thus anticipating Trotsky's dedication to "world revolution." And he was also at odds with Karl Marx. The latter excoriated him for failing to understand that progress depended on the material base of a society's production, i.e., on the economy, stupid. Bakunin, in turn, warned that state power vested in any group, even the proletariat, would always bear the seeds of tyranny.

The *Narodniki* or Populists appearing in Stoppard's play also harbored the belief that the renewal of Russia must look for models not in the capitalist West, but in the Russian countryside. They were self-consciously classless, and went to the people to teach the Russian peasant the truth of his own strength and wisdom. But the Russian peasant distrusted their woolly exhortations and more often than not, turned them in to the police as subversives.

Despairing at their failure to set into motion a society they saw stuck in the mire of despotism, a branch of the Populists turned to terrorism. The assassination in 1881 of Alexander II, the tsar who had liberated the serfs in 1861, proved a historical turning point. His son Alexander III, a Strong Man (who loved to unbend horse shoes with his bare hands) presided over a Russia where all channels of opposition were blocked. At the same time, he promoted state-sponsored industrialization. This double bind prepared the ground for a revolutionary explosion.

***

CHAPTER 14

THREE RUSSIANS FROM SIMBIRSK

The ten-day cruise down the Volga was supposed to give American and Soviet delegates the occasion and time to address the barriers that divided them. I knew little of my Quaker companions' tradition and admired the fact that it led them to venture into a strange land to seek peace – a land much vilified be official opinion. They would get together first thing in the morning, and practice silence for a whole hour. I tried to join them at first, but like with my earlier attempts at meditation, the experience proved unpromising.

Our Soviet counterparts were a group of men who called themselves "peace workers." They too were an unknown quantity: would I be able to talk to them, or would they behave like the Soviets I had met in Prague? But the word got around that I was fluent in Russian, and I was invited to join the Soviets in the evenings. My failure to practice silence with the Quakers was mirrored by my reluctance to keep up with the Russians in downing vodka. But I was, after all, a woman, and we found a compromise: they ordered Georgian champagne, and things worked out.

They worked out so much so, that they loosened enough to ask me who the "spooks" were in the American delegation. They pointed out one Russian who always ate alone, and no one spoke to. "This is "ours," they said. I was innocently startled by the assumption that we might have "observers" among us as well, and tried not to look too sheepish. Just the same, how "open" could our conversations be? I knew all about the burst of creative energy after the Revolution in literature and the arts – but I also knew about the suicide of poets and the withdrawal into silence by many more writers because they did not want to be corralled into the Writers' Union and forced to fit into the strait jacket of Socialist Realism. Perhaps it did make sense to make the arts "more accessible" to the ordinary people, but the results proved conventional.

And then there was the "thaw" of the '60s, and *Solzhenitsyn's Day in the Life of Ivan Denisovich*. But then the reins of control were pulled back again, resulting in a number of writers seeking or condemned to exile. At least they were not sent to the Gulag, which had presumably been dismantled. In the 70s there was an increased exit from the public sphere with its obligatory enthusiasm for the victories of Socialism. This retreat into the private circles of family and friends also fostered the ferment of political dissent. And now we were in the mid-80s, and dialogue on all fronts was clearly encouraged.

Our goodwill cruise proceeded down the Volga, the great, sluggish river, and eventually came to a stop in Ulyanovsk. That town was named after Vladimir Ulyanov, better known as Lenin. My notion of the man was as mummified as the likeness of him sleeping, like Snow White, under glass cover in Red Square. Yet I was meeting him everywhere, carved in stone or on giant billboards. Leery of all strenuous and monolithic appeals, but also of the automatic demonization on which I was raised, I looked forward to visiting the family home of his childhood, now a museum. But this too proved a pilgrimage destination. The earnest, plain-looking woman, who tip-toed through the comfortably furnished rooms as if they were hallowed ground, was a vestal guarding a sacred fire.

After the visit I sat on the bus, which was taking us through the quiet streets of Ulyanovsk to some other Lenin landmark. My moody thoughts about the elusive Father of the Russian Revolution were suddenly scattered by one word in the guide's speech, the word "Simbirsk." I had not realized that Ulyanovsk was the new name of the old town of Simbirsk. I jumped up and explained to one of the Soviet "peace workers" that Simbirsk was the town where my father had gone to military school. If that school still existed, I very much wanted to find it. He offered to go with me, and we got off the bus.

I looked at Ulyanovsk with new eyes. Instead of retracing the steps of Lenin, I now imagined Dad as an adolescent walking these very streets. The first man we asked about an old military school told us, with a half-smile, that it was now the "new" military school. We followed his directions and soon enough, behind tall trees and a wrought-iron fence, I saw a set of reddish brick buildings. An armed sentry was posted at the gate, and I assumed that taking a picture would be verboten, but my companion told me to go ahead. We came closer and I snapped a couple of pictures. The young sentry looked alarmed, and we moved on.

Later I discovered that Alexander Kerensky, the man brought forward by the February or Democratic Revolution (as opposed to the later Bolshevik October one), was also a native of Simbirsk. If my sense of Lenin's historical role was distorted through the magnifying lens of myth, Kerensky's name was associated with ridicule. Dad had told me that the man had fled the Winter Palace disguised as a woman. Did he really believe what I later discovered to be a canard?

I knew Dad so well, yet I had a hard time wrapping my mind around his political convictions. He was now an old factory hand in Sydney who could have used the worker benefits the Australian Labor Party championed, yet he never voted the Labor ticket. When I asked him why he did not vote his class interests, he just shook his head and changed the subject.

Even when I brought back to him the snapshots of his alma mater, all he said, after a while, was that it made him recall his first dance. It must have been a big deal, a stepping out into a world of bright lights and bright young girls fluttering in gauze and satin who had invaded the school's familiar territory of endless classes and drills.

Did the past have such a hold on Dad because it was wonderful, or because it was terrible? It must have been such a tight knot of both these extremes that his life's course was set once and for all. And yet it was not the ease and privilege he seemed to regret. I never heard him complain about our poverty or uncertain circumstances. It was something else. He seemed to carry a wound of violent severance, as if he had been cut off from the very roots of life.

Being alive for him had been about fields and woods and horses and dogs, sleigh rides in winter, the promise of spring as the ice breaks on the frozen rivers, fishing and swimming in summer, and the golden harvest in fall. And it had been about old-fashioned hospitality when family and friends gathered to enjoy hearty food and strong drink.

That's when he must have heard the story about the hunting party. They were stalking a big wolf when one of Dad's uncles felt the urge to attend to nature's call. He was thus occupied when the wolf appeared before him catching him quite literally with his pants down. He grabbed his rifle and fired... and got the wolf, but the recoil was powerful, and the rest of the party came upon him sitting in a pile of his own shit. The story was too juicy not to make the rounds ever after.

And so, they had gathered, and had their fun, and rendered thanks to God on high and to His representative on earth, the Tsar, for holding it all together. It was all about taking things for granted because it had always been that way – at least for them...

Alexander Kerensky, the second man from Simbirsk, had chosen a different path. His father had exchanged his priestly calling for that of a secular educator. In the very first paragraph of Kerensky's memoir, the town of Simbirsk appears as a vision of apple trees in blossom sloping down from the high bank all the way to the Volga. This emblematic vision of a Russian landscape is immediately recognizable in the popular World War II song "Katiusha" (diminutive for Yekaterina). It too begins with apple blossoms and mists rising from the river, and the girl Katiusha stepping out on the high bank to sing her faith in the return of the soldier she loves.

It happened that Lenin's father was also a member of the educational system in Simbirsk and that the two families knew each other. Kerensky wrote in his memoir that in 1887 news from the capital shook the provincial town. A gifted and promising young man, who had been sent to Saint Petersburg to pursue his higher education, had been implicated in a terrorist plot against Tsar Alexander III. The name of the young man was Alexander Ulyanov. The impact on Alexander's younger brother Vladimir remains incalculable, for his older brother was summarily tried and executed.

Alexander Kerensky also went on to pursue his studies in Saint Petersburg. Unlike the Ulyanov brothers, however, he turned to politics to pursue his goals. There was mounting agitation to wrest a parliament and a constitution from the unwilling monarch. Tsar Nicholas II had made a deathbed promise to his father, the "strong man" Alexander III, to safeguard absolutism. He was also influenced by his beautiful wife, a German princess raised by Queen Victoria. The Tsarina became a convert to Russia's ancient ways and fell under the spell of the "man of God" Rasputin. Her son, the young Tsarevich Aleksei, suffered from hemophilia, and Rasputin was reputed to have the power to talk the boy's blood flow to a stop.

The Tsar had ignored increasing unrest in cities and the countryside. The 1905 war with Japan, which resulted in Russia's defeat, aggravated an already unstable situation. The events of Bloody Sunday, when the police opened fire on a huge peaceful demonstration led by a priest, precipitated the Revolution of 1905. This finally caused Nicholas II to allow the formation of a parliament or Duma. And Alexander Kerensky was elected to this First Duma by the Trudoviki, or Labor Party, while the Socialist Revolutionaries and the Social Democrats boycotted the election.

The issue of land redistribution was staunchly opposed by the imperial regime, and Nicholas II dissolved the First Duma. The Second Duma was also dissolved on the initiative of the minister Piotr Stolypin. There had been a rash of Left terrorist attacks and Stolypin was assassinated in 1911. His reform attempts were also opposed by the extreme Right, which resorted to the scapegoating of minorities, especially Jews and Poles.

Russia's foreign policy, particularly its support of the Orthodox populations in the Balkans, gradually led to its involvement in World War I. And yet, Nicholas II had sponsored an international peace conference in 1899 at The Hague. He had been influenced by a book, *The Future of War*, written by a Jewish entrepreneur named Ivan Bloch. The author warned that the application of emergent technology to warfare would place overwhelming demands on future warring parties and result in the destruction of their social, economic, and political orders.

Kaiser Wilhelm II of Germany dismissed the Russian Tsar's initiative as "humanitarian nonsense." He felt quite confident in Germany's capacity to gain the upper hand in any military conflict. The result was the slaughter of millions in World War I and the collapse of the Prussian Hohenzollern dynasty as well as that of the Russian Romanovs and Austrian Habsburgs.

If World War I had not erupted in August of 1914, who knows how the social and political struggles within the Russian Empire would have played out? The various Dumas had succeeded in wresting a number of concessions from the wavering Russian monarch. But World War I did erupt and events took on the disheveled plot of a Dostoyevsky novel. There were rumors that the German woman on the throne and the black magician Rasputin were plotting to sell Russia to the Germans; a group of courtiers assassinated the monk. There were rumors that the Germans also financed the Bolsheviks. There were bread riots and strikes - and the soldiers garrisoned in the capital were persuaded to join the insurgents. This led to the Tsar's abdication and Kerensky's premiership in the Provisional Government.

At first things looked promising. The February Revolution of 1917, after all, was a bloodless one. Kerensky was a consensus candidate because he was trusted by both the parliamentarians and the soviets. The latter were people's councils, rapidly formed during the first days of the February uprising in Petrograd (renamed from Petersburg during the war). At this initial stage the revolutionaries cooperated with Kerensky, as the Mensheviks in particular made their peace with what they saw as the inevitable bourgeois phase of Russia's political and economic development. As a matter of fact, a Bolshevik uprising attempted in July of 1917 failed, and Lenin fled to Finland.

What catapulted Lenin's triumphal return and takeover of power in October of the same year was the attempt by would-be dictator General Kornilov to depose Kerensky. In the ensuing power struggle Kerensky's bid for democracy in Russia was defeated, and he did have to flee, but dressed as a sailor, not as a woman.

෬෧

The third man from Simbirsk, who gave the town his family's name (Ulyanovsk), took Russia in a radically new direction. In this man's writings we find no idyllic description of Simbirsk wreathed in apple blossoms or associated with Proustian memories of first dances with *jeunes filles en fleur*. Yet Vladimir Ulyanov's childhood in Simbirsk did not seem all that different from Dad's or Kerensky's - until that fatal year of 1887 when his brother Alexander was executed for political terrorism.

Vladimir entered Kazan University, but was dismissed during some student unrests on the sole suspicion of his name. Banished to the countryside, where his mother's family owned a small estate, he immersed himself in the reading of the revolutionary classics. He also pursued a law degree by correspondence and passed the bar exam in 1891. Thanks to the tireless petitioning of his mother, he was allowed to practice law in Samara, a river town further down on the Volga. His clients were petty thieves and a notorious wife beater. Only in hindsight can we see how these unpromising beginnings forged the determined character of Vladimir Ulyanov and his stubborn dedication to lay the foundations of a revolutionary movement that could not be defeated.

There was no disagreement among Russian revolutionaries about Marx's general critique of the status quo. Feuerbach had demonstrated the invention of gods by men. Hegel had demonstrated the dialectical law of history. Marx saw in the new class of the proletariat the lever needed to marshal all these ideas for the liberation of mankind. Crowded in alien cities and bonded by common suffering, they could rise in solidarity and break the chains of oppression. But because of lack of proletarians in their society, Marx's Russian followers tended to adapt his ideas to local agrarian terms.

The draconian regime of Alexander III had wiped out the oppositional movements in Russia. The severe famine of 1891, however, reawakened social concerns, and a new generation of Russians prepared to renew the struggle. When Vladimir Ulyanov arrived in Saint Petersburg in 1893, he was already known thanks to the publication of a couple of early articles. Among his admirers was Nadezhda Krupskaia.

Anxious to observe revolutionary movements in Western Europe as a possible model for Russia, Vladimir Ulyanov traveled abroad in 1895. He returned to Saint Petersburg reaffirmed in his convictions and ready to begin organizing a disciplined revolutionary movement. Before the year was up, however, he and his collaborators, while attempting to start a printing press, were arrested. His prison sentence was commuted to exile in Siberia two years later, and it was there, where the river Lena runs its mighty course, that Vladimir Ulyanov became "Lenin."

After his first year in Siberia, Lenin was joined by Nadezhda Krupskaia, and they were married. He formulated his plan to issue a newspaper from abroad as Herzen had done earlier in the century. However, frustrated by the dissensions among all the revolutionaries, Lenin did not intend his paper to be a "debating rag." It would be the rallying point around the foundation of Marxist theory. And through the agents of its smuggling and distribution in Russia, the organizational tool of a conspiratorial revolutionary movement.

In 1899, the year my father was born, Lenin began his long exile abroad, and the struggle to define and control the direction of the Russian Revolution. In the West, revolutionary theory and practice had moved on since Marx's death in 1883. The Labor Movement in England, the Socialists in France, and the Social Democrats in Germany had made some advances in their bid for economic and political inclusion in the lives of their countries. As a result, a revisionist or soft form of Marxism, intent on immediate and practical results, had become the norm.

Was this the right path for Russia? At the Second International Congress of 1903 Russian Social Democrats gathered in Brussels to hammer out their platform. A split occurred between Bolsheviks and Mensheviks. The latter argued that revolutionary initiative had to be developed from the workers themselves. Lenin, the leader of the Bolsheviks, argued that a well-organized group of professional revolutionaries was the only way to revolutionary success. The Bolshevik position was in the minority, but this did not prevent Lenin from pursuing his goal.

Despite the failure of the 1905 revolutions, Lenin struggled on, forging new alliances. A fearless young man from Georgia made his appearance to pay his respects to Lenin. He was willing to rob banks to finance the work of the Revolution, and Lenin made sure that he was elected to the Central Committee of the Party. His name, Yosif Djugashvili, was later to be generally known as Stalin, the Man of Steel.

But World War I erupted, and not a day too soon for Lenin's purposes. Everywhere in Europe nationalist fervor swept the field. In France a socialist member of Parliament, the pacifist Jean Jaurès, was assassinated by a "patriot." In Germany the Social Democrats joined other members of the Reichstag in voting for the Kaiser's war budget. In Russia the police looked on as mobs vandalized German stores in Saint Petersburg and Moscow. As usual, Lenin held fast in the midst of general confusion.

Conceding that the Russian proletariat was still not strong enough to carry the World Revolution, he too turned to Russia's real popular masses, the peasants: after all, the war was being fought with their bodies. He sent his emissaries to the soldiers and told them to go home and take over the land. This is just what Dad witnessed upon returning from the battlefield.

Kerensky, instead, toured the front in person, exhorting the soldiers to fight on for the Motherland. He promised that the land transfer would be properly legislated as soon as the war was won. He reports one soldier's response: "But if I get killed first, how is the land going to be mine?" This was pretty basic logic, and Lenin understood it while Kerensky did not. On October 25, 1917, Lenin, Trotsky, Stalin, and their associates, seized power in Petrograd and Moscow. They were intent on building a society that was no longer based on the foundations of autocracy, class, private property, and the authority of the church.

These radical changes were not to be rammed through without a bloody fight. Dad wanted a social system where his family's orchard could not be chopped down just because some commissar said so. Those he joined, however, were not in agreement about the future order of things. Among the Whites there were monarchists and constitutionalists and democrats and socialists and would-be military dictators and allied troops from abroad.

But there were other challenges as well. A large swath of the country was still under German occupation. The Polish leader Józef Piłsudski attempted to reclaim historical lands going back to the 16th and 17th centuries, which included portions of Ukraine and Belarus. This Polish-Soviet war lasted from 1919 to 1921. There were other independence movements from the Baltics to Trans-Caucasia to some Central Asian Muslim Republics. In Ukraine, the Rada or "central council" proclaimed an independent Ukrainian republic, but then was subjected by invasions from Germany, Denikin's White Army, the Red Army, then partly incorporated into Poland.

Faced by resistance on all these fronts, the Reds appealed to the peasantry. Afraid that the Whites would take away the land the Revolution had given them, they tipped the balance and saved the Communist Revolution. Initially taking a page from the French Communards, Lenin had told the peasant delegations and the worker unions to take matters into their own hands and count on their own initiative. But the chaos and desolation visited on the country by World War I, the Civil War and other conflicts had taken the tall of 20 million lives. The population was starving. The experimenting with popular-initiative policies turned into its opposite - War Communism. The methods of control from above, with the inevitable coercion this entails, became the rule of Soviet life.

As part of the struggle, Tsar Nicholas II and his family were murdered in 1918 in Yekaterinburg, renamed Sverdlovsk for the name of the murderer. The Civil War and the death from starvation of his mother remained a deep, life-long wound to my Dad. Alexander Kerensky joined the 2 million emigres abroad. And Vladimir Lenin, the third man from Simbirsk, without whom the Bolshevik Revolution could not have taken its successful turn, died of a stroke in 1924. My homework on all these complicated issues and past events was far from advanced when the Peace Cruise navigated down the Volga in 1984. But the Volga just kept rolling along like *Ole Man River*, and carried us to our next major stop at Volgograd (renamed from Stalingrad of World War II fame). As we prepared to disembark, everyone was handed a red rose, and our Soviet

214

companions grew quiet and reflective. This day was going to be dedicated to visiting a collection of monuments to the heroic defenders of Stalingrad.

I did not look forward to visiting a Soviet war memorial. Judging from the typical pattern institutionalized by Socialist Realism, I braced myself for an irritating mix of the monumental and the hyperbolic. We began to ascend the huge multi-level complex on Mamai's Kurgan, a hill named after a Tatar warlord. One of the Soviets explained to me that the hill had initially been half its current size. The charred remains of the entire city of half a million people, which had been completely reduced to rubble during the battle, had been hoisted up that hill.

I looked up. Way on top, the statue of an enormous woman, Mother Russia no doubt, towered among moving clouds. Half-turning away as if to summon out of the open vastness at her back an army of her invisible children, she held aloft a huge sword. My Soviet companion added, not without a touch of challenge in his voice, that the tip of the risen sward made the statue taller than the Statue of Liberty. I picked up on the challenge and retorted that the Statue of Liberty held up a light, not a sword. His counter-retort was just as quick: "So were we supposed to sit pretty and let the Germans turn us into slaves?" We went on in silence, each keeping our own counsel about the price of liberty.

The strenuous climb was relieved by a series of landings. One of them opened into a hall carved out of the mountain side. One of the men from the Soviet delegation drew my attention to the lists of fallen soldiers on the circular wall around us: "There," he said, "I knew my uncle was mentioned here somewhere, that's him right here." This man, as later events would highlight the irony, was a Chechen.

We went on, and were accompanied all along by stone soldiers in various poses of Herculean effort. A man's torso, his muscles defined in realistic tension, rose out of a slab of granite, each powerful fist locked on a grenade. Another soldier held up his wounded comrade, both unconquered and unconquerable giants. There was a pieta: a mother, her peasant kerchief framing her face like the traditional veil of the Virgin, was bending over the body of her fallen son. We passed many group sculptures in postures of coordinated combat: crouching hulks in tense anticipation, frozen leaps forward, shoulder to shoulder resistance of immovable men, their heavy pedestals holding them forever to their common resolve.

As we climbed higher the wide staircase narrowed down and we walked between two sheer walls of rock out of which a whole army of soldiers looked down on us. Gouged out of the rock they were roughly pitted as if molded by bursts of shrapnel, and their collective stare was the hollow stare of death.

I thought back to the Presidents at Mt. Rushmore. It occurred to me that Mt. Rushmore was about presidents, while Volgograd was about soldiers – ordinary people. Were the giants on Mt. Rushmore, and the giants of Volgograd proclaiming incompatible messages? Is that why there had been a Cold War as soon as the "hot" war had ended? Is that why we were now in a nuclear arms race which threatened to bring the whole world to extinction?

I began to look at the actual people surrounding me. Men with weathered faces, women in summery print dresses, children wide-eyed as adults bent over them, speaking softly. What were they saying about us, the American visitors - were we not just like them, ordinary people with something to say? We had come all this way to learn, and prepared to go home to tell everyone what we had seen and heard.

***

CHAPTER 15

THE WAGES OF WAR

If the remarkable memorial of Volgograd proclaimed the indomitable defense of the Fatherland, it also witnessed the perils and ravages of war. Like everywhere else in Europe, the Soviet Union had faced a blitzkrieg. German panzer divisions broke through Soviet defense lines. Airfields, caught by surprise as the U.S. Navy was at Pearl Harbor, were destroyed before aircraft could lift. By the fall of 1941 Leningrad was encircled and Moscow threatened. U.S. Secretary of State Stinson, in briefing FDR, estimated that the Soviets had a month to surrender.

How was it that despite its herculean efforts to prepare, the Soviet Union seemed taken by surprise?

After Maxim Litvinov's failure to rally the West against Hitler, Stalin had counted on the Molotov-Ribbentrop Pact to divert German aggression from the Soviet Union. But the West had caved in, and Hitler turned on the Soviet Union. He had always known that the Slavs were an inferior race fit to be lorded over by Teutons. An upstart like Vlasov was, at best, to be used. Moreover, this was an opportunity to dispose of the Jews of Eastern Europe. He equated Jews with Bolsheviks. The civilization of Europe was being saved from the Red Threat and gloriously renewed under its new order of Nazi discipline.

And now it looked like he was proven right. Two million Soviet soldiers had been taken prisoner and seven million of the occupied populations were being shipped to Germany for slave labor. To spread Nazi discipline among the newly conquered populations, Hitler undertook preliminary experiments in mass extermination. A group of mental patients was dynamited in Minsk, but that proved messy. Another group of mental patients was locked in a room in Mogilev and car exhaust fumes were piped in; this worked in minutes and became the preferred killing option. Its further technical refinements would prove invaluable toward the final disposition of the Jews and other undesirables. For now, starvation and old-fashioned executions did the job.

How was it that so many people were rounded up in the first place? As mentioned earlier, Ukrainians had borne the brunt of Stalin's collectivization, and the buried dream of national independence was ever ready to flare up. But Hitler despised his potential allies. The Nazis exterminated the Ukrainian and Polish nationalists. They starved three million Red Army prisoners. They waged colonial war on the entire occupied population.

In the meantime, desperate efforts to hold on were made in Leningrad and Moscow. Hitler was planning to raze Moscow to the ground and to submerge it under an artificial lake. He ordered his forces to hold off occupying Leningrad in order to concentrate on Moscow. In Moscow, the Man of Steel flinched. It was do or die, and he became more receptive to professional military advice. The call to stand firm for Soviet Communism became a call to save the Fatherland. Churches had been closed and vandalized by the Bolsheviks. They were now reopened and people were called upon to pray for victory.

Groups of partisans began to form in occupied territory. In Leningrad, the blockaded population was rescued from total starvation by a supply route improvised once Lake Ladoga froze. Industrial centers were dismounted, shipped east, and reconstructed. Shifts around the clock, 'manned' by women, began to re-supply the troops with war materiel. Land-lease supplies from Britain and the United States began to arrive as well.

Still, Stalin fumed because his Western Allies failed to open a second front. Hitler fumed because Moscow and Leningrad had not yet fallen. Since the war promised to last, both Stalin and Hitler began to concentrate their attention on the strategic lower basin of the Volga, the country's bread basket. Because Stalingrad bore the Soviet leader's name, it became a magnet for a cataclysmic showdown.

Field Marshal Zhukov convinced Stalin that headlong sacrificial thrusts against a better armed, better organized enemy were not going to win the war. By September of 1942 the Germans under General Paulus had already entered the boundaries of Stalingrad, yet Zhukov insisted that the rescue of the city needed more preparation. Bombed and shelled night and day, Stalingrad was collapsing around Mamai Kurgan. Still awaiting rescue, the defenders struggled on. Men crawled through the rubble under cover of darkness and attacked the enemy with grenades and bayonets. They were ground down by German batteries, and still they attacked. It is to these men that a grateful posterity erected the monuments on Mamayev Kurgan. The inscription by Vassily Grossman on a wall reads: "Was it mere men who were attacking? Were they mortal?"

They were mortal. They kept dying until Field Marshal Zhukov assembled a formidable force of men, tanks, heavy guns, and aircraft. The Soviet counter-offensive, launched in November of 1942, was not expected. Hitler had underestimated the will and capacity of the Soviets to regroup. He forbade Paulus to break out of encirclement, and it was now the turn of the Germans to suffer cold, hunger, fear, and defeat. General Paulus surrendered on January 31, 1943. In Germany, every radio broadcast Siegfried's funeral march from Wagner's *Die Götterdämmerung*.

The war did not end at Stalingrad, but the tide had turned at last. For nearly two more years bitter battles would be fought on all five continents. But before the smoke had lifted from the ruins of Dresden and Berlin, the former Allies meeting at Potsdam in 1945 were locked in a Cold War.

Once again, my homework was cut out for me: what exactly was the issue between East and West? Of course, I had grown up with my family's 'White' version of the story, much reinforced by my American experience. But now I had crossed the line into 'enemy' territory, and it was clear that the Soviet 'peace workers' we met represented not just their individual positions as those of the American delegation, but their government's position. I had noticed that the country looked poor: was their Communist system at fault, or the relentless arms race between us? That is the question. Clearly, the East - West alliance had been but a shotgun wedding. Once Germany was defeated, the parties proved incompatible, and divorce followed.

Stalin knew that their situations were widely unequal. The Soviet Union had sacrificed 27 million people in the showdown. The Soviets and the Germans had both practiced a scorched-earth policy, and the land was devastated. The US, on the other hand, had not been invaded, and their body count was maybe 400,000. Who was the real winner? Moreover, newly-elected President Truman came to the meeting with the BOMB in his back pocket. Was it back to the post-World War I situation, when Socialism and Capitalism were facing off, and the Soviet Union had to go it alone? Harry Truman had shown his colors back in 1941 while still a senator. He had stated: "If the Germans are winning, we will support the Soviets; if the Soviets are winning, we will support the Germans."

So, Stalin held onto the Eastern European countries the Soviet armies had liberated as a buffer zone. Earlier on, following the Yalta agreement, Stalin had turned his back on the Greek Communist movement, which had been in the forefront of the anti-Nazi resistance. And he had tried to control Tito, who had supported the Greeks. But now, instead of allowing open elections in Eastern Europe, he made sure that the Communist parties gained control. Winston Churchill announced that an "iron curtain" had fallen between East and West.

Following the Soviet lead, the countries of Eastern Europe introduced economic plans, industrialization, and collectivization in agriculture. This last policy met the most resistance. In Roman Catholic countries like Hungary and Poland, there was persistent opposition from the Church. These resistance movement met with severe repression.

But the British and the Americans were doing the same thing in their liberation zones. When the Greek National Liberation Front was about to reconquer Athens, the British stopped them. And then there was the Turkish problem. The Soviets were pressuring Turkey for free passage through the Dardanelles. The Mediterranean had always been Franco-British territory, and so now the Brits were worried about the Dardanelles again in 1946, and turned to the U.S. for help.

Truman, who had been promoted ahead of George Wallace, a much more progressive candidate, to the vice-presidency under FDR, now turned to more conservative advisers. George Kennan advised that the Soviets only understood force, and the needed policy was "containment." Dean Acheson was the first to articulate the since familiar notion of the "domino theory": if Turkey yielded and if Greece "fell," the Mediterranean was lost. George Marshall proposed massive economic aid to Western Europe to head off its vulnerability to Communist influence. After all, not just Greece, but Italy and even France had large Communist movements. His rescue plan, subsequently known as the Marshall Plan, included the former enemy, Germany.

Thus, the Truman Doctrine was born: the initial version of the CIA and the NSA were created, and in April of 1948, the North Atlantic Treaty Organization was signed. The stated intention of NATO was "to settle... international disputes by peaceful means... and to refrain ... from the threat or use of force." Famous last words...

The British journalist Richard Cottrell, however, has a different interpretation of events. In his book *Gladio*, he calls it "NATO's Dagger at the Heart of Europe," and documents in great detail the Pentagon-Nazi-Mafia connection. He explains the 'left behind' phenomenon. Apparently, there were people and caches of ammunition 'left behind' to resist the Germans. But Germany had lost, and instead of the various anti-Nazi resistance movements, another set of resisters sprang up. They were all those that were disappointed BECAUSE Germany lost. These were the foot soldiers NATO turned to and financed to organize a "strategy of tension."

For example, the French 'gladiators' came from earlier Vichy collaborators, but more recently from the ranks of disappointed *colons* ejected from Vietnam and Algeria. One of them, Colonel Guérin-Sérac, was a mastermind of the 'strategy of tension': "The destruction of the state must be carried out under the cover of 'Communist activities.' Popular opinion must be polarized...they must understand that we are the only instrument capable of saving the nation." President De Gaulle who, they felt, betrayed them in Algeria, survived four assassination attempts. No wonder the French pulled out of NATO, which found its new home in Brussels.

Stalin died in 1953, and in 1954 the Soviet Union actually expressed an interest in joining NATO. This overture was rebuffed as West Germany was invited to join NATO in 1955. The same year, the Soviets created the Warsaw Pact and in 1956 suppressed the Hungarian uprising. This happened despite Nikita Khrushchev's 'de-Stalinization' at home and escalated into the Cuban crisis of 1962. And under President Eisenhower, the Vietnam War still followed the 'domino theory.'

Khrushchev's attempts at political reform were replaced by the Brezhnev era, which lasted from 1964 to Brezhnev's death in 1982. His team reverted to old patterns of stabilization at home and abroad – hence the suppression of the 1968 revolt in Czechoslovakia. But then successes in economic development allowed the formation of a loyal managerial class, as well as spreading benefits to the larger population. There was free medical care for all, guaranteed pensions at retirement, more housing, subsidized prices for essential food products, and full employment.

These positive circumstances, and the underground pressure of the dissident movement, were conducive to the policy of *détente* with the West, which resulted in the 1975 Helsinki Accords. But no trade relations developed and the arms race escalated. Zbigniew Brzezinski, President Carter's National Security Adviser, boasted entrapping Brezhnev into a "Soviet Vietnam" in Afghanistan. As Vietnam had undermined President Johnson's "Great Society", so would the Soviet war in Afghanistan undermine the economic advances they had achieved.

All these struggles, whether military or economic, eventually led to the rise of Gorbachev and *perestroika*. My trip to the Prague peace conference in 1983 and the 'peace cruise' down the Volga in 1954 happened just before Gorbachev's appearance on the scene. But even then, the longing for peace was palpable everywhere in Europe, both East and West. After all, that's where World War II had taken its deadly toll, and the unrelenting arms race was experienced as the ultimate doomsday machine.

***

CHAPTER 16

PIETA

Home at last. That night I woke up, instantly lucid: it was 3 a.m. I was jet-lagged and my brain was still processing film clips of the Russian trip. But now I tried to reconstruct in the dark the bits and pieces of a different script. Rick had told me some of this on the way home from the airport, and I had muted it as we mute an intrusive commercial. But no matter how you suppress them, they come back and this one was an animated poster of Peter's Jamaican vacation. However, instead of pale sand and aquamarine waters and palms swaying to the strands of calypso music, it showed Peter behind bars, the only white body in a crowded jail.

The tape stops at this point, and the sequel of what could have happened next is deleted. The voice-over goes on. During Peter's stay in Jamaica, his friends, confident of his white skin, had entrusted him with their stash of dope. But his white skin proved useless after all, and he was arrested for possession. Luckily, his friends knew the system and "bought him out." Hence a happy end. I rewind and play over, rewind and play over, always breaking off at what could have happened next.

I got up and stood by the window, observing the outline of the roofs of Village Greens as they began to emerge from the night's shadows. I walked over to the dresser and picked up our wedding picture, put it back, picked up the picture with Peter and Muriel, aged seven and three respectively. It had been taken on the day Bibi the Beagle had entered our lives. It was a favorite picture of mine, and I had retrieved it from Peter's room some time back. Now I looked at it closely. There was a whitish film over it, not the even layer of dust, but a cloudy substance more concentrated at the center and diminishing toward the edges. In double exposure over the idyllic picture of the kids with the dog, there now appeared a collage of memory flashes. I knock, then open the door to Peter's room… he is bending over something, then quickly shuts a drawer… I look for something or other in Peter's room later on, open that drawer, and there's the picture with the dog in it... I decide to take it back... And now in the silent pre-dawn hours it all adds up: Peter bending over the now clouded picture of his childhood, razor in hand, using the glass surface to prepare a dose of cocaine.

How "flat and unprofitable" the light of day. I put the desecrated picture back on the dresser, leaving the film of coke untouched, as one of those nightmare clues that lead nowhere. When Rick wakes up, we talk. He asks me about my trip, but his interest is lukewarm, and we drop the subject. Neither do we talk about Peter's Jamaican interlude: it happened, and now it is over. We simply do not know what to do.

The nuclear arms race had achieved front-page rating, and my peace work took on new dimensions. A forum on the Strategic Defense Initiative was jointly organized by Rutgers at Newark where I worked, and the New Jersey Institute of Technology. My job was to pick up at the airport and bring to the auditorium a noted scientist flying in from Washington. He was to make the case for President Reagan's famous "space umbrella." When I tried to engage our guest on the topic of the forum, he proved unwilling to waste a scientific explanation on me.

As we drove on in silence, a recent dream of Peter's came to mind. *He and his friends are exploring the Arden Woods across from our subdivision of Village Greens... they are not exactly lost, but something ominous is in the air... they peer through the dark... ahead in a clearing and surrounded by an eerie light, ALIENS ARE LANDING! Peter freezes with terror... but then President Reagan appears and Peter feels safe again.* I considered telling the man from Washington about my son's dream. I was even tempted to add a touch of the surrealist Belgian painter Magritte to the picture by having the President hold an open umbrella. But the man seemed too humorless to recognize in my son's fears and childlike faith in President Reagan any childishness of his own.

Similar engagements absorbed me, and Rick grumbled. He grumbled that the phone rang too much. He grumbled that I ran to meetings or church instead of going to the movies with him. Then Staten Island and our household were visited by the Nuclear Homeport issue. The Battleship S/S IOWA was being taken out of mothballs, armed with nuclear tipped cruise missiles, and about to be docked off Staten Island. The local newspaper sported a red-white-and-blue border and quoted our congressman to the effect that the Battleship S/S IOWA was bringing our borough 900 jobs.

My peacenik friends, however, were concerned that nuclear missiles were a patent hazard in busy New York harbor with its high record of accidents. Moreover, an investigation discovered that the 900 jobs proved to be a red herring. But who was interested in hearing OUR point of view? Not the congressman's office and not the newspaper. At our gatherings people began to say that the only way to get attention was to create a media event. The construction crews were getting ready to break ground and we voted for a peaceful protest.

At the news that I planned to participate in the action, Rick blew his top. If I was going to go through with this fool thing, he said, I need not bother coming home. I did go through with the fool thing. Some twenty of us entered the construction zone. As the bulldozer advanced, we held hands and sang "we are a gentle, angry people..." Unlike the one that killed Rachel Corrie in Gaza in later years, this bulldozer did stop, and we were all arrested. I was not feeling in the least heroic; it was as if I had washed yet another load of the family's laundry. Rick showed up after all, bailed me out, and we drove home in silence.

I did not think that my peace activities were at odds with motherhood and apple pie while Rick took care of the Chevrolet side of things. But something about this cooperative contract of ours no longer worked. President Eisenhower's Military-Industrial Complex had come home to roost.

We were also at odds about dealing with the kids. Peter stayed out a lot, and one time I heard him arriving in the wee hours of the morning. I came down to find him as high as a kite. Before I knew what I was doing, I attacked him with a coat hanger, the weapon nearest at hand. With a sad, embarrassed smile, he just put up his arms in defense. Rick slept right through the commotion, and when I shook him awake, he mumbled something about an important presentation and went back to sleep.

A counselor suggested that coat hangers were not what parenting was all about. He said that I had to get Peter into a rehab. Really? We were respectable, intelligent, loving parents, and we could not send our son to some dump with desperate low-lives. A friend of a friend recommended a brilliant psychiatrist, and Peter went along. The psychiatrist-patient relationship being privileged, we stood aside. Time passed, the psychiatrist's bills came in like clockwork, and just as regularly, Peter drugged out.

The counselor kept insisting that we had to get Peter into a rehab. Alright already. The Caron Foundation in Pennsylvania looked promising. Peter said, "No way." I was told I had to put him out of the house until he agreed to go to the rehab. I told Peter so and he disappeared for three days and three nights. During those three days and sleepless nights I had vivid visions of him in jail, lying in the street mugged, under the wheels of the subway, at the bottom of the East River. Then he reappeared. He HAD been mugged and he HAD considered jumping off a bridge.

But here he was, and we took him to the rehab facility in Pennsylvania. The people there said to leave it to them and to stay away. Summer break had come around in the meantime, and we took Muriel to a horse camp in Vermont. We were both exhausted. Rick had some business in Paris, and asked me to come along.

I was not up to meeting with my friends, and Paris was a big, noisy, endless labyrinth. Rick took care of business. This included a fancy reception in a fancy palace. I had imagined just such occasions before. I had imagined standing by Rick's side and sharing the glamor. Here I was at last but the pomp and circumstance felt oppressive. I wandered through the streets of Paris, looking for something, but couldn't find it.

Then one evening there was a phone call from the Caron Foundation in Pennsylvania. It appeared that Peter had "decompressed." This, the long-distance voice explained, meant that Peter was having a mental breakdown and that they had transferred him to a psychiatric hospital. And no, we should not rush back home; he would most likely not recognize us. These words pushed me to the vanishing point of some ever-receding, ever narrowing path. The voice kept saying to give it time.

So, we decided to stay put in France. We visited some cathedrals, and this proved a boon. As I entered each cathedral, I looked for the most tortured crucifix, lit a candle, and kneeled. I searched the face of Jesus, trying to find in his features a clue to what Peter must be going through: alone with his voices in some unfamiliar room, voices which whispered and taunted and crucified him. Or I would search out a *pieta*, and just sit there, looking at my own plight. Sobs rose from deep in my chest, and I did not try to hold them back. I could see that my behavior unnerved Rick. So, I acted pretty normal most of the time, but the minute we entered another cathedral I lit a candle, kneeled, looked up to Jesus or Mary, and began to shake with sobs.

The crying helped. I was grateful to this ancient wisdom of the Catholic tradition which did not shy away from displaying the contortions and spasms of human pain. Yet when I looked at Jesus on the Cross and at Mary with the broken body of her son across her lap - I saw no redemption through suffering.

It was Yahweh of the Old Testament who visited me now, he who had once tested Abraham. But unlike Abraham, who knew who was boss then and prepared to kill his own son, I did not bow my head in obeisance. After all, no Hollywood angel had appeared in the nick of time to avert the sacrificial knife when Jesus cried out on the Cross.

Sure, everyone suffers and everyone dies. But there is time to die and there is time to live. As to the violent logic of transgression and redemption – that the Lamb of God has to drip human blood to satisfy the Father's authority – thanks, but no thanks. Some man, made in His image, some childless cleric who had neither suffered birth pangs, nor watched a son walk off to war or twitch on an electric chair, dreamed up the notion of instant salvation. But I saw my own son up there on the cross, and where was the salvation in that?

❧

On our homeward journey we went to pick up Muriel at her camp in Vermont. She did not know what had happened to Peter. Her world now centered on horses, and she took us around the stables. She knew the name and character of every horse. She loved not just riding them, but feeding them, scrubbing them, braiding their manes, getting the crud from under their hooves, and yes, shoveling the manure. I sighed with relief. If I had ever harbored hidden worries about hereditary repercussions because of Mother's mental breakdown, I had harbored them for Muriel. She was the one who had been colicky as a baby and fussy as a child, while happy-go-lucky Peter had been good-natured and easy-going from day one. Except for the mysterious school phobia episode at age seven.

We were now to be given the key to that mystery. The long crying spell at the time had nothing to do with school phobia. An older boy had raped him while other boys looked on. He had cried for help, but they didn't lift a finger. Peter interpreted this to mean that what was happening to him was somehow "normal," and was not able to confide in me.

We were now told to control our emotions and did so, at least during our visits with Peter. He looked skinny and shy and younger than his nineteen years. He told us how he had been visited by a man cloaked in black, how he had recognized him as Darth Vader, and how he had sat across from him, looking into the empty holes of his eyes. This time no President Star Warrior appeared to save him.

The doctor at Fairmount Hospital said that Peter did have an addiction problem, and that drugs could trigger a psychosis. On the other hand, Peter could be suffering from mental illness, and his resort to drugs could have been self-medication. He needed time. The doctor referred Peter to a half-way house in Albany, N.Y.

Peter held out a few weeks, then ran away. We drove him back and he ran away again. He claimed he had been sexually harassed. We tried local facilities: a combination of psychiatric visits and outpatient workshops. I tried to consult the psychiatrist, but he refused to meet with me. When Peter reported that his therapy workshop consisted of basket weaving, I went to see for myself. There they were, a group of heavily sedated citizens, weaving baskets.

Neighbors had had results with a local daytime rehab program called Daytop, and we signed Peter up. We were told that the house of the addict had to be completely free of drugs and alcohol. Rick, however, objected to being judged on what he saw as his moderate alcohol consumption. This became a bone of contention between us. One time he was pouring himself another glass of wine when I heard Peter coming down the stairs. I nudged Rick to put the bottle away, which he ignored. As Peter approached I grabbed the bottle, the bottle flew against the kitchen wall, glass splinters bounced all over, and Peter entered the kitchen to witness the wine splashing on the wall in a bloody starburst.

I continued at Daytop alone. We were a pretty desolate bunch of parents sitting in a circle, trying to figure out what had happened to us. Once I observed Peter staring at himself in the mirror. He turned to me and asked me if he was black. I was bewildered. I remembered seeing an African crucifix during our French pilgrimage. The rigid body of the black Christ, his arms outspread, was itself the ebony cross. But the whole tough method at Daytop was too much for Peter, and he had another psychotic break.

That summer of 1987 the news was bad again; Dad had passed away. Sitting on the plane which was taking me to Sydney, I thought of my last visit with him. It had taken place when he was already living in a nursing home. His general health had been good, but undiagnosed glaucoma had caused a steady loss of sight, until he was no longer able to exercise his much-treasured independence. Thanks to the large Russian community in Sydney, Mom had arranged to place him in a Russian nursing home with Russian-style food and Russian Orthodox religious services. I had had a chance to visit him there, and was impressed.

As I sat on the plane to Sydney now, I thought of what turned out to be our last conversation together. Dad had asked me whether a daughter, if she found out that her father was not her father, would still be his daughter. I realized then that our family secret, the one revealed to me by his relatives in France, had been no secret to him. I did not hesitate. I said that there could only be one father for a daughter: the father who raised her. Our conversation took another turn as if all that needed to be said had been said. As we embraced for what turned out to be our last farewell, Dad seemed at peace.

I, however, was not at peace now. I wondered how a daughter worthy of the name could have abandoned her father to a lonely death thousands of miles away. It wasn't just that he had seen to it that I was fed and clothed and protected. He had handed down to me a way of being – a model of decency and fortitude and kindness and forbearance – and his love of books and poetry, which has lasted me a lifetime. So, when I placed my farewell kiss on Dad's forehead, the chill of death overwhelmed me.

But once again my sorrow was mediated by the wisdom of an ancient tradition. The Russian Orthodox liturgy has a thousand-year practice of cradling human misery. As the choir beseeched God to receive His servant Constantine into eternal peace, it gathered my helpless grief into its circular harmonies, and by and by, brought peace to me.

It never occurred to us at the time that my visit with Mom would also prove final. Only six months later Maurice called: Mom too had passed away. Once again I flew over the Pacific. Mom's struggle with mental illness had changed her, but now I thought back to the indomitable woman she had once been.

I recalled how she had turned her back on the German soldier in Belgrade. How she had convinced Frau Doppner to take me into her school in Blankenbug. How she had made dolls from scraps of cloth and trudged to German farms to barter them for milk and eggs. How she had stayed up nights sewing those American surplus blankets into warm clothes for us. How she had created Christmas celebrations and birthday parties out of nothing. How she had pushed me to study in all languages. How she had taught me to swim and hike and play tennis. How she had rescued me from a premature commitment to marriage. How she had taught me to be unafraid. And when she had had to start surviving all over again in Australia, it was no wonder that she crashed at last.

As the flight hours to Sydney passed and I watched the curve of the horizon light up at dawn, I thought of how the interlocking circles of my parents' lives had each closed. Dad had passed away unobtrusively at age 87 after a long, self-effacing life. Mom had exited life as she had lived it, with a flourish. Maurice had taken her out on the town to celebrate her 76th birthday. They had wined and dined and danced. Back home Mom suffered a heart attack and the rush to the hospital did not save her.

***

CHAPTER 17

A THOUSAND YEARS OF CHRISTIANITY

During the academic year of 1984/85 my dissertation had been accepted, and I was granted my Ph.D. The spring of 1988, however, proved to be the last term of my employment by Rutgers University at Newark. A tenure-track line had become available. My peers seemed pleased with the way I straddled two disciplines and my teaching evaluations were consistently good - but I had not done much about publishing. Rick blamed my peace work. We could also blame Peter, but we had not brought him into the world to be blamed. Surely the young man with his degree from Oxford and publications who was my competition for the position was not to blame. The administration was bowled over by his credentials and I was history.

When the Unitarian Universalist United Nations Office approached me to be a consultant with a peace mission to the Soviet Union that summer of 1988, I seized the opportunity. Kievan Rus had renounced its pagan ways in the Year of our Lord 988, and now the Evil Empire was preparing to renounce its godlessness as well; they were celebrating their first millennium of Christianity.

Our travel arrangements were much less constrained than during the cruise of 1984. Aside from the usual stints in Moscow and Leningrad, this trip took us to Transcaucasia. One of our Georgian excursions took us to Gori, the birthplace of Stalin. As we walked through the small house which had witnessed his troubled childhood, I noticed a young Georgian girl, aged fifteen or so, among the visitors. I asked her what she thought of Stalin. She seemed surprised: she loved him, of course. I asked her why. She flashed a smile both shy and radiant: "Because he is ours."

Stalin had also been ours to reckon with. Who was really the man behind those once ubiquitous portraits? His ghost rose from these humble rooms and I felt pulled into the nightmare of history once again. So, this sad place was his starting point, the place where his mother had taken her drunken husband's beatings as she tried to shield her only remaining boy. Two other sons had died in early childhood.

The Orthodox spiritual seminary of Tbilisi was the only education available for free. His mother's pious hopes for her son seemed realized when Yosif was admitted. But the Russian Empire was seething with dissent. The sterile rigidity of the seminary was no match for the message of Marx and Lenin, whom the streetwise young rebel was reading in secret. After a passing association with Georgian nationalists and Mensheviks, Yosif Dzhugashvili opted for the maximalism of the Bolshevik faction. His organizing efforts among the workers of Tbilisi, Batumi, and Baku, his hold-ups to replenish the Party's coffers, his repeated internments in the Far North and Siberia, earned him the respect of fellow revolutionaries and the nickname of Stalin, "the man of steel."

Stalin followed Lenin and Trotsky in opposing Kerensky's Provisional Government and participated in the October Revolution of 1917. The Bolsheviks had inherited a vast Russian empire, and some of the national groups had used the Revolution to rebel. One of Stalin's early jobs was commissar of nationalities. The policy he pursued was one of "national form and socialist content." This meant tolerating, even encouraging local linguistic and cultural traditions, but by including the participation and promotion of local leaders into the Communist Party, it also created the bonds holding the Soviet Union together.

Stalin went along with Lenin when he instituted the New Economic Policy (NEP). Its purpose was to mitigate the rigors of War Communism. It allowed the peasants to sell their produce after taxes, which encouraged production, and it allowed small-scale industry and retail trade. When Lenin died in 1924, a power struggle ensued to define and control the future of the Revolution. Trotsky had argued against NEP as a step backward from the active implementation of Socialism, which needed rapid industrialization. Nikolai

Bukharin called this a "Genghis Khan plan" and insisted that industrialization should be promoted not on the production but on the consumption model.

As the general secretary of the Party, Stalin had been promoting his own people at key levels of the party's apparatus. Allying himself with Bukharin, he defeated Trotsky in the '20s, as representing the Left Opposition, or doctrinaire incapable of assessing the realities of the USSR in a hostile world: the much-expected World Revolution had not taken place. And after Hitler came to power, he had made his intentions quite clear. Germany's future consisted in *Drang nach Osten* ("drive to the East") and the German war machine was in full swing.

Stalin figured he had about 10 years to prepare and proceeded to implement some of Trotsky's plans after all - all-out industrialization regardless of human cost. When the atrocities this entailed caused Bukharin to advise restraint, Stalin turned on Bukharin and his supporters. In the show trials of the late '30s, they were condemned as Right Deviationists or traitors to the revolutionary cause.

Clearly, the tightly controlled one-party system which had been Lenin's life work suffered just one dominant personality at the top. It turned out that Stalin was the one to possess the patience, lucky timing, and ruthlessness to replace Lenin at the helm. In his 1924 book *Foundations of Leninism*, Stalin identified himself with Lenin's legacy. He promoted the optimistic message that it was up to the Soviet people to show the world how to build 'Socialism in one country.'

"Scientific Marxism" had offered no blueprint on how to industrialize a basically agrarian society. Stalin's five-year plans took the lead in practicing "the dictatorship of the proletariat" from above. The collectivization of agriculture was one of its major priorities, and it proved problematical. The kulaks, or farmers who had prospered under NEP, were reluctant to give up on their gains. In Ukraine, the forced creation of kolkhozes or cooperative farms, was especially resisted. Massive transfers of people (the numbers are still actively contested) to Siberia or Kazakhstan took place. Many perished from the starvation these disruptions created.

In time, the five-year plans concentrated on the need to create a modern armament industry to "catch up to the West." The competition with Western Capitalism became a life-or-death race to match the German war machine. This sense of "do or die" created the atmosphere in which the "purges" of the late 30s were conducted. Were the excesses this engendered to be blamed on Stalin's personal paranoia, or were there oppositional movements (such as the Vlasov movement I briefly discussed earlier) which justified the paranoia?

All these demands and emergencies created a painfully regimented society. Any individual interests, whether access to consumer goods or freedom of thought and expression, were discounted, and created what the dissident Alexander Zinoviev called *homo Sovieticus*. But *homo Sovieticus* was not just an apparatchik or a Gulag guard. Many were true believers. They were like the Christian martyrs of old, who had believed in the imminence of the Second Coming, but had to live with the realities of the Roman Empire. The Soviet latter-day martyrs were resigned and even exulted to be the stepping stones of History in its inevitable march to Communism, or the realization of heaven on earth.

Those who escaped from the Soviet crucible, like some members of my family, to alert the outside world, tended to play into the hands of reaction. The "shining example of the Soviet Union," especially considering the depressions of the 30s which swept the West, became an article of faith for the Left. They pointed to class leveling and the rapid strides in urbanization, literacy, and industrial power achieved in the USSR. But it is easy to glorify the sacrifices of others.

As to the emerging peoples of the Third World, they had good reason to equate colonialism with capitalist exploitation rather than the benefits of democracy. They welcomed the promise of Soviet support. World War II intervened and clinched the matter. Although Churchill had earlier characterized Russians as "baboons," in December 1941 Stalin appeared on the *Time* magazine cover as Man of the Year.

On my visit to Georgia during my trip with the Unitarian Universalists in 1988, I witnessed some of the changes taking place in Soviet society. We were visiting a church in Tbilisi, the capital of Georgia, and I found myself mediating a theological debate. The priest, finding out that one of the women in the group was a minister, pressed her about the Second Coming of Christ. Being a Unitarian, she demurred, and the priest was outraged. How was her position any different from the bloody Communists who had persecuted them for last 70 years!?

I was allowed to take breakaway groups to schools and hospitals and parks. People would gather around us, and discovering that I could interpret, showered us with questions. They wanted to know how Americans lived, and announced that they too would be free one day. In Baku, the capital of Azerbaijan, a young woman took us proudly to visit the temple where the sacred fire of the Zoroastrian faith was burning. On the other hand, we were invited to go skinny-dipping in the Caspian Sea by a young man. Short of that, we were invited to appear on the local TV.

The last leg of our trip was an overnight train ride from Leningrad to Moscow. The attendant, who brought in some tea, looked pale with fright. She had just heard a radio broadcast in which President Reagan had announced that "the bombing [of the Soviet Union] begins in five minutes." He had not been aware that the microphones were still on. Our train attendant could not be reassured. How could we use the power of our vote to elect a man given to such jokes? Once again, I recalled that Stalin's paranoia was not without foundation. Some thirty-five years after the passing of the great tyrant, international brinkmanship was still the order of the day.

And twenty years later still, in the fall of 2008, Gori was in the news once more. It was the Cuban missile crisis all over again, only in reverse. Stalin's Georgia was now an outpost of the American Empire and had made the mistake of challenging the wounded giant to the north over their competing claim to the little enclave of Ossetia. Russian tanks had gone into action, and this played handily into the presidential campaigns of John McCain and Barack Obama.

The elections of 2020 in the US are too self-absorbed to make much of the current war between Armenia and Azerbaijan over the Armenian enclave of Nagorno-Karabakh. And who knows where Turkey stands these days? They have been repeatedly humiliated by their rejection from joining the European Union - although they are still part of NATO.

And Erdoğan's power has been challenged by the Gülen movement. The movement's leader, Fethullah Gülen, has lived in the US since 1999, not far from the CIA headquarter in Langley, Virginia. Is there competition between Erdoğan's drive to revive the glories of a Turkish empire in Central Asia and Gülen's more "acceptable" way? Does it not suit US policy that the Gülen organization lavishes financial support to newly-founded Islamic schools all over the 'Stans,' formerly part of the Soviet Union?

***

CHAPTER 18

GOODBYE TO ALL THAT

The time that followed my return from the Soviet Union in 1988 had some of the qualities of other lost, transitional times. Maybe overcharged brain cells need to dim their signals in order to reshuffle life's mixed messages. Maybe it's all about how far we can bend to the laws of reality without breaking. The loss of my position at Rutgers, if hardly a lucky break, had opened up a breathing space. But how do you breathe under water? I was in that sunken ship at the bottom again, the heavy steel doors were locked, and I was afraid to push them open. Would the waters not rush in to crush me?

Our quest for Peter's cure finally led us to Regent Hospital in Manhattan. For the first time a doctor practiced a comprehensive approach, addressing mental illness and drug use – and included the family as well. It transpired that Peter's drug of choice was cannabis. We were relieved that it wasn't something more severe, like heroin. One of his new friends in the therapy group, a handsome, well-mannered and engaging young man struggled with that unforgiving addiction. Once again, we were told to wait and see.

In the meantime, Muriel too began to show "attitude." She must have been not quite fifteen when she announced that she was the only virgin in her group - and wasn't that "too weird?" She and I were lounging among the pillows and shams and comforters of our Victorian bed when she broached the subject of her disposable virginity. I looked at my daughter. She was not a chick yet, but well on her way. Matching her large honey-colored eyes, light brown hair streaked with sun-bleached highlights and unblemished skin, her body was already defined where it counted. On the other hand, she still wore braces. I seized on those little metal wires designed to push back her teeth the way medieval knights leaving for the Crusades had counted on the chastity belt to safeguard their wives' sacred receptacles. I don't know whether their contraptions had worked then, but I guessed it WAS possible to lose your virginity with braces on.

I took a deep breath and agreed that her interest in sex was in the natural order of things. She flashed her braces at me, and her eyes went dreamy. "It's not about sex, Mom, boys gross me out. It's about babies. Wouldn't a cuddly little baby be SO cool?" The massive oak bed felt like a boat taking on water. She was evidently outgrowing puppies and kittens. I braced myself against the stiff headboard and told her that if she had a baby, neither she nor her baby would be welcome in my house.

Her eyes opened wide in shock and disbelief. We talked some more. She wondered why boys were so rough and always after the girls. I promised her that in time she could expect better in lovemaking than what boys her age had to offer. We kept on talking. She volunteered at last that she was prepared to tell the boys off until she herself was good and ready. And yes, it made sense to wait until she could actually take care of a baby herself. Holding and kissing and having a baby together, wasn't that what it was all about? I held and kissed my baby, and we made up.

And then, I don't know how it happened, Muriel was seventeen, and she WAS ready. The boy was good looking in an intense Sicilian sort of way and they were in love. I proceeded with caution. She knew about protection, didn't she? "DERRR, Mom!" Next question: what were his plans for the future? No, he was not planning to go to college. He was going to be an actor. I couldn't help thinking of the boy's slurred street speech - but didn't Sylvester Stallone, the Italian Stallion, speak just like that? Muriel, to my intense relief, did not see herself on the silver screen. We did the college rounds together, and Muriel and Hood College near Washington D.C. opted for each other. I figured things would sort themselves out now that she would move away.

The situation that was not sorting itself out was the situation between Rick and me. We seemed way past talking things out. So, I wrote him a letter. I wrote that I was unhappy. I wrote that he objected to my church and peace activities, but that it was the one place I felt useful and validated. I wrote that

I figured he loved the kids in his own way, but that I felt I was raising them alone. I wrote that I just couldn't go on like this if nothing changed. I placed the letter on Rick's pillow, and waited. Then I waited some more. The letter disappeared but there was no reply. It was as if I had never written it.

Gradually, I began to think the unthinkable: that our life together was over, and that we might as well make it official. I began to buy books on divorce. The book *Crazy Time* by Abigail Trafford really hit the spot. I recognized in its descriptions the erratic feelings I was going through. I would sit and stare at the furnishings of our cozy house, go over the agony and ecstasy of all the little decisions of buying this dresser or that chair, and then visualize all of it piled up at the curb ready for the Salvation Army.

Salvation? Was there no way back to the confident beginnings, the boisterous lovemaking, and the inspired labor of birthing and caring? I imagined Rick reading my letter, I imagined... I could not imagine past that blind spot - that he had simply put the letter away as if I had never written it. Tears were a relief, and I would sit and cry in the empty house. But after a while there was a hot feeling rising from the pit of my stomach and I felt ready to ambush Rick when he came home and to attack him with my two fists.

My mind was made up. I would pack up and be out of there. But where would I go? I had been holding on to see Muriel enter college. But what about Peter? So, it was back to nostalgia, and regrets, and feeble hopes of salvaging things - followed by distrust and anger all over again. I was on the roller-coaster of "crazy time."

I read how men hid their financial affairs and managed to get out of supporting divorced wives and families, often starting over with younger women. I knew there wasn't much left over from our running expenses, but Rick was enrolled in some company investment plans, and I was out of the loop. I better plan my exit carefully. What were my options? Not another man. Our sex life was not exactly sizzling, but whatever outside temptations had come along - had not been all that tempting.

My friends were also struggling. Foster had moved out and Jane finally turned her back on the past and began to date again. While I had my hands full with my teenagers, Nancy had had a struggle of it as well. Luco's quiet ways turned out to be a form of depression associated with secret drinking. None of our men had been willing to resort to counseling. Nancy and I met and counseled each other. I did have a Ph.D., but it had not exactly secured me a career thus far. Maybe the time had come to look for job opportunities away from New York? I looked into it, and was offered a one-year position in Russian at Michigan State University in the Fall Semester of 1989.

Muriel was ready to graduate from high school, and we prepared to celebrate even though Rick was in one of his funks. I did not know the people at the Staten Island Academy. The days when it had seemed of the utmost importance to rush to PTA meetings and do fund-raisers for enrichment programs were long gone. We sat among strangers, ourselves estranged. The kids had taken off, leaving the dance floor to the parents. Rick and I had enjoyed dancing together in the past, but now he was not interested. Truth be told, those middle-aged, dressed up people did not look too hot. It occurred to me that I was one of them. No wonder Rick was not in the mood for romance.

As we drove home, I watched the telephone poles float by. Some were leftovers from days gone by, old tree trunks with a mess of wires and white ceramic transmitters looking like old-fashioned hair curlers. Most, however, were huge steel towers, Babels reaching for the sky in an international confusion of tongues. As they stretched their wires across oceans and continents, millions of people talked to each other. And here we were, sitting just inches apart, and nothing could breach the silence between us.

Peter was off street drugs, or so it seemed. We had run out of insurance money, and Peter now worked his program with Regent Hospital on an outpatient basis. But then a terrible thing happened. His friend, the one with the heroin addiction, relapsed and died of an overdose. Could we trust Peter to stick to his program? Could I leave for Michigan? I was sitting in my study, and Peter stood before me. He too was a good-looking kid. His hair was a shade darker than Muriel's and as I spoke, he kept his eyes downcast. I was telling him about my plans at Michigan State, and asking him about Regent Hospital, but he just stood there, saying nothing.

When he finally looked up, it was to say that he wanted to die. I thought I was prepared for anything by now, but I was not prepared for this. I looked into his eyes and it was like looking into a dark pool of water, with Peter already at the bottom of it, lost forever. Then he smiled an apologetic little smile; he was seven years old again, and we were both utterly helpless.

I tried, as I had been repeatedly advised, to "detach with love." Struggling to keep my voice from shaking, I repeated a statement current at the time which I myself believed. It asserted that more scientists lived in our day than had ever lived since the beginning of history, and therefore there was hope for an understanding and eventual cure for what ailed Peter. Could he not hold out a little longer? Was there nothing in his life to hold on to – not even the tiniest spark? He had to look for that spark - I could not do it for him. If he wanted to opt out, either through drugs or suicide, I could not really stop him. I had already lined up all the available resources, such as they were. It was up to him to use them. The time had come for me to move on to a struggle of my own. Life was a struggle: his lot was especially hard, but I was absolutely counting on him to struggle on.

So, I said good bye to Rick and the kids and took off. The campus of the Michigan State University in East Lansing is quite beautiful. Its large size is softened by plenty of trees and a river running through a wood grove, which buffers the campus from the edge of town. I was able to use an apartment reserved for visiting scholars right on campus. It felt great to be on my own. I still remember the change of seasons: the burst of fall colors, the web of ice-sparkling branches fanning out against a pale sky, and the first trickle of water in spring from beneath the ice cap of the still frozen river.

I was now mercifully teaching only Russian. A novelty at Michigan State was visiting scholars from the Soviet Union. A Russian language specialist had been housed for the semester near my own apartment, and I was asked to shepherd her during her stay. She turned out to be a delightful woman and we got along famously.

My duties of hospitality toward our Soviet guest took me to a basketball game. The local team was playing a visiting Soviet team and my new friend Zoya had been eager to go. We found our places in the huge stadium and I got my first experience of the rituals of cheering and doing the wave. The whole auditorium cheered as one for the local team, and this struck me as unsportsmanlike. When Zoya jumped to her feet and began to yell for the Soviet team, I felt duty bound as her host to support her. Here we were, standing up and doing a counter-wave of two. It was only a sports event, but the undercurrent of frenzy around me felt like I was taking my life in my hands.

I was enjoying my stay in Michigan, but my position there was only a one-year appointment. For once, luck was on my side. Mikhail Gorbachev was charming his way around the world, and Russian Studies programs were filling up nationwide. In response to my applications, I had twelve interviews lined up at the Modern Languages Association's yearly convention, which was held in Chicago that year.

My work at Michigan State presented me with a challenge I had been reluctant to face. It had to do with learning to use computers. I bellyached to one of my classes, and one of the students offered to help out. Ray was remarkably patient for a young man and convinced me by and by that the magic box behind the screen was actually dumb. All I had to do was humor it with step-by-step instructions. I discovered that my mindset was not at all linear and indulged in a few tantrums. Eventually, however, I began to get the hang of it. Just as well, since Ray was due to graduate at the end of the fall semester, and that time was quickly approaching.

Late one evening there was a knock on my door; it was Ray. I had known him all along as a quiet, even shy young man. We had become good friends, he had been at my place before, so I let him in. Classes were over, he had been out celebrating with his friends, and on his way home had noticed the light in my window. I wasn't sure what to do, so I offered him the proverbial cup of coffee. He, however, knew very well what to do.

One hears of campus shenanigans, lecherous old professors and students with crushes on them. I myself had weathered some of this as a graduate student. As a professor, however, I had felt neither lecherous nor aware of any student hormones flowing my way. But now Ray put his arms around me and, to my utter dismay, all my defenses crumbled.

His touch on my skin was as sure as if I had been so many computer keys. My starved body absorbed his tenderness and know-how and I opened up to him. He stayed the night, and we woke up in each other's arms. So much for quiet, shy young men. After Ray left, I just sat there in a complete daze, wondering what had happened to me. I had a body after all - and what was I going to do with it now?

Ray took off for England while I remained in a lingering state of after-glow. All the same, I took myself and my after-glow to the conference in Chicago to face prospective employers. Six interviewers asked me to follow-up meetings at their home institutions. Thus, spring semester zoomed by as I kept flying off to my on-site job interviews.

Unexpectedly, I received a letter from Ray and decided to write him back. On Valentine Day I received a stunning arrangement of tropical flowers from Hawaii. I assumed it came from Rick, but it was from Ray. Later that day there was a delivery from Rick as well: a little basket of daisies. I love daisies, and was even touched that he had sent them, but it was too late. Now I felt as rare and exotic as the flowers Ray had sent me. I was flattered that a one-night stand with me held his memory in the midst of what London had to offer. I was pretty sure that Rick had had someone in London, and this was a bit of pay-back. I began to watch my diet and to haunt little boutiques in the neighborhood.

As job offers began to come in, Michigan State was among them. And there was now a fair chance that Rick would be transferred to Detroit, which was less than an hour's drive from East Lansing. Maybe there was a chance for us after all? He was, however, holding out for a position in Switzerland. Wouldn't I LOVE to live in Switzerland? Maybe so once upon a time, but

NOW - when I was finally on track for a career? Another nail in the coffin of our partnership, if more nails were needed to hammer shut a dialogue as dead as ours. I opted for the place that would take me away the farthest, the University of Arizona.

In the meantime, Ray and I kept up our correspondence. Actually, I wrote more than he did. Words were MY forte, and I used words the way Ray had used his sense of touch. I did fantasize seeing him again just as I knew that it would never happen, nor, on the face of it, SHOULD happen. The age difference between us totally precluded a viable relationship. Perhaps the unreality of it all was part of the attraction. They do say that love is a mild state of insanity.

Rick must have sensed something, for he appeared more attentive when I returned to New York that summer. He invited me to join him on a business trip to Greece. The kids were busy with their own lives, and the conference in Moscow I planned to attend was not scheduled until late July. The news from Ray was vague. Ray was a mirage, and I was a fool. To get over it I decided to go to Greece with Rick.

Greece is as beautiful as everyone says it is, except for Athens. I thought the famous Acropolis pitiful in the midst of smog and urban sprawl. And that's how I felt as well in the midst of all the beauty: a ruined dream. After Greece Rick was due to attend a conference in Italy. I opted, instead, to visit my dear friends the Mandrykas, who had retired to Nice.

Then something happened to upset the flow of events. There was a phone call. A wave of panic swept over me as I thought of Peter, and it took me some time to take in the fact that the voice was Ray's. I thought he was calling from England, but no, he was in Nice, and waiting for me at the train station. The shy young man certainly knew how to create a sense of drama. So, we met in secret. The Mandrykas must have guessed something, but remained discreet. An early breakfast in a little waterfront café after a night of intense love, while daylight broke slowly over the Mediterranean, is my own private snapshot of Nice.

But then Rick returned from Italy, Ray returned to London, and I prepared to fly to my Moscow conference – as it happened, by way of London. And that's where Ray stood waiting for me at the airport gate - and my seat on the plane to Moscow remained empty. We took off on a tour of England, saw the sights on our modest budget during the day, and pursued the immodest exploration of our bodies during the night.

Soon enough, however, we had to part, and I flew back to New York. But New York, the Big Apple of so many years, was home no longer. I packed a couple of suitcases and prepared to fly out to Tucson. Rick offered to drive out later with some more stuff. It was business as usual. I wondered whether this helpful, affectless state of neutrality was the desired norm for him. To me it felt like death-in-life, and I couldn't wait to get away. The kids wished me well, and I took off.

***

CHAPTER 19

ARIZONA MONSOONS

The monsoon season in Arizona, which was already in full swing when I arrived in Mid-August of 1990, was a perfect harbinger of change. Overcharged heat waves exploded daily into fantastic storms. Dark clouds ripped open with lighting, churned and collided in a crash of thunder, and poured out sheets of water. Then, drawing apart like a stage curtain, revealed stupendous rainbows arching over a newly washed earth.

When Rick arrived in September with some odds and ends, I played it close to the vest. I had a job and a modest income now, but no savings or a personal credit history. In those days no bank would have given me a mortgage loan. I feared Rick's power of financial retaliation over me if I showed my hand too soon, so we presented ourselves to the real estate brokers as a couple.

This murky chemistry of deception was like the compressed waves of Arizona heat. It was bound to erupt into a stormy show-down sooner or later. And now one more ingredient was added to the unstable mix. Once again Ray showed up on my doorstep. At the same time, my family began to make plans to come to Arizona. Rick's mom, Francine, began to discuss the option of assisted living in Tucson. Then it was Muriel's turn. It no longer made sense to pay for a college education at Hood when she could get one for free at the University of Arizona. Tony, her Staten Island boyfriend, was thrilled by the relative proximity to Hollywood, and the two of them announced their arrival at Christmas time. Rick and Peter also decided to join us for the holidays.

Verily, stepping outside the bonds of matrimony is easier for men than it is for women. I had run away from all of them, and now they were all due to arrive. Ray moved out of my apartment for the duration and proprieties were maintained. After Rick and Peter left and Muriel and Tony found a place of their own, Ray returned. I don't know what Ray got out of our life together. To me it was all about not being dependent on a man wielding implicit historic and economic power, and not having the primary responsibility for offspring. To know, instead, in every fiber of my aging body that time was short and yet to glory in it with reckless abandon.

The Department of Russian Studies was throwing all the advanced courses at me, and I took them on with relish. I also began work on my tenure book. While I prepared my classes or researched my book, Ray found a job working with computers in one of the University's departments. Our nights were our own.

I settled my choice on one of the houses Rick and I had looked at and the purchase was finalized. Rick did not know that I did not move in alone. At some point that spring I confided in Muriel. She seemed to take the news in stride, looked Ray over and pronounced him O.K.

Summer came, and Rick put our house on Staten Island up for sale. His bid for the Swiss position had not worked out, and he and Peter were preparing to move to Detroit after all. He expected me to lend a hand with the move. This could have been as good a time as any to make a clean breast of things, but I worried about Peter. He would be cut off from his support systems - would Rick know how to rebuild them in Detroit?

I told Ray that I needed to attend to family matters back east, and he looked touchingly glum as he drove me to the Tucson airport. Once in Detroit, I noticed that without me to run interference between them, Rick and Peter were learning to build a relationship with each other. Rick promised to take care of things, so I stayed long enough to help them settle in, and returned to Tucson.

Ray met me at the airport and drove me home. Next morning, he took off for work while I slept in. I was still in my nightgown and robe lingering over a cup of coffee and a literary review, when the doorbell rang. I opened the door to a young woman in her early '30s: she was looking for Ray. She just stood there, looking ME over. How did SHE know to look for him HERE? I told her he was at work, and closed the door.

So, what I had always known would happen had already happened. And yet I was not prepared. When Ray came home that night, however, I was ready and asked him to move out. He said, "What did you expect, leaving me for your husband?" O.K., perhaps I had failed to consider his feelings, but he had clearly landed on his feet, and was now free to enjoy his consolation prize. Ray was not big on talk, and proceeded to show me; we made stormy love. I gave him time to make up his mind one way or the other. I began to get strange phone calls from the young woman in question. Next thing there was a call from Rick: he was coming down. She had evidently found a way to contact him and warned him that his wife was losing it with "a man half her age."

Rick arrived. My rival faded out of focus while the camera zoomed in on Rick and Ray. They faced off like two characters in a movie. Rick attempted to throw Ray bodily out of the house and a scuffle ensued. I moved out with Ray and into an apartment which was crawling with *cucarachas*. We lay on our bed and counted them.

But then Rick had to return to Detroit, and Ray and I moved back into the house. Classes resumed. I remember the look on my students' faces when a messenger walked into class with two dozen red roses. Rick was wooing me long-distance; he had realized that mere daisies would no longer do. I enjoyed the roses because they upset Ray. But we had each won our battle. Rick and the girl-friend were out of the picture, and our life together resumed its course.

Muriel dropped in from time to time and we celebrated Christmas together. After the park-like alleys, colonial buildings and small classes of Hood College she felt lost in the sheer size of the University of Arizona. It took some time to reorient herself and pick a major. Eventually, she chose wildlife management, dreaming of a life of running with wolves. I thought Tony was wolf enough, but my own example was hardly a model of common sense. Until the big time in Hollywood, Tony was hired to fall off roofs during mock fights at Old Tucson. The place is an abandoned set for cowboy movies and carries on the traditions of the Wild West as a tourist attraction.

In the summer of 1992 Ray took off for a trip to Russia and I settled down to write my tenure book. That same summer, however, Rick and Peter arrived in Tucson. Following the dramatic disclosure of a rival, Rick had decided on early retirement. Francine had already moved to Tucson, and Rick bought his own house. The whole family reconstituted itself in the Old Pueblo, as Tucson is affectionately known. We were all on our best behavior now, and I was profoundly grateful to Rick for keeping up with his parenting. Peter was clearly unable to fend for himself. They were all evidently prepared to wait until the Indian summer of my folly burned itself out.

Summer lasts pretty much all year-round in Arizona, and Ray and I entered another year of life together. Yet Ray was a young man who had not even begun to make his mark in the world, as the world and he both expected. His computer job at the University was a job, not a career. Ray was interested in using his Russian in international business, and the Thunderbird Business School in Phoenix, the capital of Arizona, offered an MBA in the field. I duly encouraged his prospects, and for the next two years we made many trips between Tucson and Phoenix to see each other. But the inevitable happened after all. Ray fell in love with a young woman in his program.

It had been five years since we had first met, and our bond was not easily loosened. Ray would come and visit, then disappear, and I sat by the proverbial phone like a love-sick teenager and waited. I watched Gloria Swanson and William Holden in *Sunset Boulevard* on TCM and tried out for the Norma Desmond part. I was visiting Ray once again and we jumped into bed as usual. But then Ray seemed to withdraw and I got the feeling that he was anxious to see me go. I figured he had a date with my competition. He assured me it was a working date: they had a class assignment due the next day. It was the sincere note in his voice that finally clued me in. He was telling the truth. He had not succeeded in getting into her pants yet... but surely not for lack of trying. I now felt that he was using my body to make love to her, and our sexual bond lost its magic. It felt driven and compulsive.

I got dressed and left. I drove home through the night. I stopped for coffee at the diner facing weirdly shaped Picacho Peak. For a moment the jagged mass of rock appeared as I had once seen it, covered with a golden blaze of Mexican poppies. But the brief season was long since over and the stony outcropping stood barren against a pale sky. My Indian summer with Ray was over at last.

Rick's forbearance with me had also run its course. We began to discuss divorce. I fully expected a power struggle over finances and was referred to a cracker-jack attorney. As I walked into the man's office, I saw on his walls obvious proof of his fitness for the job. Instead of a set of framed diplomas I was staring at a series of stuffed animal heads: elk, stag, long horn, mountain goat... Then one of those heads with glassy eyes morphed into the familiar features of Rick's head; I did get the point. But I shook off this momentary surrender to blood lust and looked with mixed feelings at my champion, who was stepping briskly forward to shake my hand. Despite the lawyer's forceful professional advice, Rick and I settled our affairs amicably.

All these more or less tumultuous events were not altogether conducive to the concentration needed to further my tenure package, but I plugged away. I had given a dozen papers at various conferences and published articles. I had also received several grants for special projects. One of them took me, in the fall of 1995, to examine archival materials in Moscow and Leningrad - now once again Saint Petersburg. I had been too busy and too distracted to follow the momentous changes taking place in what was no longer the Soviet Union.

And now, in 1995, the place was hard to recognize. It must have been past 10 p.m. in Moscow when I passed the construction site of the Cathedral of Christ the Savior. The site was lit up, and buzzed like a beehive with construction workers. They were building an exact replica of the church built in 1883 and famously dynamited by Stalin in 1931.

In a Saint Petersburg library, I asked for materials on early writings by Russian Tsarinas who had been sequestered in convents. The specialist turned out to be an elderly woman surrounded not just by stacks of books, but by pictures of Tsars and Tsarinas and great-duchesses and grand-dukes displayed like icons complete with votive lights. But this keeper of the pre-revolutionary flame misunderstood the feminist premises of my research and I left with empty hands.

Outside, a group of middle-aged, ill-shaven men, their chests covered with war medals, stood at a corner and sang patriotic songs to the strains of an accordion. Free enterprise, by the looks of it, was in full swing, but my own coin was their only profit thus far.

Further down the street, a poorly-dressed but genteel-looking woman stood on the sidewalk, displaying on a towel at her feet three silver spoons, an alarm clock, an ornate picture frame, and an old calendar. Upon discovering that I knew Russian, she poured forth a torrent of grievances. She said that her pension barely covered her utility bills. She said that her niece was a teacher in Simbirsk (now no longer Ulyanovsk) and that she and her colleagues were on a hunger strike because they had not been paid in months. She said she knew elderly people who were killed by gangsters after they had been conned into signing over their apartment to some 'entrepreneurs.'

I also caught some of the going action on TV. It was a medley of scandal disclosures, high-minded discourse on liberty, and rowdy politicians coming to literal blows. This lively eruption of *glasnost* exhibited the agony and extasy of Gorbachev's *perestroika*. A 'coup' to unseat him took place in the summer of 1991.

But it was too late. Yeltsin, who was not going to dilly-dally like Gorbachev, and had full support from the West, defied the "Communist die-hards" and, memorably standing on a tank, won the day. And all those who, inspired by the Voice of America and Radio Free Europe, had yearned for change, poured out into the streets to support him: free at last!

They had no idea that the way to freedom (or sanity), to borrow Naomi Klein's formula, was "shock therapy." She quotes John Williamson, a senior fellow at the Peterson Institute for International Economics, in 1993: "One will have to ask whether it could conceivably make sense to think of deliberately provoking a crisis so as to remove the political logjam to reform."

As Michael Hudson explains as well, the International Monetary Fund and the World Bank met in Houston in 1991 and "laid out in advance" how to make Russian banking dependent on foreign loans through hyperinflation. He describes how specialists in economics from the Harvard Institute were bankrolled to advise the Russians on how to solve their problems. As he suggests, "the Russians didn't understand that industrial capitalism that Marx described had metamorphosed into finance capitalism and was completely different."

No one was concerned about the problems of the general public, whose savings had been wiped out. It was the problems of those who had access to the country's resources that mattered. These "leaders" were easily convinced to save themselves by appropriating these resources, then cashing them out to foreign investors at giveaway prices. Because of routine recourse to Mafia-like 'protection,' the process was characterized as "gangster Capitalism." And while the oligarchs squirreled their ill-gotten gains abroad, the majority of the population was left jobless and hungry.

Serhii Plokhy, the director of the Ukrainian Institute at Harvard University, documents the parallel process of the dissolution of the Soviet Union in his book, *The Last Empire*. He describes how Yeltsin and George H. Bush were in frequent phone contact, as Yeltsin sought much needed personal advice. Gorbachev had also called President Bush for mutual dialogue. He was known to believe in "the European destiny of the Soviet Union."

We love to characterize Putin as a sinister KGB asset. He was a minor player while President George H. Bush had headed the CIA under President Ford. At any rate, these 'heart-to-heart' relationships gave President Bush ready access to the conflict between Gorbachev and Yeltsin: the former was intent on salvaging the Soviet Union, while the latter was ready to write off the Central Asian Republics, which, as he put it, "we feed all the time."

Yeltsin found a way around Gorbachev by getting together with President Kravchuk of Ukraine and Stanislav Shushkevich of Belarus. They met at the Belovezha Hunting Lodge in Belarus on December 8, 1991. At that meeting they put together a document creating a Commonwealth of the three Slavic republics. This initiated the dissolution of the Soviet Union and caused Gorbachev to resign. This kind of analysis would catch up with me later. Upon returning home, my main focus was on my book manuscript. As the tenure clock ticked away, I was advised to take a leave of absence, even an unpaid leave of absence, to ensure meeting my deadline. My department granted my request for the spring term of 1996, and I buckled down for the final stretch.

Rick was presumably watching over Peter, but this did not seem to include any professional back-up. What Peter had thought of my romantic involvement with Ray, he kept to himself. Under normal circumstances it would have been his season to sow wild oats, not that of his aging mother. Now, however, at the very time when I was counting on full and undivided concentration to meet my deadline, Peter was experiencing another downturn. He was seriously and unmistakably suicidal.

His chosen time to call me from his Dad's house was 3 a.m. He needed someone to help him tell off his voices. They kept urging him to drive off the highway, or explained in minute detail how to make a noose to hang himself in his Dad's garage. It got so that I would wake seconds before the phone rang, then the phone would ring, and it would start. I tried to sound upbeat but I couldn't have sounded too convincing, as my own hope in promised breakthroughs in mental health was now quite shaken. I undertook once again to figure out what the profession, the research, and local resources had to offer.

Psychiatrists remained as aloof as ever. After a ten-minute consultation they prescribed an ever-changing set of pills. Peter had already tried most of them and was quite familiar with the side-effects they produced. Some of them gave him what he called the "heebie-jeebies," forcing him into restless, involuntary motion. Others subdued him into a zombie-like state without erasing the mocking, obscene, threatening voices.

Rick was willing to pitch in, and we attended a parents' training program. We were told that the scientists were working hard on testing their findings, and new and improved neuroleptics, not the clumsy old-fashioned ones, but finely tuned atypicals were already coming down the pike. We watched optimistic videos. Famous stars testified to their new lives thanks to the wonder drugs.

I was surprised that the other parents in the group were so easily persuaded. I realized that they were content with just sedating their "loved ones," and we quit the group.

The urgency of my research in the mental health field competed with the urgency of my scholarly research. I was working on the penultimate chapter of my manuscript, had submitted a prospectus and early chapters to various university presses, and a couple of them had expressed an interest. Since the unpaid leave of absence entitled me, in principle, to a one-year extension, I was on track. My book would be published and peer reviewed by the following spring, and my chances for tenure would be good at that point.

But it did not work out that way. When I applied for my extension in that fall of 1996, it was refused, and I found myself inside Kafka's novel *The Trial*. I had felt competent and appreciated by both peers and students until then, but now what had seemed so straightforward in the rule books became a quicksand of theological casuistry.

As I walked the corridors of academe looking for redress, they narrowed visibly. I kept knocking on doors, but the sound rang hollow. When a door would swing open at last and I stepped in, giants of radical advocacy shrank into absolute dwarfs before my very eyes as the desks behind which they crouched filled the room. The gate, as Kafka knew, was closed all along; this was the gate assigned to me, but it was the very gate I could not enter.

Popular notions of entrenched oldsters who shuffle to classes on their last tenured legs are not groundless. But gate keepers take care of their own, and I was not one of them. As a junior, middle-aged, female faculty member I was of little use to anyone in the academic survival of the fittest. And international politics, which had helped me to land my job during Gorbachev's triumphs, now helped to take it away. The Cold War had petered out and grant money for Russian had dried up, shifting to Arabic studies.

I recalled a low moment when some of the best among my graduate students confessed that Tolstoy and Dostoyevsky left them cold, and that they saw their life's future in the intelligence field. Did I really want tenure to lock me into training spies? The tenure fiasco began to feel like a ticket to freedom. I had visited Puerto Peñasco in Mexico (also known as Rocky Point), a small fishing port on the Sea of Cortez. I likely had enough equity in my property for a small house in Puerto Peñasco, and the meager pension I would glean from my spotty academic career would see me through south of the border. I decided not to fight for tenure and not to look for a position elsewhere. Instead, I would move to Mexico and revive my early dream of writing.

I set my sights on a little house in Puerto Peñasco, and invited the family to check it out. There it stood, my vision of a future life of liberty. Sure, the house needed patching up, but what I saw before me was the way it would look after I fixed it. The pile of debris in front was gone, there were plants on the tiny front porch, and the rusty water pipes had been replaced. I ignored the primitive kitchen corner: it would do. The back room was to be lined with mysterious masks, and the Indian blanket on my bed was woven in rainbow stripes of vivid color. And above my desk in the back room, the window opened to the sea.

Rick looked the house over and said nothing. Then he finally took a deep breath and said o.k., if I did not want to get back together, so be it. He was sorry, but so be it. But he would still see to it that I had a decent place to live in, not the sorry shack before us. I was stunned. Stunned, after all the wrangling, by his impulse of generosity. I waited for the other shoe to drop, for him to take it all back, but he didn't. Could it be that he HAD changed after all?

While Rick and I lingered in this new phase of separate peace, Peter and Muriel began to enter their own attempts at adult relationships. Muriel was now dating a lot, and various young men came to ring our door bell. Her latest summer job was with Parks and Recreation. It entailed taking risk kids from the south side of Tucson on wilderness trips. She would come back telling stories of mountain rappelling and white-water rafting on the Salt River. When I raised the question of the possible danger of these expeditions, she explained that danger was precisely the point. The idea was to replicate gang-member bonding in life-threatening situations.

She now met someone she was ready to settle down with for life. He turned out, once again, not to be a fellow student. Nor was he a wilderness companion, but a long-haired rocker. I had been diplomatic with Tony, but lost my cool with Robert. How did he propose to feed my grand-children, I asked him. This put a damper on the occasion, but sometime later Muriel announced that Robert had enrolled at the University of Arizona, and was acing everything.

Peter too had met someone after all. Catie had been subjected to a number of spine operations which had left her body impaired. Yet she had a pretty face and a ready wit. Tall, good-looking, sad Peter and lively Catie who seemed to carry her handicap with such spirit looked ill matched, yet they had found each other. Hope springs eternal.

Soon enough it was time for wedding bells. Muriel wanted a traditional wedding with all the trimmings, and with Francine's financial help, we were able to give her one. Nancy and her son Lew flew in from New Jersey. Luis was conspicuously absent; they too were no longer together, and had taken the final step of divorce. We celebrated and danced to Rob's rock group. Although my ears had trouble picking anything out of the high-decibel mass of noise, what mattered was that Muriel was magnificent in her wedding dress and that she looked so happy.

Peter's wedding followed soon thereafter. Catie's family was Mormon, so we all drove to Phoenix to a sober celebration officiated by a Mormon elder. But I was just as thrilled watching Peter make his solemn promises as he looked down at misshapen Catie, as I had been watching Muriel look up into Rob's eyes from under her bridal veil.

Our kids' entering into their commitments recalled our own hopeful beginnings, Rick's and mine. We had cooperated pretty seamlessly through these latest family events. Maybe Rick had REALLY changed? Maybe my dream house in Puerto Peñasco WAS a sorry shack? Maybe instead of blissfully writing I would spend my days struggling with ever-rusting pipes and cucarachas? I no longer knew what I felt or did not feel. I had trouble sleeping. One night I jumped out of bed, threw on my raincoat, got into my car and drove over to Rick's house. He tells me that when he opened his door what first struck him was the weirdness of my wearing a raincoat: it was not raining. Then he realized that I was wearing nothing underneath.

**

CHAPTER 20

LUZ DE PLATA

If I didn't know what I was doing that night, I had done it anyway. Rick and I were back together. We sat together at the movies again and we no longer looked past each other at meal time. At night, our bodies took nothing for granted. We wanted to touch lightly on old wounds and took our time exploring hidden patches of skin memory, which we wanted to rewrite anew.

And we talked. I asked him about the unanswered letter. He drew a blank. He figured he had been scared. He told me about discovering his abandonment issues. He told me that his distancing ways were not about me but about his own childhood struggles. We promised to be gentle with each other's struggles. What about the women? Yes, there had been women, but he had never ever considered leaving me. On that score I had paid him back with interest, and we were even.

We recalled how we had promised to take turns supporting each other's dreams. My dream of writing my own stuff was still only a dream, and Rick promised to back me up all the way this time. I did not have to run away to Mexico. Mindful of our new ways, we pooled our resources and looked for a house unburdened by unwelcome memories.

As soon as Rick and I were settled in our new house, we decided to celebrate our reunion. The outline of mountain crags and the wild profusion of cactuses which surrounded us would provide the enchanted backdrop to our new, new beginnings. I had missed out on a real wedding gown the first time around, so I now made my appearance in white lace and wide-brimmed hat to match. Rick looked young and happy as we stood before a Unitarian Universalist minister this time and renewed our vows. The sun was sinking behind the Tucson Mountains. Its rays, filtered through a mass of clouds, threw a mantle of burnished silver over us. This lingering, subdued glow became the emblem of our reconstructed life together. In deference to the Hispanic traditions which surround us, our gate greeted the outside world with the words *"Luz de Plata"* – silver light.

Francine had never offered criticism or even advice during our years of estrangement. She advanced a down payment to Peter and Catie for a modest little house. She had also come to feel isolated and confined in her assisted living quarters and entered into a partnership with Rob and Muriel. We found them a combination property with a house for the young couple and a guest house for Francine.

Peter and Catie both received Social Security disability benefits, but this was hardly enough to live on, and we helped out. Catie was often sick, however. Time and again she needed to be rushed to the hospital, and Peter was dutiful and attentive to her needs. The phone rang at 5:00 a.m. one day. Catie was in the emergency room, so I rushed to the hospital. But when I got there Catie was blissfully "out," and they told me they had given her some morphine for pain. But what was her illness? She had come down with the flu. The FLU? And they had given her MORPHINE? Peter came clean at last: he said he was sick and tired of taking Catie to the hospital for a fix. For a FIX? What was going on? It turned out that Catie was severely addicted to morphine, and that she was sending Peter out to get whatever he could on the street when the hospitals didn't come through.

We urged them both to enter some form of counseling. Catie was unwilling - Peter agreed, and took off for a clinic in Los Angeles. When he returned, he was no longer willing to get back together with Catie. She moved into a motel, where Peter continued to check in on her. He brought her food and looked after her cat. And then on one of those visits, he found her dead. Whether from withdrawal or an overdose, Catie's young and troubled life had been cut short with brutal suddenness.

Since my move to the Southwest, I had been so preoccupied by personal priorities that little mind space had been left open to the wider world. This being Arizona, however, the action was on the border with Mexico. I had been vaguely aware of the Sanctuary Movement back in the '80s. But, mostly absorbed by East-West relations, I had failed, as they say, to connect the dots.

I now discovered how those "dots" of East and West and North and South were coming together, of all places, in Tucson. Several churches here had originated the Sanctuary Movement by opening their doors to refugees from Central America. Civil wars there had been inspired by the Cuban Revolution of 1959 and the U.S. response to it. The School of the Americas (SOA) was founded in Panama by President Kennedy in 1963. Its mission was to train counter-insurgency troops to stem the spread of Communism.

I had never heard of the School of the Americas, but now I kept hearing of it as of the "School of Assassins." In 1984 President Carter had relocated SOA to Fort Benning in Columbus, Ga. A United Nations Truth Commission had listed some of the names associated with the atrocities in Central America, and there was a telling overlap with names of graduates from the SOA, renamed to the Western Hemisphere Institute for Security Cooperation (or WHISC) in 2000.

Gradually, a protest movement gathered around Father Roy Bourgeois. Born in Louisiana in 1938, he had opted for a military career. But his service in Vietnam turned him around, and he entered the priesthood. His pastoral work in Bolivia made him a witness of local events: anyone who would be calling for improvement to the population's poverty would be silenced. He was banned, and brought his witness back home to the United States. He moved to the vicinity of Fort Benning and began daily vigils at the Fort's entrance. In time he was joined by other priests and then nuns, and pastors, and friends, and the protest movement against the School of the Americas began to grow.

When a busload of Sanctuary veterans prepared to trek from Tucson to Georgia in November of 1998 for the yearly protest at Fort Benning, I decided to ride along. The marchers at Fort Benning bore a sea of white crosses, each inscribed with the name of an assassination or massacre victim. Some eight thousand people gathered at Fort Benning in 1998, and a couple of thousand defied the prohibition by "crossing the line" onto Ft. Benning property. I was among them. But a decision had been made that year not to make any arrests.

I did not regret escaping the attentions of Federal Judge J. Robert Elliott, who had made his reputation issuing injunctions against Martin Luther King, Jr.

Yet Central and South America were still just exotic places in my mind, filled with jungles and pampas and Andean heights, places of magic realism, sultry tangos, and wild carnivals. I had lived in many lands and remembered that you don't know a country until you see the color of its skies, hear the sound of its songs, and break bread with its people. When the director of a local organization called BorderLinks organized a trip to El Salvador in the spring of 2000, I jumped on the bandwagon.

The occasion of the trip to El Salvador was the commemoration of the 1980 assassination of Archbishop Romero. The BorderLinks people were experienced in taking "gringos" south of the border. I stayed with a Salvadoran family, in their home with tiny rooms, concrete floors and primitive bath and kitchen facilities. Their outside wall bore traces of bullet holes.

My poor Spanish was not conducive to advanced dialogue and we were not lectured much on the history of El Salvador during our stay. Rather, as doubting Thomas is said to have done upon encountering the risen Savior, we were taken to touch the still open wounds inflicted by history on the body of El Salvador. Our first visit took us to the church where Archbishop Oscar Romero had been assassinated. There we listened to an old nun who told us how the Archbishop had been celebrating Mass, how one of those bullets which explode upon hitting its target felled him, and how she had sat there, trying to hold pieces of him together.

Another visit took us to the University of Central America, on whose campus seven Jesuits had been murdered. The latter had been contaminated by the movement known as liberation theology, which related neo-Marxist social analysis to Jesus' teachings on behalf of the poor. But the powers-that-be preferred to inherit the earth themselves. When I entered the now empty back room where the Jesuits' housekeeper Julia Elba and her daughter Celina had also been killed, something happened to me. I was overcome by an overwhelming feeling of mortal danger.

As to Archbishop Romero, he had attained his eminent position precisely because he was a modest, bookish man, and could be counted on to know his place. Yet there were guerrillas in the hills denouncing exploitation and calling for justice. Father Rutilio Grande, an old friend of the Archbishop's, had sided with their cause. Archbishop Romero was a man of peace and chided his friend for being a hothead. Then one day they killed the trouble-making priest and the Archbishop began, however reluctantly, to walk in his friend's shoes.

He went to the villages and witnessed the depredations of the security forces. He began to speak out against the violence privately, then publicly. One by one his friends, relatives, and fellow-clerics turned away. Pope John-Paul II condemned him, claiming separation of church and state. And eventually, as he fully expected, a gunman killed him in broad daylight while he was celebrating Mass. An official 1993 U.N. report identified the man who had ordered the killing as former Major and SOA graduate Roberto d'Aubuisson.

Next, we were driven to the province of Chalatenango. We were on our way to visit the graves of American nuns who had also been murdered in El Salvador. Their families had sought redress with the State Department back home, but in vain. A military patrol stopped our bus, and made us disembark. The soldiers, very young and heavily armed, had us line up outside, and our American passports felt very light.

Our final destination was the village of Flores. We walked on a dirt road surrounded by jungle-overgrown hills. It had rained, and the smell of the earth was strong. Something about the place felt strangely familiar. We visited a pre-school. Lovely children played on grass mats. Later we listened to testimonials. Women spoke of round-ups, of hiding in caves, of burned crops and dry wells, and of lost children - children snatched away by soldiers and sold into adoption.

The next day, we were taken to the river Sunpul. We had been told to bring our bathing suits, and we jumped into the river and splashed merrily. But our moment of tourist indulgence was not to last. We were gathered on the edge of the river, and were told that six hundred women, children, and old men had been driven into the river and massacred on this very spot. Then one of the young Salvadorans who were accompanying us bent down and scooped up some of the mud which must still hold particles of the spilled blood. He reminded us that the day was Ash Wednesday, and with his thumb he traced a mud cross on our foreheads. Our river frolic turned out to be a baptism of earth and blood.

As we stood transfixed by the River Sumpul, there was a rumble up above. It was a convoy of U.S. troops lumbering way up on the lip of the canyon. I looked up, and perhaps because our encounters had had all these religious overtones, I found myself in a strange, almost hallucinatory state... I was by the River Jordan, John the Baptist was about to pour water over my head, and up above the resounding, all-powerful voice of the Almighty...

But what were American troops doing in El Salvador? I was quite ignorant of the country's history. As I immersed myself in this history upon returning home, I discovered how much there was to learn. The country's development from the days of the Spanish *Conquista* was typical of other Latin American countries: the taking over of the land from the indigenous population in order to create a rich landowner elite. In time they abolished the native communal lands, developed large plantations and forced the peasants to work on them to produce cash crops like coffee. They rationalized their exploitation by the natural inferiority of the exploited.

Sporadic rebellions by the impoverished population had caused these elites to develop a strong military to keep them in check, and the head of the government was usually a colonel or a general. One of the more notorious ones was General Maximiliano Hernandez Martinez. He modeled his behavior on Franco, Mussolini, and Hitler, and relied on them for police training and the supply of weapons. He suppressed a peasant uprising with a terrible massacre known as the Matanza. He was replaced in 1944, but El Salvador continued to be ruled by military men.

In his *The Open Veins of Latin America*, Eduardo Galeano explains the Capitalist system introduced by the British after the Spanish empire's withdrawal. Instead of occupying the land, or investing into its development, they relied on the existing elites to supply raw materials in exchange for manufactured goods. And when the British Empire lost its power, the United

States stepped in. Increasingly, this included military involvement to support compliant regimes.

But this handy partnership between local strong men and foreign powers caused people to rebel. The example of the successful Cuban Revolution of 1959 became a hopeful model. In El Salvador, a mass movement overthrew President Lemus in October of 1960. The United States, however, sponsored a counter-coup, and this power struggle took on an ever-escalating pattern. Special forces fresh from Vietnam proceeded to organize a centralized intelligence agency for all of Central America, linking the police, the military, and the National Guard.

To balance out the activities of the counter-insurgency forces, President Kennedy had founded the Alliance for Progress: its purpose was to facilitate reform and development. But the funds intended to such goals were regularly side-tracked. The election of President Reagan was celebrated by the officials in El Salvador. He believed in neo-liberal politics, worked to erase the "Vietnam syndrome," and eventually poured 6 billion dollars into funding the war of repression.

It seems amazing that despite the local tradition of power politics, and the massive support of the United States, the popular resistance held out. Apparently, people left destitute in the countryside, or knowing that they were on the extermination lists in the cities, were ready, since death was inevitable, to die fighting. In time, the various guerrilla factions formed a coalition and became known as the FMLN. The Civil War had lasted 10 years, and in 1992 a piece agreement was finally signed.

The '90s, however, saw the famous LA headlines about gangs from El Salvador. President Clinton implemented massive repatriation, and as always with "gangs," the Mafia and the CIA were part of the picture. Gang wars made El Salvador "the murder capital of the world."

During my visit in 2000, I knew something of the School of the Americas as the headquarter for training counter-insurgency, and its methods of assassination and torture. I was now learning something of the resistance, particularly the involvement of the clergy in liberation theology.

Upon our return to the capital, we took part in the march which commemorated the assassination of Archbishop Romero. It was a fiesta. Young people chanted with hopeful, expectant faces: *Que viva Monsignor Romero! Que viva!* As we rested afterward, my hosts treated me to the delicious Salvadoran tortillas called *pupusas*. "What do people in North America think of Monsignor Romero?" they wanted to know. How was I to tell them that most people in North America never heard of Monsignor Romero? And now we had seen enough, and we were on our way home. Soon we were landing at Houston Airport and stepping back into the din, glut and glitter which characterize our way of life. I touched my forehead, as if to test whether the mud cross traced by the River Sumpul was still there. I wondered if I deserved to bear it.

***

CHAPTER 21

EL DORADO

As with my earlier journeys of discovery, I came home with a sense of purpose. First, I would do my homework, and then I would do my best to share my newly acquired understanding. Upon moving to Arizona, I had reconnected with the local Unitarian Universalist congregations. I had been much absorbed in my academic work, and less involved than on Staten Island. Just the same, I was invited to give "lay sermons" on occasion, and became chair of the Social Action Committee. This would be the place to start.

In the meantime, I visited with the family, and we caught up. Muriel had given birth to her first child, Chloe, and was expecting again. Rob had found a job with Raytheon. While his earlier plans to become a Rock Star had been a matter of concern, we had all been reassured when he enrolled in school. Yet his college experience took a surprising turn. His family had been traditional Democrats, but now Rob's economics teacher converted him to a conservative libertarian point of view. But whether Democrat or libertarian, what were the options to make a living in Tucson, Arizona? Who was I, peacenik that I was, to quibble?

Alex was doing well enough. Francine had given him a down payment for a modest house, and we helped with the mortgage. The really important thing was that he stuck to his drugs and alcohol support systems, and this made his mental illness more manageable.

The one that was not doing too well was Francine. She was not sick exactly, but weak and despondent. Muriel called one day: something was wrong with Francine. Muriel had already called the ambulance and we met Francine at the hospital. She had suffered a heat stroke. She recovered somewhat, but not enough to go home. She had become disoriented and we had to come to terms with the fact that only a nursing home would keep her safe. We found a small, family-like facility, and visited her often. For some time now she had made her peace with leaving this world, and insisted that she did not want intensive life-support systems. When another health crisis developed in the spring of 2001, Rick felt that he was following her wishes by letting her die peacefully in her bed.

Francine had wanted to be cremated without further ado, her ashes mingled with Frank's ashes, which she had kept all these years, and cast into the sea. It did not have to be the moody North Sea on whose shores she had been born 88 years ago. The sun shone brightly, as it always does over the Sea of Cortez, and we scattered Frank and Francine's ashes over the waters.

My trip to El Salvador had only intensified my urge to understand "the big picture" of world affairs. I sat among family or friends, I listened to my granddaughter Chloe's teething problems or to how the church canvass at my Unitarian Church needed more push. And without warning I stood again by the River Sumpul, and the water was reflecting all that light, and the young Salvadoran was scooping up some mud and lifting his hand to my forehead, and the American convoy was rumbling up above.

Was the Cold War not over and had we not won it? But a different kind of war had been in progress for a long time south of the border, and I prepared to learn all about it. But when I shared my excitement with my friends at the Unitarian Church, their response was lukewarm. Some of them were worried that my earlier talk about the School of the Americas and now more talk on the subject would jeopardize our tax-exempt status.

I seemed no longer at home with my UU friends as I used to be... Where are the days when someone threw a rock through a window when John Murray, the Universalist, preached the "heresy" of universal salvation? Nowadays it seemed all about New Age uplift... We rinse our mouths with our proud principles, gurgling and regurgitating them as if we were on a wine tasting junket in Sonoma Valley. Look at the Evangelicals: they at least have the passion of their convictions, benighted as they may be, and the guts to fight for them... "Benighted," what a word – like holding on to each other and stumbling along in the dark of night..

I recalled how the Unitarian Church of Staten Island had sent me as a delegate to the peace conference in Prague. I thought of the picture with Peter and Muriel and the dog Bibi, and the residue of white powder over it. President Clinton had dedicated large sums to deal with that scourge of cocaine at its source in Colombia. I decided to go to Colombia.

The organization Witness for Peace was preparing a trip to Colombia, and I signed up. Rick and the kids were appalled. Staying put to baby sit and to tend cactuses and to write if I must, would have better answered their expectations, especially now that Muriel was expecting again. Nancy argued against my undertaking as well. She had lived in Colombia, and was familiar with the then forty-year history of *la violencia*. The Witness for Peace people suggested that a way to involve my church would be to ask them to support my trip with financial contributions. When I did ask, the response was one of outrage: who did I think I was?

But neither Rick nor my kids nor my friends knew the little girl I had once been in Yugoslavia and Germany: cold and hungry and grateful for scraps of food and clothing and terrified of planes. I did, of course, enjoy my position of security in these my years of "silver light." But even now I wake up with a start in the middle of the night at the sound of planes flying overhead. I don't want to turn my back on that little girl I still carry inside because she is my bridge to other little girls and boys cowering somewhere in fields or refugee camps.

And now there was another thread, a trail of white powder connecting those kids to my own in that picture with the dog. I went ahead with my traveling plans. A man from one of the local papers, the *Arizona Daily Star,* showed up at the house wanting to take my picture. He took an inordinate amount of time as I was asked to strike various poses. The result was a piece about the professor, wife, mother, and grandmother undertaking a trip to Colombia to see where her tax dollars were going.

The planners of our trip gathered a hundred or so of us in Miami. They conceded that Colombia was indeed a dangerous place, and they made it quite plain that they could not guarantee our safety. They gave us the choice to go home or to write a letter of farewell to our loved ones, should the worst happen. We wrote our letters and boarded our plane to Colombia.

In Bogotá, the capital of Colombia, a Mennonite Church near our hotel became our general headquarters. The parents of the minister of that church had come to Colombia to work in a leprosy. Che Guevara, who was a doctor, had also worked at that leprosy in his youth. The minister's parents stayed in Colombia, and that's where he grew up and engaged in his own ministry. During our stay in Bogota the people at the church kindly prepared all our meals.

Unlike the earlier trip in El Salvador, the Witness for Peace team organized for us back-to-back meetings with a diverse group of people: business groups, ranchers, women's groups, labor representatives, U.S. Embassy staff, educators, governors, peasant delegations, indigenous groups, peace workers, and church people. I had not realized that our trip had profited from a ceasefire, and was impressed by the open access to dialogue we were offered. We even visited a military base, where we spoke to three SOA-trained officers.

El Salvador's curse had been that it was a poor country. Colombia's curse seemed to be that it was a rich one. Was it not one of the contenders for the mythical location of El Dorado? But there was something both countries had in common, an unequal distribution of their resources. It was still true that a few families controlled Colombia's mineral wealth, its crops, its business, its media, and its politics. These were the people our own government counted on for 'stability.' But this was not working, hence *la violencia*.

The oldest and most powerful revolutionary movement in Colombia, going back to the 60s, was the FARC (*Fuerzas Armadas Revolucionarias de Colombia*). It began as a peasant movement. When the price of coffee went down on the world market, and day-laborers on the large plantations were dismissed, they went south to claim new land parcels. They had eventually formed an alliance with urban intellectuals and workers in the '80s, and attempted to promote their combined agendas as a political movement. But repeatedly, their attempt at participating in public life was met with violent opposition and many of their leaders were assassinated. They then retreated to their southern strongholds and to retaliatory tactics of kidnapping and counter-assassination.

The second largest guerrilla group is the ELN (National Liberation Army). They are primarily active in the Northeast, and their specialty is blowing up oil pipes. They protest the suppression of the right of labor to organize, which is granted by the Colombian Constitution. We met with a labor group which claimed that two thousand labor leaders had been killed in the previous year alone. President George W. Bush, who owned substantial oil interests in Colombia (the Harken Energy Corporation), would not take kindly to the blowing up of oil pipes. This would explain the subsequent renaming of U.S. involvement in Colombia from the War on Drugs to the War on Terror.

At the time of our trip in the spring of 2001, however, it was still all about drugs. When coffee prices dropped on the world market, everybody had switched to coca. It is a weed that grows up in the Andes and down in the Amazon. And it is a plant whose refined product is in much demand up north. It allows the campesinos to get a little cash, the FARC to keep up the civil war, the middle-men to feed their families, the banks to move money, and the big cartels to buy up large tracts of land, build sky-scrapers, become business moguls and political bosses. And it allows the financing of paramilitary security forces, the AUC.

This makes the drug lords the new power brokers in Colombia, and creates the following situation. Funds appropriated in the U.S. Congress for the War on Drugs go overwhelmingly to train and supply the Colombian army with our weapons. The Colombian army works with the security forces. The security forces work for the drug lords. Thus the U.S. War on Drugs supports the most conspicuous narco traffickers of them all.

As it became increasingly clear during our trip, the War on Drugs was a fig leaf. Everybody told us that fumigation does not work. But the ecological implications of aerial spraying of chemicals (glyphosate happens to be produced by the same company that gave us Agent Orange in Vietnam), are incalculable. And while coca is fairly resistant to fumigation, regular food crops are decimated. Fumigation poisons rivers and wells, and it causes skin and pulmonary diseases. Chickens and goats and little children alike are born with birth defects.

The real purpose of the War on Drugs appeared to be about taking sides in Colombia's civil war. This is why we did not fumigate the vast coca areas in the Northwest under army or paramilitary control. We only fumigated the coca areas of the Southwest which is under the control of the FARC.

The American colonel in charge of military operations who was delegated from the U.S. Consulate to speak to us, expressed frustration with having to be limited to fumigation sorties. At the time SEVEN new American bases were being built in Colombia – now we are up to NINE bases. Why is Colombia so important to U.S. policy? Why the massive subsidies, the formal U.S. support, and increasingly privatized mercenary armies?

These policies have been the rule for all US administrations. Colombia's geographical position makes it the "gateway" to the rest of Latin America. And the Colombian elites have been willing to be Washington's surrogates in fighting all oppositional forces – whether the FARK or the ELN, or more centrist or democratic movements.

The colonel who spoke to us was also chafing to take a crack at the loudmouth across the border - Hugo Chavez, who had been recently elected to the presidency of Venezuela. His example, although his Bolivarian Revolution was not grounded in Communism, was nevertheless problematical to both the Venezuelan elites and their allies in the U.S. But as we know, the April 2002 coup and subsequent attempts to unseat Chavez had failed. And after this charismatic, popular leader died in 2013, the much more pedestrian Nicolas Maduro also turned out to have enough popular support to withstand attempts to overthrow him.

As it happens, Colombian mercenaries were involved in this effort. Apparently, they had rescued our presidential candidate, Juan Guaido, in 2019, and spirited him across the border to the safety of Colombia. Now that there is alarming talk from the likes of China and Russia of a "multi-polar" world, Central and Latin America need more than ever reflect the declaration of the Monroe Doctrine – as strictly under North American control.

Back in 2001, our group was subdivided, and my sub-group was taken to Caqueta, nominally under FARC control – the same province where

Ingrid Betancourt was abducted, as she told us in her memoir. From Florencia, the capital of Caqueta, we were taken to a sprawling shanty town called, with appropriate irony, Nueva Colombia. Our host welcomed three of us Americans into a tiny bodega. I was to share the narrow bed with another woman, while he and his grandson and an American man were to sleep on the floor.

Using the bathroom at night turned out to be a challenge. I had to grope my way in the dark first over the sleeping bodies, then out the door held together by twisted wires, then down a rickety ladder, then down some slippery boulders to where the outhouse stood in oozing sewage. As a climax to this perilous journey, an angry rooster on whose territory I was evidently trespassing, attacked me. Comic relief is welcome even in a place like Nueva Colombia.

But there was not much to laugh about as we listened the next day to the people who had been displaced by civil war and fumigation. One woman was struggling to take care of nine children: four of her own, and five of her neighbor's, who was killed before her very eyes by the AUC or "security forces." An old man asked us point blank: "If you don't like us to grow coca, why don't you help us plant crops we can live on? Why do you just spray us like cockroaches?" Is fumigation, then, a deliberate policy of flushing out guerrilla supporters as in Vietnam? Are the peasants and their families and the indigenous peoples just collateral damage? Or is it all a territorial battle over who is going to profit from the lucrative coca business?

We had one last meeting upon our return to Bogotá. A man stood before us, shaking slightly. He said he had been tortured, hence the shakes. He said that there were many people like him in Colombia who believe in peace and dignity and democracy. But thus far official peace talks had been but a "pantomime." The government and its allies want peace without concessions to social change. The guerillas, burned by earlier attempts, will only negotiate from a position of strength. Thus, conflict intensifies beyond endurance for some while others ride the narco-boom.

His parting words were, "When you go home and drive your beautiful car again, just remember that a body is burning in its exhaust pipe."

When our group of Tucsonans held a press conference upon our return, the *Star*, which had been so eager to take my picture and to quote my naïve pronouncements before the trip to Colombia, was not interested. An article on Colombia did, however, appear in the *Star* around that time. It turned out that Republican Congressman Kolbe, then the Chair of the Armed Services Committee, had briefly traveled to Colombia while we were there. An authoritative interview with him related how he found glyphosate to be perfectly harmless, something like the can of Roundup some use to spray their weeds.

My friends at the Unitarian Church relented, and I did give them a report back. It went well enough, I thought, except that one friend surprised me by promising to visit me in jail. Another friend's comments were truly revealing. She said that she really appreciated my "jumping up and down" in front of the congregation… But didn't I get it? "Can't you tell that we are too middle-class to budge"?

I had not dwelled on the concept of class much. I had never read any of Karl Marx's writings, even though Rick had the three volumes of *Das Kapital* on one of our book shelves. But he never got around to reading them either. I mentioned the class thing to one of our friends, who defined himself as a Marxist. Well yes, he said, Marx had insisted that capitalists would always support each other – even across borders – because that's how they supported their own elite positions around the world.

I thought of my own "class" position. My parents (both my Dads) had been born with a silver spoon in their mouths, but this hadn't done me any good. Just the same, the silver sugar prongs of Babushka's mythical dowery had been a secret talisman, like Ariadne's thread that would guide me through the labyrinth of life. Of course, Mom made sure that I followed that thread by insisting on schoolwork… which did lend me, against all odds, at the University of Sydney – and there I met Rick. And marrying Rick, had I not climbed back - a least into the middle-class?

It finally dawned on me — especially after my latest journeys stepping gingerly down from the first world into the third: it was being American that qualified me for a place among the ultimate world elite. But my American friends lacked my early un-American training of running from bombs: no wonder they simply cannot hear what I have to say. And my academic friends, their vaunted "liberal biases" notwithstanding, were no different.

When the whole Yugoslavia affair began in the '90s, I had raised questions about the concept of "humanitarian intervention" with one of my colleagues. She immediately became a staunch defender of our "standing up for democracy." She repeatedly traveled to Bulgaria and Macedonia. I knew the paltry nature of our salaries... Surely, she must have received grants? From the same sources my students had admitted to receiving with the view of becoming spies?

Nancy mentioned how a colleague of hers had been approached when planning a trip to a conference in Argentina: she had been asked to report back — to sort of observe her colleagues and general proceedings... Still, even Nancy and I began to experience some discomfort when our long phone conversations strayed from family and literature - to politics. She told me that I was changing, and that I was pressing her to step out of her comfort zone. Was I?

I must have been changing. I remembered the crazy Norseman on the street corner of Manhattan when I first set foot in New York. Had I become him? Was my peace and justice 'hectoring' like his waving of his ancient pike? My interfaith trip to Israel/Palestine in 2012 and report-back became a point of no return. My Unitarian fellow-congregants were willing to prepare meals for the homeless, and they were certainly "on the side of love" for the LGBTQ movement. But making questionable distinctions between anti-Zionism vs. anti-Semitism was too much to ask. With some regret, and after 30 years of involvement with Unitarian Universalism, I quit.

***

CHAPTER 22

TAMO DALEKO

Rick was frustrated. Here he was putting his best foot forward, acting supportive... but Ft. Benning? El Salvador? Colombia? What next? Were my elaborate multinational journeys taking me anywhere? Had I stayed in Dostoyevsky's cellar too long, keeping my "spite" in cold storage, so that it was now frozen stiff? It was 2003, and was it not high time to add it all up?

It was. But the inner journey which the bombing of Belgrade had precipitated in 1999 needed one last real-time trip, all the way back to former Yugoslavia. That country had been obliterated from the world map just as I had banned it from my own consciousness. But can one delete the past? An episode from my D.P. camp days in Schleissheim, Germany, illustrates the dilemma.

I am ten years old and sitting at a table doing my homework. The door opens, and visitors step in. Mom calls me over to meet them. The lady says something to me, but I don't understand her. It seems that in the last four years I have learned German but have forgotten Serbo-Croatian. Mom apologizes and sends me back to my homework. Later, after I've gone to bed in the little enclave Babushka and I have together, I hear them singing in that language I no longer understand: *"Tamo daleko, daleko od mora"* ("Over there, far away, far away from the sea")... That faraway place whose language I no longer recognized was the place where I was born. But under those forgotten words associated with a forgotten place the melody lingers on, hovering over my sleep.

Of course, I did not know the family secret at the time – and even when the war in Bosnia screamed from the headlines in the 1990s, I was too absorbed in family and work to keep up with world events. But then there was the struggle over Kosovo and the bombing of Belgrade in 1999. Those missiles came to seek me out personally, and whether I liked it or not, dragged me out of hiding. The question was not only where I came from as partly Yugoslav or Montenegrin, but where I was going as an American.

Yet when I thought back to that bombing on April 6, 1941 in Belgrade, what came back to me now was how well that day had started. I knew it was a Sunday because Dad was home. He was not always there even on Sundays because he was driving a big truck and that took him all over the country. So, Dad was home, I was still in my pajamas, and we were having our breakfast. I distinctly remember the way Dad's spoon tinkled against the sides of his cup as he stirred his coffee. Then everybody jumped up because of the strange, vibrating noise outside and I followed them to our balcony. We lived in an apartment building, and down below in the street people were running. Then the noise changed and grew, and I put my fingers in my ears, and Dad scooped me into a blanket, and we too started running.

We ran down the stairs, round and round, and it was like a merry chase, because Babushka ran behind us, repeating, "But the child doesn't have her shoes on!" Father ignored her, and it was the funniest thing the way she held out this pair of booties. They hovered above my nose, but she couldn't catch us. Then we all sat in a dark cellar with other people. They were listening for something, and there were strange rumbling noises, but Babushka got hold of my feet at last and got my booties on. I felt warm and snuggly against Dad's chest. After quite some time we climbed out of the cellar, and stepped out into the street. I looked up. Where I would wave to Babushka up on our balcony sometimes, there was no balcony. The balcony was gone, and the wall was gone, and you could see into our apartment like into that doll house my friend Mira had.

Then we went somewhere. As we passed a bridge, there was a woman asleep on the ground. She wore a white gown and she had the most beautiful black hair. I asked Babushka why she was sleeping by the bridge and Babushka said she was an angel in heaven now. I was a little puzzled because I saw no wings, but she was so beautiful, she had to be an angel. We walked a long while. Then we arrived in a house full of people and we kids had a slumber party on the floor.

We found another place to live in, the house with the big porch. Wild grape grew on the wall of the porch, and I fed them to Pavlik. Pavlik was a stuffed rabbit dressed like people, but he didn't have a tie. He developed a belly ache from the wild grape, and I had to nurse him. The wild grape leaves turned dull with frost. The sky was gray. Dad's face, when we said good bye to him at the train station had looked gray like that.

"Ma, where's Daddy?"

"Out there somewhere making a fool of himself."

Babushka took me by the hand, we both knelt in front of her icon of the Virgin and Child, and prayed for Daddy. I prayed to the Holy Virgin Mother of God, and to Our Father Who Art in Heaven… and to Father Christmas… How could there be Christmas without Father? He hadn't come home on Sunday, and not on the next Sunday either, and I had lost count. One two, three, five, six… No: one two three, five… No: one, two, three, FOUR, five, six… Six icicles were hanging outside the window. Christmas any day now.

Mom too disappeared for long days, then returned hauling in big bags of coal or potatoes. We had a neighbor, Mme. May. Mom said she was a lady and would rather die of cold than carry coal and rather die of hunger than eat beans. That's why Mom had to haul her coal in for her as well. She was broken-hearted because her husband had disappeared too and now her daughter was dancing with the German soldiers. As we weren't going to have beans for Christmas Eve, Mme. May and her daughter were invited to join us for the occasion.

So, Christmas Eve was going to happen after all. I had prayed to Father Christmas to PLEASE wait just a little, little longer. But as I feared, the day had come and half-gone already. I stood by the window, watching the glass pane frost over into a leafy forest. Now my job was to look out for the first star, and that would signal the beginning of Christmas Eve. Maybe the star of Bethlehem would forget to show up? But there she was already, hovering on the edge of the crystal forest.

I prepared to make the announcement, turned around - and stopped in amazement. A Christmas tree stood there, shimmering softly with candle light. It was a surprise. I had heard some goings on in the back of the house, but Babushka kept me busy getting washed up. They really fooled me. And what was UNDER the Christmas tree? Sitting there and all dressed up was the most beautiful doll in the whole world! Oh yes, Mother and Babushka and Mme. May nodded, she was mine. I had to be careful with her though, she was no stuffed animal like Pavlik; her head was made of delicate porcelain. Mme. May had bought her in Vienna many years ago when her daughter was a little girl just like me, and now she was dancing with the German soldiers even on Christmas Eve.

Mme. May was crying, and I began to cry too. Everything was wrong. Father Christmas hadn't really come... And why was Mme. May's daughter dancing with the soldiers and WHERE WAS DADDY? Then there was a loud knock, the door flew open and Dad, shaking the snow from his boots, said: "Will you put up a deserter?"

The war situation was pretty confused in Yugoslavia in those days. You didn't have to be a child to be mixed up. Yugoslavia was surrounded by Axis-allied countries. Regent Prince Paul had signed a treaty of neutrality with Germany, but a group of Serb officers rebelled, ousted him, and promoted young Prince Peter, still under age, to the throne. The furious Germans then bombed Belgrade and overran the country.

But the occupation of Yugoslavia meant different things to different people. Dad's disappearance and Mr. May's disappearance, as it turned out, were quite different. Dad had joined a movement of White Russians who associated themselves with Vlasov's efforts of regime change in the Soviet Union, even if this meant collaboration with Germany. Mom had tried to talk Dad out of the "harebrained idea," but he had joined up anyway. But when the Germans prepared to move those recruits to the Western front instead of sending them to liberate Mother Russia, Father had walked away, making his fairy-tale appearance on Christmas Eve. Mr. May, however, did not return. He was Jewish, and I learned later that he had ended his life in a concentration camp.

Mom and I were going somewhere in Belgrade one day, and we happened to pass a bakery. Somebody opened the door and the smell of warm bread enveloped us and pulled us in. We entered and sat down at a table. But instead of ordering something to eat, Mom ordered tea for herself and a lemonade for me. My mouth had already watered with imaginary tidbits and I was struggling with my disappointment when a platter monumentally laden with poppy buns and fruit tarts landed on our table. Mom looked surprised. A German soldier walked over, and as Mom explained later, told her that he had just such a daughter as me back home in Germany, and that Mom would be doing him a favor in allowing him to treat us. But Mother said nothing, and to my utter dismay rose from her chair, took me by the hand, and we walked out.

People in Yugoslavia were definitely taking sides. Young King Peter had taken his government into exile to London. Colonel Draža Mihailović withdrew with his troops into the mountainous forest on the western edge of Serbia, where they became "Chetnik," i.e., guerillas. In Croatia the Germans found a staunch ally in Ante Pavelić. His Ustasha became the nominal rulers of "independent" Croatia and proceeded to exterminate the Jewish and Roma populations - and even more Orthodox Serbs, whom they saw as Schismatics. Josip Broz (Tito) gathered his Communist followers and retreated into the Bosnian highlands. In Sarajevo the Grand Mufti of Jerusalem came in person to review the Bosnian division of Muslim SS.

Dad, having given up on any further military involvement, resumed his truck driving job. This also proved pretty dangerous. The Resistance, whether Draža's Chetniks or Tito's Partisans, had grown apace and occupied large swaths of the countryside. The Germans controlled the larger cities and patrolled roads and railway lines. Truckers could be held up by any party or caught in cross-fires. A man in Father's company had been killed in an ambush in a town south of Belgrade.

One day Dad failed to return. Once again, we waited. And waited. Tempers flared. Mom lost her temper with me and I lost my temper with dolly Natasha. I placed her for time out against the glass door. Somebody pushed the door open, and Natasha fell and broke her head. As the dream which haunted me even in adulthood suggests, I took this very hard. Mom told me I cried for hours. Perhaps the doll's entrance into my life was associated with Dad's miraculous return on that Christmas Eve, and now her broken head announced that this time he would not return.

But he did return. He had been captured by one of the resistance groups. They confiscated his truck, and kept him for several weeks. Dad pleaded an old wound and family commitments and they let him go at last. Dad had described them as "hairy," and I suspect that they were Chetniks. Tito's Partisans would have been less lenient.

Allied support had been directed to Draža, the official resistance leader sanctioned by exiled King Peter. Tito and Draža met to discuss the terms of an alliance, but failed to come to an understanding. Serbia was, after all, the main target of German reprisals. Every time a German unit was attacked, a Serb village was burned to the ground; some 25,000 civilians perished in 1941 alone. As Draža put it, the Brits wanted to fight the Germans to the last Serb. He was not wrong: compare Yugoslavia's war casualties of about a million people to World War II casualties of some 300,000 of the British and the Americans put together. Tito, however, had committed himself to an all-out resistance, and Churchill switched Allied support from Draža to Tito.

Those were the paradoxes we lived with. And now that we were under German occupation, it was our friends who bombed us. There was no cellar in the house with the big porch. When the sirens announced a bombing raid, we ran to a vacant lot nearby where a primitive shelter had been dug. One time, Babushka refused to run to the shelter. She had a meat pie in the oven, and it had cost so much standing in line that she simply refused to abandon it. Mom tried to pry her away from the stove, but Babushka held fast. Mom then grabbed me instead and dragged me, fighting and screaming for Babushka, to the shelter. After the raid was over, we ran home. The house was still there, Babushka was there, and the pie was ready to eat.

The closest call came on the day we went swimming in the Danube. Our neighborhood was within walking distance of the river, whose banks was a favorite picnic spot. It must have been a Sunday again, because Dad was home, and friends had gathered to spend the day together. I was playing in the sand by the river when a hush settled all around. The adults stood around, looking up. When I too looked up, I saw silvery stars dancing in the sun-lit sky - stars in broad daylight!

Then those stars grew bigger and bigger, turned into black birds and began to swoop down at us. I heard Dad cry: "Hey, they're after the bridge!" He grabbed me, and we began to run. When the noise above us reached a breaking point of sound, he yelled "DOWN!" and everybody went down. As he threw me to the ground and covered me with his body, the earth shook and the river boiled over. Then he jumped up, grabbed me again, yelled "RUN!" and everybody ran. And then "DOWN!" and down we went. At one point I landed in an ant hill and watched the little critters run in confusion. I felt very sorry for them.

After that episode my parents sent Babushka and me into a nearby village for safety. We stayed with a peasant family, and the floor of our small room was made of plain, hard-trampled earth. The taste of black bread and the weight of the old farmer's rough hand patting me on the head seem all saved up in the smell of that earthen floor. And as I write this it all comes back to me: the smell of that earthen floor in a Serb village, and the smell of the earth in the Salvadoran village of Flores – and children playing on those mats, and me playing in that farm house, long ago, far away...

And now they were bombing Belgrade again. WE were bombing Belgrade. Some jarhead computer whiz kids were holed up in the bowels of mammoth carriers floating off the Adriatic coast, and they were punching keys or pressing joy sticks as if they were in some gaming arcade. And those "smart rockets" hovered just above ground and swished down streets and turned corners as they searched out their targets. In addition to arms depots and factories they hit a civilian train (and the Chinese embassy, why not?). Were the guys at the controls "just" having fun, or were they "just" following orders?

But I no longer believe that a dead woman lying by a bridge is "an angel in heaven." And Milošević, whatever he was, was not the devil incarnate. For better, for worse, there are only people. I had managed to forget what it was like to be bombed because it now happened in faraway places. But what we like to think of as far away turns out to be unexpectedly close to home.

When Rick and I prepared to undertake our trip to former Yugoslavia, my first tentative steps were to make myself useful to some Bosnian refugees who were beginning to arrive in Tucson. Whatever Serbo-Croatian still lay buried in my brain cells became activated by and by and I managed to function well enough in the language.

We decided to start with Belgrade, and chose a hotel near Kalemegdan Park. I remembered the name because of being taken to the zoo there, and because of the story of how one of the bombings had let the elephants and tigers loose in the neighborhood. But the park is also a historical landmark. It surrounds the rocky promontory where the Romans first established a foothold and where the Turks later built a fortress to overlook the point where two mighty rivers, the Danube and the Sava, come together.

The hotel had a stolid 1950s feel, but it was perfectly serviceable. When Rick indulged in a couple of disparaging remarks about the accommodations and the service, I dissolved into tears. I instructed him that this was not an expense-account trip like the ones he used to take as the international economist for General Motors. This was a journey in search of my roots and the secret motives of war and peace.

Now that he had been properly briefed about our mission, he promised to behave, and did so. When we tried to rent a car and were charged an exorbitant insurance fee, he said nothing. They explained that if we planned to take a car with Belgrade plates to Bosnia and Croatia, it was sure to be vandalized. So, we changed our plans and decided to use trains and buses instead, and my prince of a husband lugged the luggage without a word of complaint from then on.

We planned to spend more time in Belgrade on the return leg of our trip, and boarded a train for Podgorica (formerly Titograd), the capital of Montenegro. Since our excursions would be local, we had no trouble renting a car the next day and began our visit with the monastery of Ostrog. Our car went up a precipitous mountainside road and took perilous hair-pin turns. The monastery of Ostrog is actually a cave carved into the mountainside, and walled off flush with the rest of the sheer cliff. The whitewashed, sun-struck gash in the grey rock is a place of pilgrimage for people of all faiths.

As I entered the cave and faced the ancient frescoes crowding the low vault, something happened to me. My chest tightened and I had trouble breathing. It was like the feeling which had overcome me under the gaze of the stone soldiers in Volgograd, and in the house where the Jesuit priests had been murdered in El Salvador. There was a sense of some terrible alien presence as if here too death hovered, invisible.

I had always thought of Orthodox icons as stylized and otherworldly, but these frescoes actually looked, with their black eyes and gaunt faces and dark hair, just like the people around me. I was face to face with my own kin, and for the first time a deep sense of mourning over the death of my unknown father was allowed to take over. Perhaps I sensed, once again, how miraculous and unmerited my own survival was in a world which for most is but the valley of the shadow of death. The monastic cave of Ostrog was a refuge as the bald rock of Montenegro rising from the sea had been a refuge from rivers of blood spilled by contending armies trampling over the Balkans.

In the main palace of King Nikola of Montenegro, we found the ballroom entirely devoted to a display of oversized portraits of Nicholas II of Russia, his wife, son, four daughters, and other members of the imperial family. Two daughters of King Nikola had married two Russian grand-dukes. The Orthodox link between Russia and Serbia goes back to Ivan III of Muscovy, and his marriage to the last heiress of Byzantium. A Serb, a refugee from the Turkish invasion, had formulated the idea of Moscow as the Third Rome. The first Rome, the Rome of the Catholics, had lapsed into heresy. Constantinople, the second Rome, had fallen to the Turks in 1453. It was up to Moscow to pick up the succession as the Third Rome.

The campaigns of Ivan IV against the Tatars and the subsequent campaigns against the Turks of a succession of Russian Tsars had turned the link with fallen Constantinople into a kind of manifest destiny for the Russian Empire. But its steady advance toward the Mediterranean alarmed France and England. They allied themselves with Turkey and fought the Crimean War of 1854-56. There Tennyson took his inspiration for *The Charge of the Light Brigade* ("Theirs is not to ask the reason why, theirs is but to do and die"). From there young Leo Tolstoy also sent his anti-patriotic *Sebastopol Sketches*. Perhaps the difference in outlook between the two writers hinged on the fact that the latter was actually on the scene to witness the mutual slaughter.

Like the French and the British, the Germans and the Austrians also worried about Turkey's condition as "the sick man of Europe." But their concern was not so much for Turkey. The example of its subject Slavic populations rebellions could lead to their rebellion against their other overlord, the Austrian Empire. The assassination of the Austrian Archduke Franz Ferdinand in Sarajevo in 1914 started World War I.

Once the Kingdom of Yugoslavia was established by the Treaty of Paris in 1919, aging King Nikola of Montenegro was left without a job – and my Montenegrin family without a patron. Mom did tell me that my birth father had grown up in France. His family must have followed King Nikola into exile. But when a Belgian company began building a railroad through Bosnia, this opened opportunities for people fluent in French. Both my fathers qualified. And thus, the historical tie between the distant Russian Empire and the rugged rock of Montenegro was repeated in Mother's and Vojislav Lukačević's romance in Bihać.

Next, we visited the Monastery of Cetinje, associated with the very foundation of Montenegro as a state. Among the notables who had struggled to maintain it was the Prince-Bishop Peter II, Njegoš. But a special museum devoted to him was in sad decay. In a rush of newly-embraced Capitalist enterprise, somebody had built tourist accommodations next to the new building. They remained empty. The naïve belief that foreign tourists would be interested in Prince-Bishop Njegoš was very much like the Salvadorans' belief that North Americans knew or cared about Monsignor Romero.

It took the writings of another Montenegrin, Milovan Đilas, to introduce me to the exceptional life and works of Njegoš. A passionate Communist in the early days with Tito, Milovan Đilas had long since been a dissident, and had all the leisure of years of imprisonment to do his work of historical reflection.

Prince-Bishop Njegoš ruled Montenegro from 1830 to 1854. He had traveled to Russia, Vienna and Italy, and expressed his admiration for France and the United States. He undertook to translate Homer's *Iliad*, the *Lay of Prince Igor* of Kievan Rus, and Milton's *Paradise Lost*. There was indeed something of ancient Homeric virtues in his people and their centuries-long resistance in their mountain fastness. And like the Battle of Kosovo, the battle of Prince Igor against the Mongols had been a defeat. Yet history had also demonstrated that overwhelming odds could be mastered.

As to Milton's *Paradise Lost*, in the historical Puritan rebellion couched in terms of universal struggle between good and evil, Njegoš could recognize something familiar as well. Heretical beliefs rooted in the Manichean idea that the world had been handed over by the Almighty to the forces of darkness from the beginning, had long existed in the Balkans. The world had not been saved by Jesus' sacrifice and only a universal clash between the forces of light and darkness could deliver the world from its plight.

Njegoš thus worked to build bridges between past and present. And using the guiding principles current in his day – of civic order, ethnic kinship, and religious identity - he sought to restore the national consciousness of his people.

We stopped briefly in Kotor, a marvelous little coastal town, then crossed the border to Croatia. Dubrovnik is very well known as a tourist destination. As we approached the fabulous historical fortress, I looked for signs of demolition. Reports in the media had heralded its bombardment by the Serbs. The place looked intact, with only a few bullet holes or perhaps shell marks on the outer wall. I was glad to see that St. Blaise, the patron saint of Dubrovnik, still had the power to protect it from its enemies.

The ancient city-state's withstanding the test of time is indeed something of a miracle, and St. Blaise no doubt shares the credit with its hardy citizens. Founded, it is said, by early refugees from Rome during the Barbarian invasions, they had managed to salvage, over the centuries, a spirit of independence, commercial savvy and glorious expressiveness in art. Byzantine overlordship, more Barbarian invasions (with the Slavs staying for good), Saracen sieges, Venetian rivalry, Turkish exactions of tribute, devastating earthquakes, French and Austro-Hungarian claims, and finally the latest contest between Serbs and Croats had failed to destroy the "jewel by the sea."

***

CHAPTER 23

BROKEN BRIDGES

There is a novel titled *A Bridge on the Drina*. Ivo Andrić received the Nobel Prize for Literature in 1961 for chronicling the happenings on a bridge in the little Bosnian town of Višegrad. That bridge is a magical place as a town's life is displayed on it to public view. People pass each other, stop to talk, transact business, come to see and be seen, negotiate family alliances, take their holiday walk, rest on a bench for a spell, and reflect on the course of history. The Sultan's Janissaries used to hang out at the inn run by the Jewish inn-keeper, and now it is the Austrian soldiers. It matters little that the day of rest is Friday for Muslims, Saturday for Jews, and Sunday for Christians.

But Tony Judd reported in Postwar that during the Bosnian war Serbs organized in militias dragged out Muslims to Ivo Andrić's famous bridge, beheaded them, and threw their bodies into the Drina. Unlike Ivo Andrić's brave vision of a bridge as a space of human encounter, the unquiet genius of Dostoyevsky had already offered a different vision of bridges. In *Crime and Punishment*, we follow Raskolnikov as he stops on a bridge, and looks into the murky waters below as if into a mirror. There a woman drowning is his soul drowning because it rationalizes murder.

The recent history of Yugoslavia is a story of broken bridges. Who would have thought that a 16th century bridge with no strategic value whatsoever would also be blown up during the latest war in Bosnia? It was built over the rapid Neretva River by the Turks and had given the town of Mostar, our next destination, its name (*mostar* means bridge guard).

From Dubrovnik our bus drove us to Mostar. Over five hundred years of Ottoman rule Mostar had acquired the typical profile of a Turkish town with its lively market, the slender columns of minarets - and Christian churches as well. In the twentieth century it had expanded into modern industrial enterprises, had become a Socialist stronghold, and was reputed as the town of most mixed marriages.

All the bridges had been rebuilt under international auspices since the war, even the famous *Stari Most* (old bridge), the venerable emblem of Mostar. We walked on the picturesque street leading to the restored arch of the bridge, and even asked a passerby to take our picture. Later we happened to pass a cemetery. Practically every tombstone had the Muslim crescent over it, and practically every tomb was dated 1993. Only much later did I find out that what I had assumed to be the doing of Serb troops had actually been the handiwork of Croats.

There had initially been an alliance between Muslims and Croats against the Serbs. But Herzegovina is a stronghold of Croat nationalism, and the alliance broke down. The JNA (the Yugoslav National Army) withdrew to the surrounding hills, taking with them most of the Serb inhabitants. What followed was an 11-month siege by the Croats of the mostly Muslim East Bank, resulting in its complete destruction. It was then that the Croats dynamited the old bridge. For good measure, to discourage any Serbs from coming back to their homes, the other historical landmark of Mostar, an Orthodox church, was also reduced to rubble.

To this day the Neretva divides two unreconciled communities. We stood on the Mostar Bridge, at least for now restored to its symbolic function of linking the two river banks, and I looked down into the emerald-green waters. I recalled my baptism by the river Sumpul in El Salvador, and wondered how long it would take for the turbulent waters to wash away the blood.

Our next destination was Sarajevo, the capital of Bosnia. We disembarked from our bus and hailed a taxi. I had by then taken to sitting in the front seat of cabs in order to test my linguistic skills on the drivers. Though the designation of "Serbo-Croatian" is no longer politically correct, I got along just fine with it in all parts of former Yugoslavia. The cabbies were quite willing to talk. They shook their heads about the war, talked of fratricide, and were nostalgic about the good old days of Tito.

Our hotel turned out to be a rather grand affair, up on a hill overlooking Sarajevo, and probably dating to when the Winter Olympics were hosted in the city in 1984. Now, however, we seemed to be the hotel's only clients. We stayed several days. We saw no obvious damage as in Mostar, probably due to reconstruction since the war.

In 2004 the center of town looked busy. The Christian, Muslim and Jewish houses of worship are all within walking distance of each other, and they were all open. The Jewish synagogue was now a neat modern museum. The Orthodox church, maybe because it was very old, gave off the haunted feeling of a catacomb. The Catholic church had been built in the late 19th century after an earlier church was destroyed in 1697 by the Austrian general Prince Eugen. In pursuing the Turks after their unsuccessful siege of Vienna, he had bombarded and pretty much destroyed Sarajevo.

Expecting that mosques would now carry the burden of public piety in Sarajevo, I approached the stately 16th century Gasi-Husrenbey mosque. The two young men who collected my entrance fee sported no beards. Rick had stayed back in the hotel and there was no one else there. The domed building was a spacious, uncomplicated structure conducive to quiet reflection. The only color came from the jigsaw puzzle of wall-to-wall Turkish rugs. If I missed the infinite presence of Allah in this sacred space, it must be because I have not been raised in the Muslim faith. But then the last two generations of Bosnians had not exactly been raised in that or any other faith either.

We walked through the Markale Market, where caravans arriving from Venice, Vienna, and Istanbul used to crowd the central square. Now flocks of pigeons had taken over the fountain, and people lounged all around in cafes. It was hard to imagine that this busy place had been the scene of terrorist attacks. It was generally accepted that these attacks had been launched from Serb positions in the surrounding hills. But a number of witnesses (British and French military personnel and State Department officials) offered detailed evidence that on at least two of the occasions, Muslim nationalists had been the perpetrators in order to derail ongoing peace talks they did not deem favorable to their side. By then the media had done its job and the "facts" were academic.

Three Pulitzer Prizes have been won reporting on the atrocities in Bosnia. Milošević was repeatedly compared to Hitler, and the Serbs to the Nazis. That language is downright Orwellian considering the sides taken during World War II, when Croatia shocked even the Germans by their Nazi fervor. Zlata, a teenage girl, was shown on TV screens around the world, and her diary about what it felt like to be trapped in Sarajevo was compared to the diary of Anne Frank. No one mentioned that the Muslim authorities had forbidden people to leave the capital.

We boarded a bus once again and began our trek to Bihać, my birthplace. It is located in the north-westernmost corner of Bosnia. Buses were not going through the northeastern bulge of Bosnia, which is now Republika Srpska. Some of the worst ethnic cleansing is said to have taken place there. How did such horrors come to be? While Western Europe was finally putting its centuries-old power struggles aside and Germany was re-integrating its long-divided eastern and western sectors, how did Yugoslavia happen to go in the opposite direction?

One obvious reason was that the mixed blessing of the historical patronage of Yugoslavia by the Northern Empire was no longer available. The Soviet Union was dealing with its own dismemberment. Afghanistan had been the last straw, and the Soviet Union found itself prone on the witch doctor's couch undergoing the shock therapy of free-market economics. As a result, the United States lost interest in Yugoslavia. As James Baker, Secretary of State under the first Bush administration put it, "We have no dog in that fight."

Yet I came to learn that Yugoslavia remained the contested territory of outside forces as it had always been. Rome and its eastern and western successors had divided up the Balkans between Orthodoxy and Catholicism. Then the Turks and the Austro-Hungarians used it as their primary battleground. But the legacy of those centuries-old occupations and of the three religious traditions they bequeathed would continue to haunt the Southern Slavs. The period between the two world wars, which gave them a chance to build a national identity on the ruins of those empires, would prove too short.

Even before World War II knocked out Germany, the colonial policy of divide and rule was cheerfully resumed. It is well known that Churchill, Stalin, and Roosevelt proceeded to divide up the Balkans at the 1943 Conference of Yalta. The new categories became simply "East" and "West" as Churchill sketched out the future of the region on "a half-sheet of paper," and Stalin nodded assent. Greece, despite its strong Communist movement, was assigned to the "West." Romania, despite its pro-Nazi credentials, was assigned to the "East," as was Bulgaria. Yugoslavia, since Tito had emerged the winner, and Hungary, were deemed a case of fifty-fifty.

To build Communism, Tito clamped down on both conservative and liberal movements. There were ruthless settlements of accounts with the Croat Ustasha and Bosnian Nazi and Serb Chetniks. Limiting political life to a one-party system, Tito maintained his leadership position by balancing local interests through a federative system of representation in the Communist League. The Muslims in Bosnia were granted the status of a separate nation NOT on the grounds of ethnicity, but of cultural (i.e., religious) traditions. In Kosovo the Albanians were granted the right, in 1966, to an independent educational system conducted in the non-Slavic language of Albanian.

On the international scene, Tito ran afoul of Stalin's caution in dealing with the West. Stalin was prepared to stand by the Yalta agreement of "hands off Greece." Tito, however, gave full support to the Greek Communists during their three-year Civil War. Then Tito met with the Bulgarian Socialist leader Georgi Dimitrov in 1947. They discussed the possibility of forming a federation, and even the unification of the Balkans.

These independent moves caused Stalin to censure Tito, an exchange of letters between them followed, resulting in the break of 1948. Thus, Tito became one of the leaders, together with Nasser of Egypt and Nehru of India, of the non-aligned bloc. Pursuing a policy of neutrality, he developed cautious relations with the West while still trying to pursue a Socialist path for his country. In particular, the government experimented with worker councils in the management of enterprises.

But exchanging the support of the Soviet Union for that of the West was to prove very costly. Like all small countries struggling to advance their development, Yugoslavia was obliged to rely on loans. The country had not benefited from the Marshall plan as Germany had, so it was putting those loans to work to rebuild its war-devastated infrastructure, to industrialize, to create an export market for its products, and to provide education and medical benefits for its population. By any objective measurement, the living standard of Yugoslavs rose, and it did so across the board. Federal subsidies to the economically disadvantaged southern regions sought to mitigate long-standing historical inequalities in wealth and development.

But then the whole world suffered the oil shocks of the '70s. I remember putting Peter on the school bus, then spending what felt like hours on gas lines, with little Muriel squirming in the car seat. Since Yugoslavia had to import all of its petroleum, the economic consequences proved especially severe. Hikes in oil prices, however, made the international banking system flush with petrodollars and money was more available than ever for loans. The banks' CEOs were motivated to offer easy terms because they got enormous up-front fees for these transactions. This practice has now become quite familiar to us from our recent problems with sub-prime loans.

Tito died in 1980, the year Ronald Reagan was elected president of the United States. From then on, the carrot of loans and the stick in the "hidden hand of market forces" prevailed. Paul Volker's hike of interest rates in the 1980s tripled the interest rates of debtor countries. Taxation laws in the U.S. allowed banks to write off any losses at home while rescheduling loans with growing penalty rates to the borrower. Would we now call this "bank bail-outs?"

Unable to keep up with interest payments Yugoslavia (like Latin American countries then, and South European countries now), sank into crisis. It was caught between the external pressures to guarantee loans with public funds and the internal resistance to austerity measures. Given the country's Socialist foundation, shoring up the international financial system on the backs of the poor was a hard sell. The government resorted to the old trick of printing money. But this only fueled inflation, which rose by 120% in 1987 and by 240% in 1988. By 1989 prices were doubling every month.

Like Milan Kučan of Slovenia and Franjo Tuđman of Croatia, Slobodan Milošević had also been willing to buy into economic liberalization. He made a number of trips to the United States, and made a good impression. He was civilized enough to prefer whiskey over šlivovica, the local plum-based drink. But on November 5, 1990, the U.S. Congress passed the Foreign Operations Appropriations Law 101-514. A section of that law cut off all aid, credits, and loans from the U.S. to Yugoslavia and dictated that the World Bank as well as the International Monetary Fund enforce this policy.

The law also demanded separate elections in each of the six republics that made up Yugoslavia. This proved the beginning of the end of the Yugoslav federation. The local winners of the elections used the economic storm to identify democracy with the ever more strident voices of local "nationalism."

Slovenia and Croatia's ambition to enter the club of the "Civilized West" rather than bearing the burdens of the less developed regions of southern Yugoslavia was supported by Germany. As David N. Gibbs documents in his *First Do No Harm*, Germany was actively involved in Slovene and Croat secessionist goals: "Germany ... was helping build an intelligence and security service, and this was done in full secrecy." There would also be arms smuggling, and a massive media campaign.

This was, of course, reminiscent of the historical hegemony over the region by the Austro-Hungarian and then the Nazi governments. Having reintegrated East Germany, and with the prospect of drawing repentant Warsaw Pact countries into its free-market sphere, why should a resurgent Germany allow Yugoslavia to hold the process back? In July of 1991 a European Commission met on the Adriatic island of Brioni and concluded an accord to forbid the JNA from interfering with Slovenian and Croat secession.

The Slovenian secession was relatively peaceful. The region was largely homogenous, no significant minorities felt threatened by its new status, and Milošević made a deal with Milan Kučan over the heads of the defenders of federalism, primarily in the JNA (the Yugoslav National Army). But this first relatively bloodless secession was to inaugurate the shedding of much blood.

Unlike Slovenia, Croatia did include a substantial number of Serbs. They lived in Zagreb, and in large pockets in Slavonia in the North-East and in Krajina in the West. Now Franjo Tuđman, who had been a Communist under Tito, revived Croatia's claims to separate nationhood and Catholic identity. In this he enjoyed the support of the Vatican and the financial and lobbying clout of expatriates. Joe Biden's memoir proudly refers to his close relationship to a Croatian-American priest, deemed a reliable source of information on events in Yugoslavia at the time.

Did this include details of how Tuđman purged Serbs from the police and the media, and required them to sign loyalty oaths to Croatia? Surely Joe Biden would be concerned when civilians were assaulted, and when the checkered symbol of the flag associated with Ante Pavelić's Nazi horrors during World War II was revived? Playing the nationalist card would be even more of a stretch for Slobodan Milošević, as Serbs were scattered throughout Yugoslavia. To be sure, the nationalist option had had its defenders in Serbia as well. As early as 1986, a group of Serbian intellectuals had drawn up a *Memorandum,* which listed Serb grievances. So, Milošević used the prevailing nationalist fervor as Kučan and Tuđman had done, but unlike them, he made a fatal mistake. He retreated from his earlier neo-liberal positions. His Socialist stand against the World Bank austerity measures won him the Serb election against the right-wing, ultra-nationalist Šešelj.

But the Western policy of tolerating Tito because he had stood up to Stalin was over. The international media aggravated all the confusions. They identified democracy with economic neo-liberalism. They spoke of religious differences as if they were ethnic differences. They evoked the Wilsonian concept of national self-determination when the basic democratic concept of individual rights was at stake. All this ignored the Federal Government of Yugoslavia, and the constitutional and security bases of its functioning. When the federal army (JNA) tried to hold the country together, the "international community" cried foul.

Extreme times give rise to extreme leaders. Radovan Karadžić, a Montenegrin who had unsuccessfully run for political office in Sarajevo on a

"Green" platform, now found his true calling. He would represent the claims of the large minority Serbs in Bosnia. And General Ratko Mladić, born in Herzegovina, whose parents had both been killed by Croat Ustasha during World War II, pledged to link up the Bosnian and Krajina Serbs - to be their "man on a white horse" and defender in the killing fields.

And the fact that 1989 happened to be the 600th anniversary year of the famous Battle of Kosovo, which the Christians (both Serb and Albanian) had lost to the Turks, played right into nationalist Serb hands. Milošević did not hesitate to milk it for all it was worth. He organized mass rallies and solemn processions with the 600-year-old remains of Prince Lazar, the hapless loser of the battle, throughout the country. These events were displayed on every TV screen.

But think of Texas as the American Kosovo. Imagine Texas gradually turning Hispanic demographically. Imagine that Concord, Liberty Bell, and Valley Forge are all associated with Texas. Imagine that the educational system in Texas had been conducted in Spanish for some years, and the now Hispanic majority of Texans wants to assert their self-determination and secede. Wouldn't every U.S. president run his campaign on the emotional fuel of "Remember the Alamo?"

Even before the formal secession of Croatia in 1991, the Krajina Serbs had declared their intent to stay within the Yugoslav Federation. As the Croat police tried to intervene, atrocities by extremists on both sides spilled over onto the civilian population. The JNA, claiming its federal Yugoslav status even as its Slovene and Croat officers and recruits defected, entered Croatia. The hostilities developed into an all-out struggle. The border town of Vukovar became the emblem of its horrors.

We did not get a chance to see Vukovar itself, but Boro Drašković's film Vukovar was made in 1993 during the last phase of the conflict. The film pares down the horror of war to the destruction of innocent lives – the Romeo and Juliet story of the Serb Tamo and the Croat Anna. Their wedding celebration takes place against a background of opposing demonstrations and nationalist propaganda from Zagreb and Belgrade on the ever-present TV screen. All this escalates into general conflict and Tamo must serve in the JNA (he naively believes that Europe will not allow the country to be dismembered) leaving Anna defenseless in a besieged city.

This abandons her to the bullying of local militia because she married a Serb and ultimately to the violence of the "dogs of war" who thrive on the chaos of all wars. They loot the house the young couple had built with such love and hope, and they gang rape Anna. When Tamo sneaks through enemy lines looking for her, his parents have gone back to Serbia, her parents have been killed by Serb shells, and Anna, now pregnant, is in a state of deep trauma. They survive the war, but by the end of the fighting they stand in separate groups boarding separate buses taking them in separate directions. Earlier on Anna and her father had tried to find Tamo and we get a glimpse of some of the landscapes of formerly peaceful former Yugoslavia. Now the camera dwells on an aerial shot of Vukovar as utterly devastated. After we have taken in this relentless and obviously documentary reality, a last shot shows us Tamo getting off his bus, and turning back to look for Anna. Do they have a future in what used to be their country?

I had trouble sleeping after that film. The horrors piled on horrors never seemed exaggerated the way action movies are hyped into sheer fantasy. The pace and acting were, if anything, muted. The sound track of Mozart and popular Yugoslav melodies of which I only recognized the elusive "Tamo daleko" of my half-forgotten childhood, keeps our heartbeats tuned to life-affirming strains despite the devastating tragedy. No wonder the film, a Serbo-Croat co-production, received many international awards. On the home front, however, the war raged on, now shifting its battlefields to Bosnia.

The Balkans had been open to Bogomil strains of Christianity which both the Byzantine Orthodox and the Roman Catholics had condemned as heretical. These "heresies" showed elements of typical skepticism about miracles and sacraments which one could define as Protestant. When the Turks arrived on the scene in the 15th century and offered the option of Islam, many Bosnians welcomed their more flexible doctrinal umbrella and took the pragmatic step of becoming Muslims.

It was, however, primarily the Bosnian land-owners who participated in the conversion to Islam, and were granted the bounty of collecting taxes for the Sultan. The disenfranchised serf population or raja took refuge in the Orthodox Church. And now once again Islam is on the world map as a contender. Alijah Izetbegović had published books in 1973 and 1984, in which he argued for the specifically religious and political aspects of Islam. Accused of planning a separate Muslim state, he was jailed by both Tito and his successors.

My Tucson friends from Tuzla, in the northeastern corner of Bosnia, had their own story to tell. The husband is a local Muslim and the wife is an Orthodox from Krajina, and neither of them is particularly religious. They told me how surprised they had been when women wearing the chador began to appear in Tuzla. Apparently, Mujahideen were showing up, marrying local girls, and making them wear the chador. Then word got around that all issue of mixed marriages would be exterminated by the Muslims in due course. If this was crude Serb propaganda, my friends did not wait to find out, and began to plan their move to the United States.

Milošević, in the meantime, had the ex-JNA backbone and most of the military hardware, and Tudman could count on outside support while Izetbegović had none of those assets yet. The Croat and Serb leaders felt confident in reaching a bilateral understanding. If Churchill and Stalin could divide up the goods scribbling things out on a scrap of paper, why couldn't Tudman and Milošević? Getting together in one of Tito's favorite retreats in Karadordevo as early as March 1991, they discussed the partition of Bosnia, apparently haggling over every town and village.

As we drove through the heart of Bosnia, we saw the results. We passed through a pristine landscape dotted by demolished farm houses. At one point I was cheered by the sound of a dog barking, and by the sight of a woman hanging out her wash on a line even though the farm was still half in shambles. But then it occurred to me that this sign of renewed life did not necessarily mean that the family claiming this farm was its original owner. They could be new people reshuffled according to "ethnic" identity.

What I did not know in 2004 was that Republika Srpska was no longer run by what I assumed to be Serb nationalist fanatics, but by a NATO "high representative." He had disqualified Radovan Karadžić, the elected representative, because he embodied the wish of his constituency to remain part of rump Yugoslavia. The notorious war criminal was out of the picture and NATO, under American leadership, made sure that the right politicians, the right security forces and the right media "represented" the people. I had thus missed a chance to see democracy in action for myself.

Maybe my irony is misplaced. Should the "international community" not intervene in local struggles? But who constitutes the International Community? If there is a moral imperative to intervene, this is precisely why the United Nations has been created more than half a century ago. It was intended to be a neutral, truly international entity, which would have no interest in taking sides in a local conflict. But just like the IMF and the World Bank, the UN has been diverted from its original purpose. Woefully underfunded, the organization has been kept on a very tight leash by the major powers.

Still, a UN peace-keeping mission (the UN Protection Force) was launched in Bosnia in 1992. Although it was sizable, its peace keeping mandate could not be enforced in the midst of ongoing fighting. And the fighting kept going on because peace efforts kept failing. David Gibbs cites evidence that the U.S. had an interest in scuttling these peace efforts. American spokespeople encouraged Izetbegović to reject the Cutileiro plan of 1992, and they insisted on certain clauses in the Vance-Owen plan of 1993 because they knew them to be unacceptable to the Serbs. It would seem that the US wished to see both the European Union and the UN fail in their efforts in order to reassert its own claim to the leadership of the International Community.

But things had had to deteriorate to the point of the Srebrenica massacre in 1995 to make the "successful" American peace initiative of Dayton possible.

Like a number of other towns, Srebrenica had been declared a safe zone policed by the UN. But it turned out that the Muslims used the cover of those safe zones to organize their own troops. In Srebrenica, Muslim commander Brigadier Naser Orić kept sallying out of the safe zone under cover of darkness in order to attack surrounding Serb villages. This provoked Serb retaliation, and the UN peacekeepers, caught between the two sides, were powerless to protect the population of Srebrenica or even themselves.

No wonder Diana Johnstone calls Western intervention in Srebrenica *A Fool's Crusade*. Apparently, a sizable number of Muslim troops were able to leave the town before the Serbs attacked and the number of Serb victims is vastly exaggerated.

Up until then the Europeans had opposed the military solution of air strikes proposed by the U.S. because their own troops were on the ground in Bosnia as part of the UN forces. But after Srebrenica they were won over to a NATO bombing operation. This displaced the UN as the principal actor in Bosnia, and shifted the initiative to the Americans. Alijah Izetbegović, Franio Tuđman, and Slobodan Milošević all signed the Dayton Accords, and the result is that Bosnia is now a NATO protectorate.

As I looked for answers in the Yugoslav dilemma, I recalled once again my encounter with the presidents on Mt. Rushmore. I knew much more about their human stories now, and the clay feet on which they had stood just as we do. Wouldn't Jefferson see "those people" in the Balkans with their "irrational quarrels" but as the Blacks and Indians of Europe? And Abe Lincoln, the heralded champion of the emancipation of the slaves - had he not actually been quite willing to compromise on the Emancipation Act? Once war had become the only option, however, he put all the tools at his disposal into winning. Why couldn't the southern Slavs hold out for their Union?

And then there is "progressive" Teddy Roosevelt, who commiserated with his friend Cabot Lodge about the emasculation of the Anglo-Saxon race, and was proud to call himself a "Jingo." He vied with Hearst in urging the "liberation" of Cuba and was determined to assert US priorities during the cutting of the Panama Canal. To that effect he issued a *Corollary to the Monroe Doctrine*: "In flagrant cases of wrongdoing or impotence [by Central and Latin-American governments] the adherence of the United States to the Monroe Doctrine may force the US, however reluctantly, [...] to the exercise of an international peace power."

This citation is taken from Stephen Kinzer's *Overthrow*. The author documents how Theodore Roosevelt's beliefs and actions paved the way for subsequent U.S. policies to take an ever more active role in international "peace keeping." Clearly, we no longer feel content with guarding our territory - which we take by God-given right to include the South-American hemisphere. As the latest hegemon, the whole world is our oyster.

Where does Yugoslavia fit into this scheme of things? We all 'know' that the flagrant wrongdoing was the vicious attack of the Serbs against 'the sovereign states' of former Yugoslavia – sovereign states created by an American Congress bill. And there was clearly impotence – not so much in the case of Slovenia and Croatia – but more tellingly, in the case of the European Union itself. After watching the Europeans 'mismanage' Bosnia, the Americans stepped in.

The Clinton administration championed the independence of Bosnia the way Germany had championed the independence of Slovenia and Croatia. They isolated Serbia, promoted sanctions and created the International Criminal Tribunal for the former Yugoslavia. American-armed and American-planned, its very name echoing the previous administration's engagement in Kuwait, Operation Storm pushed back the initial successes of the JNA forces. Now the earlier atrocities at Srebrenica and elsewhere were matched by the atrocities around Knin in Krajina.

How does one distinguish humanitarian intervention from *Realpolitik*? Indispensable access to oil and control of oil pipes, as Kevin Phillips documents in minute detail in his books, was a factor here as everywhere else. Did President Clinton not take advantage of the newly 'liberated' Central Asian 'Stans,' so seductively reeking of gas and oil? Would American presence in Kosovo not be handy to distribute the goods? And then there was NATO, which had been created after World War II to "keep the Soviets out, Germany down, and America in." Was it not appropriate to rein in the Europeans when they made moves to wiggle out from under NATO?

Surely, there is plenty of blame to go around. The 'international community' has used Yugoslavia to further its own strategic and economic goals much as Kučan, Tuđman, Milošević, and Izetbegović had striven to further theirs. The Catholic Slovenes and Croats started the split, the Orthodox Serbs entered the fight, and the Muslim Bosnians played catch-up. But shelling, sniping, rape, burning of villages, holding camps, and wholesale expropriations were committed by all parties.

Certain age groups, especially under conditions of unemployment, nationalist propaganda, and increasing disintegration of civil order, thrive on the excitement, gain opportunities, and power lust afforded by war. Our own kids at Guantanamo, Abu Ghraib, and Bagram, and running loose in private mercenary companies, are no different. To use the ironical title of one of Chris Hedges' books, "war is the thing that gives us meaning."

***

CHAPTER 24

DOORS

We arrived in Bihać at long last. The town itself did not seem to have suffered much damage, except for signs warning of mine fields as our bus approached. Yet the region around Bihać had been another contested area. A different alliance, this time of Muslims and Serbs, had tried to maintain itself as the Autonomous Province of Western Bosnia. The leader of the movement was Fikret Abdić, a Muslim who had been elected president of Bosnia but was later also "disqualified" in Alijah Izetbegović's favor. The region had been overtaken by the latest Croat-Muslim alliance in 1995 and was now officially a part of Muslim Bosnia.

Our little hotel was located on the right bank of the river Una. As we looked across the river, we saw a European-style town dominated by a tall tower in a verdant landscape. The hotel had some postcards, and I was surprised to find one dating back to 1939. The town had grown outward but the center, with the tall trees of its park and the ever-present Una whose banks were dotted with cafes and restaurants, looked pretty much unchanged. Except that in the postcard the tall tower was covered by a pointed roof. It must have been the steeple of a Catholic church once and was likely a war casualty.

Still, as we crossed the bridge into the center of town the next morning, it was like stepping into that postcard. The wild thought of finding the house of my birth, with a pattern of light and shadow over the waters and Dad's fish stories as my only guidance, no longer seemed altogether fantastic.

We decided to stroll up and down the banks of the river, looking for a likely house. I had at first ignored a house which stood on the edge of the river right by the bridge we crossed, but then we decided to check it out. It was not a suburban house, but one of those plain, solid two-story structures with gray stucco facing. It was, in fact, three houses built as a unit, and could be accessed from the street by three separate doors. The middle segment, on closer inspection, was cracked, the likely result of a stray mortar shell. But the other portions stood as solid as ever. There even was a date on the façade: I believe it was 1896.

The house was not fenced off, and I ventured down its left side, which led to the river. Then I stopped, my heart in my mouth. I now saw that the house vaulted over a branch of the Una. There was a window just above the turbulent stream of water and Father may very well have cast for trout right out of it. And the back of the house stood on an island shaded by tall trees. It was, I was now sure of it, the erstwhile Eden which had welcomed me to this earth.

But what followed broke the enchantment. I knocked on the nearest street door and a young woman opened it. I tried to explain to her that I had been born in this house, but this seemed to frighten her, and she shut the door in my face. I then remembered that I was in a country where masses of people had been chased from their homes and just about anyone could set forth doubtful claims to property. No wonder my abrupt and somewhat emotional appearance at her door had scared the young woman off.

As I stood there, two hands blackened with some stuff, maybe coal dust, floated out of some well-guarded corner of my memory. Those hands belonged to our landlord *Čika Stive* (Uncle Steve) and they were proffering a *kiflica*, (a crescent-shaped treat the consistency of a pretzel). I was hesitant to accept it, however, because I didn't like his "dirty" hands. And a voice, probably Dad's, told me that if Chika Stive's hands had not been dirtied by hard work, they would not have been able to buy me a *kiflica*. I wondered whether the young woman who had slammed the door in my face was a great-granddaughter of Chika Stive, or whether she was a newcomer to Chika Stive's house on the Una. I have no idea whether Chika Stive was Muslim, Orthodox, Catholic, Jewish, or atheist; the question had never come up. And now I had come so far and so close, only to face a closed door.

But it was only a wooden door, and all I needed to do was push it open in my mind. What I saw then was a young Russian couple, the way my parents look in old family photos. Mom is pretty and fashionably dressed. Her hair is bobbed and she wears one of those small hats one sees in flapper movies. Dad looks dapper in a dark suit and tie. They have been married for five years, but they are still childless. They do have a dog. It's a frisky white Spitz and they both dote on him.

Then there is the whole fishing saga. Apparently, Dad does not just cast for trout out of the window, but disappears on long fishing expeditions while Mom stays home. And sooner or later, a "tall, dark and handsome" visitor knocks on her door. Since I had refused to question Aunt Natasha, I don't know how it all came about. Was Mom lonely? Or did Dad go off on those fishing trips as an escape into his own loneliness? And when Mom becomes pregnant, what then? These are women's secrets, and that's why they used to stone adulterous women, and still do in some parts of the world.

So, I develop and grow in Mom's womb, but the life-giving fluids which surround me also bubble with the anxieties of our position. If Dad stays out fishing, if it is true that sex is not his thing, then he must know that I am not his? What happens then? Will he walk out on us?

Or maybe Mother will try to get rid of me. Will she jump up and down, trying to loosen me from the wall of her womb? Will she drink foul-smelling potions to poison me? Will she lie on her back, lift her legs up, insert a tube between her legs and pour water into herself to flush me out? Will they insert wires into her cavity to pull me out? And if all fails and I come out screaming just the same, will they wrap me into a blanket and deposit me at the priest's door in the dark of night? Or will Mom take me into her arms and jump with me into the transparent Una? No wonder I had avoided opening that door.

But they did none of those things. It could not have been easy for Dad to know and accept back then, when he and Mom were young in Bihać. Nor could it have been easy for lively, sexy Mom to go on living with a half-measure of human love. Yet they stayed together, and here I am, with Peter and Muriel and Muriel's own offspring.

But what of the mysterious stranger, the "tall, dark, and handsome" lover? Maybe Voja Lukačević was not available. Maybe he had a family of his own, and I have siblings living somewhere in Podgorica or Chicago. Or maybe Mom judged him to be unpromising husband material. One thing she did eventually tell me: Voja Lukačević never knew that I was his child.

Yet, despite my life-long devotion to the gentle father who raised me, there is something in my makeup that bears witness to my birth father's less tractable genetic strain. I am sturdier, more heavy-boned than either of my Russian parents. Unlike their resigned abdication from politics, I can't help getting worked up about them. I harbor a fatal attraction to lost causes – not to king and country to be sure, but to the causes of peace and justice and democracy, which seem just as orphaned these days. There is something of the Montenegrin fighter in me and I seem to be cursed with a touch of Serb *inat*, a doubtful mix of pig-headedness, defiance and loyalty. Is this what Dostoyevsky called "spite" or a "higher consciousness?"

We were sitting in yet another bus, and it was taking us to Zagreb, the capital of Croatia. A cabbie picked us up on the city's periphery by the Sava River and drove us to our hotel, which was located at the foot of the medieval upper town. It seemed he was taking us back in time as we traversed a succession of historical Zagrebs. First, in the distance and toward the eastward flow of the Sava, there loomed the skyline of exurban high-rise apartments probably dating back to Tito's time. Next, we crossed a 19th century city with broad avenues, impressive squares, well-developed parks, and imposing, ornate buildings. This portion of Zagreb looked very much like certain parts of Vienna. As we neared our hotel, streets became narrower, concrete pavement turned to cobblestone, and houses displayed the patina of time.

Our hotel was charming, the food tasty, and the service discreet and efficient. Rick had no complaints. One can readily see why the Croats are proud of Zagreb's 900-year stone testimonial to their lives. The proximity to Rome ensured a deep link to Roman Catholicism, and the distance from Constantinople guaranteed safety when Constantinople became Istanbul. That safety, however, was bought at the cost of a problematic alliance with the Kingdom of Hungary, and later, Imperial Austria.

The basic issues of language, religion, and the seat of power were at the center of Croatia's historical contests. When both the Turkish and the Austro-Hungarian Empires collapsed after World War I, the Catholic Croats and the Orthodox Serbs seized their chance to form a country of South Slavs (Yugoslavia). But because the Serbs had achieved a head start toward independence, the Croats were relegated once again to the position of junior partner. Under the German-Italian occupation of World War II some of the most reactionary dreams of the Croat nationalists came to the fore.

It fell to an internationalist, the Communist Josip Broz, born of a Croatian father and a Slovene mother, to repair the rift. The historical record shows that Tito and his allies did succeed in much that they undertook despite the devastation of World War II. To be sure, there were those who were disadvantaged by the changes. Large estates, religious holdings, and the properties of expelled Germans and known Partisan enemies were either nationalized or redistributed to poor peasants. Some lost their lives, my birth father among them. And there was a general curtailment of civil liberties. Everything had to be channeled toward the common good, as defined by Tito and his associates.

The writings of Slavenka Drakulić, who grew up under "the system," describe well the weight of what she calls "WE" on the sensitive individual. She talks of the mass parades and obligatory enthusiasms of her youth, the self-censoring of speech and the irritation and dreary struggle of doing without when the West was flaunting its own parade of abundant goods.

What she did not understand, and I had not quite come to understand either – although my stint in colonial Morocco did offer some early insights - is that the consumer comforts so readily enjoyed in the West were based on the exploitation of old and now new, neo-liberal, colonial deals.

Just the same, if I did not add up these insights in my head, there was a sense of inner resistance, a "gut feeling" against being shepherded into the latest, now American, "obligatory enthusiasms." Ever since the September 11 attacks in the United States, the season at the Tucson Symphony Hall was began with an imperious flourish of the conductor's baton to signal everybody to jump to their feet, and with the rousing lead of the orchestra, to sing the National Anthem.

One understands the shock of the September 11 events, and the instinctive need to hold together in solidarity. And even if we did not understand that this event would open the door to our blood-brother relationship to Saudi Arabia, and bombing of everyone else in the Middle East, Rick and I stopped jumping to our feet at the given signal, and sat it out while everyone around us stood to attention, their hand on their heart...

So now Croatia is on its own: they too are free at last! They are no longer bound by their gunshot wedding to the Balkans. They are part of "Europa." Milošević and Tuđman are dead, Croatia can move on. Perhaps the next Pope will be a Croat. As we walked in Zagreb, there was much to admire: the quaint old upper town, the well-stocked museums and the parks with their great Meštrović sculptures. Still, all this gave a feeling, somehow, of *trompe l'oeil*. There seemed few people around. Maybe tourists have simply not discovered Zagreb yet. It remains a beautiful place, but somehow melancholy, like a wall flower waiting to be asked to dance.

The time had come to undertake the last leg of our trip, and we boarded the train to Belgrade. Just as I had known earlier that Bihać was not just the dot on the map where I was born but a place overtaken by the travails of history, I now approached Belgrade with the same mix of anticipation and anxiety. I was hoping that the house with the big porch still existed somewhere as a material witness to my own existence, but I already knew that Belgrade would be a sad place.

As we approached the city, and the characteristic beat of the wheels passing over railroad ties slowed its rhythm, an old memory came out of nowhere: my first arrival in Belgrade in the winter of 1941. Mom and Dad had left ahead of time to look for work and accommodations in Belgrade while Babushka and I had stayed behind in Bihać. Babushka had only just arrived from Egypt, and was still a stranger to me. My parents' disappearance had been pretty unsettling, and my whole being, tense with expectation, was preparing for the big event of our reunion.

I was looking out the compartment window as we entered the Belgrade station at last, scanning the crowd of strangers, and all of a sudden, there she was, my Mom. She wore a wide-brimmed hat I had never seen before, and she was looking for us. I started jumping on my seat and calling and waving from our window, and the way she held her hat with one hand and looked up and smiled is as vivid to me now as on that day so many years ago.

The train was still moving at its slowed pace. I looked out the window, and noticed that we were passing some kind of shanty town. It looked even more ramshackle than Nueva Colombia. And as in Colombia, ragged children played in the dirt. The train moved on, and depot-like buildings masked the view. It had been a momentary vision, the way scenes follow each other in a movie. But we were the ones moving, leaving behind a real place with real people. Could refugees from Knin or Kosovo still be living in such appalling conditions? Or maybe they were Roma? I noticed that some of our fellow-passengers looked away with embarrassment, and I too said nothing.

This was not a promising re-introduction to Belgrade, especially after the decorous streets of Zagreb. We stopped in the same hotel near the Kalemegdan Park. This time we visited the Turkish-named fortress above the meeting of the rivers. During its construction the severed heads of rebellious Serb chieftains had ornamented the top of its walls. Belgrade too has wide avenues, but their squarish buildings point to the stern 1950s of the twentieth century rather than to the ornate Viennese style of earlier days. Belgrade, the White City, had been repeatedly bombed and reconstructed. It clearly earned its other name, "the House of War."

The vaunted capacity for surgical precision exercised in the bombings of 1999 was still evident. We saw official-looking buildings showing big open gashes, yet still standing. We visited the TV broadcasting complex whose transmission center had been taken out. I remember General Wesley Clark explaining on TV how media were of necessity strategic military targets. He did not mention that the Children's Cultural Center and its Little Theater were also part of the complex.

But then there were bridges, industrial installations, power stations, pharmaceutical, tobacco and food factories - and cities far removed from

Belgrade, that were also hit. Perhaps the unstated strategy there was to simply wipe out the country's infrastructure so that everything could be rebuilt more efficiently. Experienced international construction companies like Brown & Root know how to conduct business instead of dilly-dallying with worker councils.

Down the hill and across a little park there was a surprise. A small Russian Orthodox church stood there, and it was only cracked. Its architecture was nothing like the traditional onion domes of Old Russia. It was a jewel in the modernist style associated with the heyday of the movement which included Kandinsky, Malevich, Lavrov, Goncharova, Chagall, Stravinsky, the *ballets russes*... People were busy doing repair work, and I exchanged a few words with the priest's wife. She told me that the church had been built in 1924 by Russian émigrés, and that clumps of earth brought from the Motherland had been placed in its foundation instead of saints' relics. I wondered whether my parents had attended.

Further up and across the little park from the Media Center there was another church, this one quite large. But there was a pile of rubble next to it, and it was fenced off. The sign read "Church of St. Mark the Evangelist," and I realized that I was looking at the church which had been bombed by the Allies back in 1944 on Orthodox Easter Day. It had been full of people celebrating Easter services and the casualties had been heavy. As far as I know, the mystery of this mistake remains unsolved to this day.

On April 23, 1999, however, the "mistake" was repeated as NATO bombed that church again. They also bombed the old Monastery of Rakovica, founded in the 14th century. Repeatedly destroyed by the Turks and rebuilt, it had housed old archives and, during World War II, an orphanage for Serb children rescued from Croatia. Perhaps it was bombed by NATO because in addition to all its other activities, it had also served as a cache for weapons of mass destruction?

I had read that the Serbs had destroyed Catholic churches and mosques in Banja Luka. Was the destruction of Orthodox churches and monasteries in Belgrade then in retaliation for those earlier destructions? Somehow, NATO's involvement in such matters of local payback seems unlikely. Yet one has to wonder. During our stay in our hotel, we kept running into a tall, portly man with sparse blond hair and a cheerful voice. We would see him at breakfast, and we kept bumping into him in the elevator. He spoke English with a British accent and we ended up engaging him in conversation. What was his business in Belgrade? He represented a Baptist mission, he told us.

I recalled a little anecdote related by Warren Zimmerman in his memoir of his tenure as ambassador to former Yugoslavia. Among the duties required by his position was having his staff arrange a meeting between Slobodan Milošević and "American religious leaders." This had struck me as odd until I read Jeff Sharlet's *The Family*, which documents the powerful role the National Prayer Breakfast (instituted by Billy Graham himself) holds in U.S. politics to this day.

But the canny Montenegrin had used the occasion to do some preaching of his own. He had lectured the Americans on his views of their country's foreign policy which, he insisted, was to turn Albania into an "unsinkable aircraft carrier." From there, together with Germany, they would proceed to rule the Balkans. The embassy could not countenance this "amazing performance" and Milošević received a dressing down.

This tidbit of inside business is revealing in ways that Warren Zimmerman seems to miss. President George W. Bush had wrested from Chairman Mao the great prize of being Albania's number one hero, and the largest U.S. base before the Green Zone in Baghdad is now located in Kosovo, named Bondsteel.

But I must not jump to conclusions just because the American ambassador thought it would do Milošević good to have some quality time with Evangelicals, or because NATO bombed a church and a monastery. After all, they could have bombed the new Belgrade Cathedral of St. Sava and didn't. St. Sava (1175-1235) was the first patriarch and legislator of Serbia. His remains were burned by order of a Turkish vizier in 1594 on the site where the cathedral is now under construction.

When we entered the huge, still unfinished structure, I was hard put to sort out my feelings. The vastness of the space rising toward the central cupola in one undifferentiated sweep, instead of inviting the spirit to rise with it, weighed me down. The 400-ton cupola and four-ton gold cross on top had been installed in 1989 for the 600th anniversary of the Battle of Kosovo.

Kosovo, of course, was the "reason" why we had bombed Serbia. My capacity to function in Serbo-Croatian would not have been much use in Kosovo, so we decided to skip the turbulent province. A territory inhabited by Albanians and Slavs, Kosovo had been claimed by Byzantium, then medieval Serbia, then Turkey, then Yugoslavia.

Serbs and Albanians still had many scores to settle and competing claims to address even at the end of the twentieth century. The Kosovar Albanians had allied themselves with fascist Italy during World War II, and post-war Yugoslavia by and large suppressed their emancipation efforts. Relations remained tense as demographics changed and Serbs became a minority. In 1987 Milošević witnessed Albanian police rough up Serb protesters – and in 1989 he introduced martial law in Kosovo.

These power struggles, however, were not necessarily insoluble. Even as late as the Dayton Accords of 1995, Kosovar Ibrahim Rugova's credentials of non-violent opposition could have been given a fair hearing at the negotiating table. Instead, the Clinton administration opted for the no-nonsense approach of the Kosovo Liberation Army (KLA). Their official standing on the international list of terrorist organizations was no object. David N. Gibbs refers to the London *Sunday Times* and to the *Wall Street Journal* to document that CIA operatives had been offering field advice to the KLA, and that the latter had received official NATO/US arms and training support.

When the KLA attacked remote Serb villages, Serb security forces retaliated with brutal counter-insurgency sweeps. As the massacre of Srebrenica had tilted the balance toward NATO air strikes, the killings in the village of Račak in Kosovo by Serb forces precipitated the Conference of Rambouillet. The jury seems to be still out on the exact circumstances of the Račak killings, but the outcome of the Rambouillet Conference is now part of history.

The UN was left out of the conference. The Serbs agreed to the regional autonomy of Kosovo and the end of repressions. Discussions as to whether the UN or NATO would oversee the settlement were proceeding when it was discovered that the final draft of the agreement contained a new element or Military Annex. NATO was not only to oversee the implementation of the Rambouillet Accords in Kosovo, but demanded the use of the air space and territory of Serbia itself – OR ELSE. In their book Yugoslavia, *Death of a Nation,* Laura Silber and Allan Little, funded by the Soros Foundation, describe how the Serbs were heard partying and singing all night in their quarters after this. Those terrible, crazy Serbs! They had chosen OR ELSE and were drinking to the inevitable countdown when all the might of NATO would come crashing down on their heads.

As I stood under the impressive cupola of the St. Sava Cathedral, its stone dream of grandeur looked terminally obsolete. Did the Serbs not see that Kosovo was no longer theirs to boss around? Nor, for that matter, was it the Kosovars'; they would find that out soon enough. Kosovo has deposits of coal, lead, zinc, cadmium, gold, and silver, and the Rambouillet agreement had duly specified that "the economy of Kosovo shall function according to free-market principles." In return, Kosovo did achieve the noteworthy privilege of being officially called Kosova.

Did the "international community" really care about the old medieval frescoes in the churches and monasteries in Kosovo/a or the minority Serbs who cherished them? Was it just another blunder that the mass exodus organized by the Serbs in Kosovo/a was actually triggered by the NATO bombing itself? Did it matter that the bombs raining down in Kosovo/a to save Kosovars had killed as many Albanians as Serbs? Did President Clinton or Wesley Clark care about the depleted uranium which they spread all over Kosovo/a? Did they worry that the Albanian KLA would become the principal conduit of Afghani heroin to Europe?

All the same, NATO bombing has been deemed a great success. The Balkans' strategic position between East and West, the East now defined as the oil-rich Middle-East, was secured. And even as the bombs rained over Kosovo/a and

Serbia, NATO celebrated its fiftieth anniversary. Will Europeans ever doubt the demonstrable efficiency of U.S. arms? Kosovo/a is now officially a NATO "protectorate" just as Morocco had been a French "protectorate" in the bad old days of colonialism. Nor does it hurt that the dollar had regained much value against the euro. After all, who would want China to dump its U.S. bonds in favor of euro-backed securities?

We prepared to leave the Cathedral of St. Sava. To the side, workers perched on high trestles were covering the concrete walls with stucco. Along another wall, women in black lit candles and kneeled in prayer. Maybe their sons had been killed – or had killed others. I remembered my own endless tears in the cathedrals of France, bought a candle, and lit a flame to universal motherhood.

When we stepped out, the alley before us led to the monument to Karađorđe ("George the Black"). A prosperous trader of pigs, he had led the first Serb rebellion against the Turks in 1804, thus founding the first Serb dynasty. Although the kings of Serbia had tried to associate their actions with the glories of medieval Serb potentates, they also had to answer to the civil society rising everywhere in Europe. As a result, they rarely died in their own beds. Yet the Serbs were the only nation in the Balkans to choose their own kings. Greece, Romania, and Bulgaria had been gifted with German rulers. Nevertheless, all the efforts of Serb rulers had come to nothing. Their country and their dreams were like the St. Sava Cathedral, a work-in-progress waiting to be bombed another day. Will the 400-ton concrete cupola and its golden cross protect them?

Serbia's latest leader, Slobodan Milošević, had also come to a sorry end. He died in a prison cell in 2006, presumably of a heart attack, still unrepentant. Has the fact that he has been exonerated in 2012 of the crime of "ethnic cleansing" by the same Tribunal at the Hague that had accused him of them? Has the news filled the headlines the way his presumably dastardly deeds had?

Rick and I had been attending the Palms Springs film festivals back home and had had a chance to see some of the films coming out of Yugoslavia at the time. They tended to have the same intense, no holds barred approach regardless of whether they came from Serbia, Croatia, Bosnia, Macedonia, or Slovenia. Their collective experience had poured itself into a tragic vision (with a dollop of surrealism and black humor) which seemed to go back to the plays of Sophocles and Euripides. Perhaps these films were trying to use the universal language of ancient tragedy to crash an invisible barrier and hand the outsider a borderless pass to local truths. We hoped to find some documentation on those films at the Belgrade Cinematheque, but it was closed. We also tried to visit the Ivo Andrić museum, but it too was closed.

Disappointed by so many closed doors, I was somewhat diffident about looking for the house with the big porch. I knew the name of the neighborhood, and remembered the name of one of the streets which formed the corner where the house had stood. We hired a cab and hoped for the best. The cabbie figured out what I was talking about, and took us to the beginning of the street I knew, coming up from the Danube.

I knew that the distance could be walked, so we got out and started walking. To my surprise we soon came up against a group of tall apartment buildings. This was disorienting, but I realized that they had been built on what used to be the vacant lot where we had run for shelter during the bombing raids. So, we would have to turn back, and I kept telling myself that everything needed to be measured in child's steps. I was too eager to look ahead and kept missing what was right in front me. I now realized that we already stood at THE corner, and the house before us was THE HOUSE. There was the porch, it was still overgrown with the wild grapes which had given Pavlik, my stuffed rabbit, such a bellyache... it just wasn't a big porch.

As we stood in front of the gate, and I was telling Rick that we had found the place, a tall elderly gentleman appeared on the porch and asked us if he could help. I asked him what he knew about the house, or about its former owner, a *Gospoda* (Mrs.) Marković. "Why yes," he said, "*Gospoda* Marković was my mother." I took a second look at the tall gentleman. Something about the still handsome features, the straight carriage and the general outline of his body looked familiar. "Are you Milorad?" I asked. "Yes I am," he answered.

Milorad, *Gospoda* Marković's youngest son, had been the one whose passion for photography had fixed some of my childhood events on film, and I had brought a package of those pictures with me. "I am Galya Litvinova," I said. "Galochka!" he cried, opened the gate, and in an instant, we were in each other's arms. I introduced Rick, and we settled for drinks and talk on the famous porch. I showed him the pictures and he smiled as he looked through them; yes, he had become a camera man. He had, in fact, traveled to many places around the world making films and documentaries.

Yet when I tried to broach more general subjects about the state of the world, all he mentioned was that he had been trained as a fighter pilot by the Soviets after they had liberated Belgrade, and sent into combat. He added that he was among a handful of his comrades who survived the effort. I would have liked to have his views on the times under Tito and the times following, and the latest with Milošević, but he clammed up. I did get the feeling that he had no love lost for the role of the United States in his country, but that a host's courtesy dictated restraint. We were, after all, Americans.

Thinking to steer away from politics, I asked him if the name of Mikica Živković meant anything to him. This was the only name I could recall from my playmates on the "big porch." Milorad did know her. She had become a doctor, a gynecologist. But things had not worked out for her. She had married a Croat, but when the troubles started, her husband became devoted to the Croat national cause and left. Their only son opted to become a Croat also and left Belgrade to join his father. Then Mikica was found dangling from a rope in her bathroom.

This piece of news stunned me. I had no pictures of Mikica, so she remained a ghostlike angular body sprouting skinny arms and legs, sharp with elbows and knobby knees, and a pale face framed by dark wavy locks. The question of freckles – whether Mikica had had freckles – seemed to become of uppermost importance. Anything rather than facing the unimaginable body of a middle-aged Mikica, her angles smoothed out by years and her locks streaked with white - hanging from a rope...

So Mikica had been a doctor, and she had watched over many a child making their entrance into this world. And she had given birth to a child of her own. She would have found out then how large the gap was between her well-intentioned ministrations as a doctor and the actual birthing of flesh and blood. And even then, the pain and hope of it could never have anticipated the opening of another, unimaginable gap between her and her child as he turned his back on her. Mikica had simply found it beyond her capacity to endure that particular, intimate, unnamable pain.

I kept obsessing about Mikica's freckles as if this could save me from falling into gaps of my own. Had I not, don't I still dread the vision of Peter's body swinging from a rope? As we knew only too well, life's stresses tend to escalate with Peter. Hamlet-like, he can be haunted by imperious ghosts and feel surrounded by lying toadies and murderous hirelings. And the realities of life had proved brutal enough to confirm some of his worst imaginings. That shifting world of imminent violence where you can't tell friend from foe was just like the civil war into which Yugoslavia had descended.

To be or not to be, that is still the question. How can our young BE in such a world? And if Peter inherited his condition, the seeds of his disquiet were already evident in the political cast of Mother's symptoms. Unlike her sister Galochka, she had survived – but only to be pursued, in the end, by Communist threats she divined in the hissing and gurgling of the heating system. Those symptoms seem no different from the symptoms of soldiers who return from Afghanistan and Iraq haunted by cries and visions of mangled bodies. Just like Mikica's son, or Cindy Sheehan's Casey, or Mary Tillman's Pat, or Cindy Corrie's Rachel, and all those others killed or mutilated in body and soul - Peter too is a war casualty. The scientists of this world still lavish their genius on making ever more lethal toys – and the healers are busy devising "modern" ways to interrogate suspected terrorists.

In her *The Cost of Living*, published in 1999 as it happens, Arundhati Roy speaks of "a point in time when human intelligence has outstripped its own instinct for survival. We think we know better. We bet on the well-fed over the hungry. We conduct proxy wars out of sight and out of mind. We bomb with god-like impunity from above. We pay mercenaries to do the fighting for us, expendable ghetto kids or impoverished global hirelings seduced by the promises of shameless commercials. But true progress is in sight: with the amazing little gadgets we call "drones" we can kill anyone anywhere. And we expect to get away with it all – actually, we expect to be loved.

The news of Mikica's fate had opened up a pause of lingering silence in our conversation with Milorad. It was hard to stay away from politics after all. I asked Milorad whether I could peek into what used to be my family's living quarters. I entered, and found things not much changed. To the left was the door that had led to Mme. May's apartment. Milorad did not know what had happened to them. Straight ahead was the tiny kitchen where Babushka had stood her ground over her meat pie. And just before me there was the glass door, still intact after all those years, against which I had stood my dolly Natasha for time out. In the left corner was the spot where the Christmas tree had hovered in a soft halo of candles. To the right was the window where I had once stood, and the star of Bethlehem appeared again, and the door opened, and Dad entered, shaking the snow off his boots.

It was time to say goodbye to Milorad and to thank him for opening the gate to the porch that was not as big as I remembered, but big enough in my life. Before turning away, I glanced at the side steps where Babushka had sat crying in the dark, and where I had joined her, defying Mom. This trip to the country of my birth, this witnessing of its wounds had been but a way to keep that door open.

***

CHAPTER 25

TAKING SIDES

Opening doors: does it take a lifetime? In that early dream triggered by the 1999 bombing of Belgrade by NATO, I was perhaps reluctant to admit that Mom and Babushka had been arguing. Perhaps I was reluctant because it put me in a position to take sides. Choose Mom, who towered over me? Or stand up to her and look for Babushka, crying out there in the dark? I did, as it happens, side with Babushka. Perhaps my life's journey was all about finding my way back to that five-year-old who instinctively, innocently, did side with the weak against the strong.

There was that other dream: now Mom was out in the dark, on the other side of the door – she had followed me all the way to my safe haven in America, and in that dream, I did all I could to put all my weight against that door to keep it closed. By then I did ask myself the question: Was I strong enough to stand up for both of us?

Not that ordinary life doesn't have its own demands. If Dad and Maurice took on the burden of Mom's illness, it had been my turn to cope with Peter's illness. And if I resented Rick's escape into his job, did he not "bring home the bacon" the family lived on?   And had I not also "escaped" into respectable career efforts? Even "literature" felt like an escape now. I had been schooled in formal approaches to literature and seduced into post-modern critical analysis. I had delved in narratology and happily "deconstructed" traditional texts.

But this didn't work out after all, and my early dream of figuring out "why the world was such a mess" took hold of me again. Hence the writing of the memoir and the various trips and the switch from literature to non-fiction. And Rick had been kind enough to take me to the places which had been the milestones of my journey – the last one all the way to Yugoslavia in 2004.

And after he took early retirement (and he also insisted on more "touristy" trips as well), we embarked on a cruise down the Mediterranean and on to the Black Sea in 2010. I had briefly visited Ukraine in 1988, and since much freedom had been allowed during that trip, I had had an interesting experience in Kiev (Kyiv). A Canadian nurse, who was a member of our delegation, expressed an interest in visiting a local hospital. I offered to take her. We received the OK of our tourist guide, and were told which bus to take. So far so good. But once we were on that bus, I couldn't figure out how to pay for our tickets. I asked a bystander, and was met with smiles all around. I explained my misgivings, and finally the bystander whispered to me: "let's make love, not war." Apparently, no tickets were needed for that project.

So now we were in Ukraine again. We visited Yalta and the former Tsarist summer palace where the famous conference had taken place. We also stopped in Sebastopol, and examined a detailed panorama of the 1854-56 Crimean War. Finally, we spent a couple of days in Odessa.

This latest trip was organized by a French company. We were visiting a remarkable museum in Odessa, exhibiting archeological findings going back to the days when Crimea was an outpost of ancient Greece. A museum guard, an elderly woman who was sitting by a window, elicited a remark from my French fellow travelers. Why, they commented, did she look so grim? Why were the people generally so unsmiling? This reminded me of exactly the same remarks my American fellow travelers had expressed during my earlier trips to the Soviet Union.

There was a free chair next to the museum guard, and I asked her permission to use it. Inevitably, once she realized I spoke Russian, we began to talk. I told her that my French companions were wondering why people were not smiling. This opened a flood gate of indignation – just as with the woman in Saint Petersburg twelve years ago. "What's there to smile about?" she exclaimed. "It is my paltry job here at the museum that feeds the whole family: my daughter and her husband are out of work; they stand in the market all day trying to sell some of the produce we get from our small plot, and whatever is left of our possessions. I would like to know how your French friends would smile if they had to live like that…"

There was another observation I made during that trip. Everywhere, people spoke Russian. In Odessa, which is not part of Crimea, they spoke

Russian as well, but all the street names were in Ukrainian. That opened up another identity issue for me. My Dad was Russian, but my Mom's family, as it happens, was from Ukraine. And in all those years the issue had never come up in the family. And it wasn't like the big secret of my Montenegrin birthfather. It just didn't seem to be a problem.

Well, there must have been a problem, even if not in my own family, and the papers had drawn attention to it back in 2004: a Revolution was happening in Ukraine - the Orange Revolution. I was too busy at the time working on some other aspects of my memoir - the Moroccan decolonization or the German camps.

At some point I consulted Wikipedia on the subject. The Orange Revolution was about the presidential elections of 2003 and the contest between the two Victors: Viktor Yushchenko (whose wife was a Ukrainian-American who had worked for the State Department) and Viktor Yanukovych. The mutual accusations of fraud and bribery seemed par for the course: they are not exactly unknown in our own elections. What did surprise me, is the claim that the opposition candidate Yushchenko to the "establishment" candidate Yanukovych was supported by the SBU (Security Service of Ukraine, a successor of the Ukrainian KGB).

Perhaps less surprising to me were the extensive references to the Western governmental and non-governmental organizations active in sponsoring the Orange Revolution movement itself. According to *The Guardian*, the foreign donors included the U.S. State Department and USAID as well as both the National Democratic and National Republican Institutes, the NGO Freedom House and George Soros' Open Society Institute. The National Endowment for Democracy, a foundation supported by the U.S. government, had been promoting "democracy building" activities since 1988.

This was not that surprising to me because I was familiar with earlier American "Cold War" initiatives. A group of Ukrainian nationalists had sided with the Nazi invaders during World War II, and their leaders had massacred Jews, Poles, and Communists. One of the most notorious among them was Stepan Bandera. But after the Soviets regained those territories, the Ukrainian nationalists ended up in exile. Scores of them were welcomed to the United

States, where the CIA financed the Ukrainian Institute in New York, and, as reported by Dan Rather in a *Sixty Minutes* program, facilitated their underground activities in Ukraine.

As the Wikipedia article suggested, the ubiquitous reference to "democracy" was the ultimate justification for the long-term involvement of foreign agencies in the affairs of Ukraine. The promise of "democracy" has held a powerful attraction to the peoples of Eastern Europe, and among them, Ukraine. As I observed during my trip to the Soviet Union in 1988, people were disappointed that the lonely "building of socialism" had put them at odds with the rest of the "civilized world," – not to mention the dead-end arms race.

They were mesmerized by the good news coming over the airways from Radio Liberty and Radio Free Europe and Voice of America. They didn't want to be left out anymore, they wanted to "turn to the West," they wanted to enjoy the benefits of democracy. Apparently, the huge funds patiently invested to promote this great vision did do the job. And there was no need for me to be so surprised that even the local security forces were conquered: follow the money, as they say.

In the meantime, some voices raised alarms about the health of democracy even in the land of the free and the home of the brave. Chalmers Johnson, naval officer during the Korean War and historian of military affairs, has written an article in 2008, titled "Military-Industrial Complex: It's Much Later Than You Think". Referring to the well-known warning by President Eisenhower, he traces the gradual evolution of the military influence on public affairs back to FDR's "arsenal of democracy" to prepare for World War II, and the fact that the arms buildup had been a boon to get the country out of the Great Depression.

President Reagan's disparagement of government as "the problem" is also well known. Chalmers Johnson describes how "the uniformed air, land, and naval forces of the country as well as its intelligence agencies… are now all dependent on hordes of private contractors." The implication is that they are unaccountable to army rules, and that the "outsourcing" of intelligence has led to rather disappointing results. This "wholesale transfer of military and intelligence functions to private, often anonymous, operatives" also proved enormously costly.

The advent of the Democrat President Bill Clinton apparently only accelerated the military and intelligence privatization process – choosing to cut costs in the public domain instead. Then during the presidency of George W. Bush we suffered the September 11 attack on the World Trade Center. The Patriot Act has given NASA, as Edward Snowden demonstrated, to treat every American citizen as a potential "terrorist."

Chalmers Johnson concludes that this "hollowing out" of government agencies in favor of a "military industrial complex" no longer answerable to them is an advanced process of de-democratization. He quotes Sheldon S. Wolin's *Democracy Incorporated* as follows: "The privatization of public services and functions manifests the steady evolution of corporate power into a political form, into an integral, even dominant partner with the state."

The question with respect to Ukraine, and our promotion of democracy there, is then whether under the guise of this hoary label of respectability – "democracy" -we are really promoting something else? The explosion of liberty sponsored by Yeltsin and his comrade Leonid Kravchuk in Ukraine opened the door to the reign of the oligarchs, not the free exercise of democracy by the people.

As other trips had done, the cruise on the Black Sea and the visit to the cities of Southern Ukraine had stimulated more questions than answers. I thought I had pretty much finished my memoir, but now I decided to catch up with Ukraine. I buckled down to serious research when something terrible and quite unexpected happened and interrupted my work. Rick and I had been having a mellow time after getting back together. I was busy writing while he had joined a hiking group and happily explored the trails in the surrounding mountains.

I also devoted time to digging and planting on our property, a love I had first developed back in the days of my life in Morocco. The climate was very similar, but there were differences. I enjoyed learning all about barrel cactuses and jumping chollas – and the coyotes and javelinas and gila monsters. We were regulars at the symphony, and Rick was involved with the Chamber

Music society. He had been a film buff all his life, and now he was happy to participate in the programs of local film theater, the Loft Cinema.

Muriel and Rob were doing well. He still worked for Raytheon while Muriel had adjusted to the responsibilities of motherhood by transferring her earlier ambition of "running with wolves" to starting a dog daycare business. I was happy to have the girls, Chloe and Astrid, over often, making our home a welcoming place for Christmas celebrations or Easter egg hunts.

Peter's life took its own, less happy, course. He attempted relationships, and the happiest three years he experienced were with a young Russian immigrant and her three kids. But like other relationships, this didn't last. Eventually, he met a woman who was intent on moving back to Champaign, Illinois, where her daughter lived, and Peter followed her. I worried that he would no longer have our support in times of recurrent crises. But we would not be around forever, and maybe he needed to find his own way in the world as best he could.

Rick and I used to go on early morning walks, and "early" in Arizona, especially in the summer, means no later than 6 a.m. On that particular morning Rick kept reminding me to get going, because he wanted to be back in time to catch his favorite news program. As we began our usual round past our gate and into the neighborhood, Rick complained about stomach discomfort. He blamed it on our supermarket having discontinued his favorite brand of bread. Then he stopped, and his knees began to buckle under him. I rushed to hold him up, but this only resulted in both of us slowly sinking to the ground. A passerby noticed our problem, and helped me lay Rick down on the ground.

This man had a phone, and called 911. The voice at the other end kept cross-examining my cry for help and the wait for the ambulance felt excruciatingly long. Rick's breath was labored and he didn't respond when I tried to talk to him. Finally, the ambulance came and I was directed to sit with the driver instead of with Rick. Again, the ambulance seemed to proceed at a nightmarishly slow pace. At some point the guys who were with Rick in the back of the ambulance started messaging to the driver and they did so in numbers... I figured that it was a set code, and that the worst had happened. When we finally reached the hospital, I was again directed away from Rick, and asked to stay in a waiting room. After a while, they came to tell me what I already knew, but still refused to believe: Rick had died on the way to the hospital.

This sense that what had happened did not, could not have happened haunted me in the next days and weeks: I still expected to see Rick sitting at his computer when I entered his study. Then the grief process took over, and Muriel and I cried together, and I finally conceded that Rick's unexpected departure was better than lingering in some hospital bed attached to invasive so-called life supports. This would have given me time to adjust to the inevitable, but the way Rick had left this earth was, I thought, rather elegant.

Peter came down from Champaign and we organized a memorial. The people who rallied around us at the time were neither my academic nor my church friends. After quitting the Unitarian church, I had joined a Tikkun group. *Tikkun olam* means "mending the world" in Hebrew, and I found myself at home with this more engaged group of people – also reminiscent of my days in Village Greens in New York, and its predominantly Jewish community. And now in my hour of need, it was these Jewish friends who helped with the memorial in a Christian church, and organized the reception.

They say not to make major decisions during the grieving period, but I just didn't want to stay in our now empty house. I also felt overwhelmed by the things that Rick had managed: I am not a detail person, and dealing with financial issues was a challenge. Muriel did help out, but all the stress affected my health and I developed heart problems. But in time things did regain some sense of equilibrium. I moved into a smaller place. The heart doctors patched me up, and fitted me out with a pacemaker. I prepared to write again.

I re-examined my memoir and wondered why the agencies I had approached earlier didn't even ask to read the manuscript. I guess it didn't meet some elusive standard or expectation. Understandably, I was not Lady Gaga or Madeleine Albright. Nor was my opus a so-called "disaster memoir," one of those spellbinding sagas about triumphing over molestation, rape and drug addiction. It was about the course of the troubled 20th century reflected in the troubled lives of my family – a hybrid approach much too complicated, no doubt.

One thing about the memoir I did want to re-examine was the chapters dealing with the Russian/Soviet issue. I felt that my White Russian origin had perhaps directed me to rely on somewhat limited, even possibly biased sources. I decided to attend a Marxist study group to attempt to examine the other side of these issues..

I dutifully read the assignments and struggled to overcome the built-in gap I saw between the theoretical claims of the Marxists and my own knowledge of what had happened to my family in Soviet Russia. As I tried to follow the heated debates of the group's participants, I began to distinguish among them those who just sounded off from those who seemed to be really grounded in the texts. One man, John Mackoviak, struck me as eminently good at articulating complicated concepts in a clear, accessible, and convincing way. I turned to him when I needed help with a reading.

Over two years had passed since Rick had died, and I found out that John had lost his wife a year before I had lost Rick. We exchanged books, we participated in various events, we became friends. I finally asked John to read my memoir. Because I was focusing on the political side of it, it only occurred to me afterward that I had invited him into my personal life – some of it quite intimate. John was discrete about the personal stuff, and his compliments about my writing style offered a neutral bridge between us, leaving in abeyance the memoir's personal as well as political aspects.

I have friends who, despite our advanced age, are looking for companionship – even on the swampy grounds of the internet. After Rick died, I told Muriel that I would absolutely NOT emulate my friends in this respect. But now, quite unexpectedly, I had met a man whose qualities of intelligence, tact, and wit were quite impressive. And on his side, he now initiated something of an old-fashioned courtship. He told me later that the day I left the keys in my car because I was too absorbed in our conversation, he knew we were meant for each other.

How is it that a Marxist-Leninist and a White Russian are "meant for each other?" Well, we were both compulsive readers intent on focusing on the "big picture" as well as "naturally" inclined to side with the underdog. He was a Chicago "Polack" raised in a "proletarian" milieu who practiced his beliefs as a union and later farm-worker organizer. I was (as it turned out) a very "mixed" Russian mostly practiced in running from bombs and surviving various other calamities. I had also "done time" in resistance movements – mostly for peace. After some four years of our common life, we still feel that we belong together, and are still absorbed in ongoing dialogue.

***

CHAPTER 26

BORDERLAND

After the inevitable trials life throws at us, but also the unexpected gifts it offers, I was ready to resume work on my memoir. I particularly wanted to continue exploring the subject of Ukraine.

The word "Ukraine" means borderland. Its geographical location on the Pontic Steppe, the region north of the Black Sea, offers no natural borders, and caused its history to reflect this permanent state of passage or contest by other powers. Herodotus mentions the Iranian-speaking Cimmerians and Scythians, which were conquered by another Iranian-speaking group from Central Asia, the Sarmatians.

The 2nd century C.E. saw the next wave of invaders, this time the Germanic Goths, who occupied the vast territory from the Baltic to the Black Sea. Two centuries later, they were confronted with another wave of nomadic invaders from Central Asia, the Huns. They were a combination of Turkic and Mongol-speaking tribes, and eventually gave Hungary its name. In the sixth century, another Mongol and Turkic-speaking federation of nomads, the Avars, passed through the territory, followed by the Magyars, whose Finno-Ugric language is still spoken in Hungary. The seventh century saw the passage of the Bulgars, (who moved on and gave Bulgaria its name) because they were displaced by the Khazars, yet another Turkic-speaking people.

What of the Slavs in this constant movement of non-Slavic peoples? During all those migrations the Greeks did refer to sedentary people who practiced agriculture in the valleys of the rivers. Over time, the nomadic invaders acquired some of the settlers' ways, but the settlers were also integrated into the nomadic confederations, and swept with them across the Danube delta in the conquest of other territories.

But as the large empires and confederations exhausted each other in colonization and warfare, the Slavs transformed themselves from colonized to colonizers. They learned to ride horses and forge strong weapons. They elected chieftains and formed tribal alliances. They offered a linguistic bridge to all the disparate populations, and their self-awareness coalesced around language use rather than a particular ethnicity.

In the 9th century a principality known as "Kievan Rus" was formed. Its name stems from a local eastern Slavic people referred to as the Ruthenes or Rusiny whose language was "Ruski," Their history is also associated with Norsemen. The Norsemen are well known in other parts of Europe as pirates, merchants, and state builders. A branch of Norsemen had established a settlement on the Volkhov River near the Baltic Sea, which in time became Novgorod (Newtown). From that northernmost position they navigated the Volga and the Dnieper rivers to trade with the Middle East by way of the Caspian Sea and with Byzantium by way of the Black Sea.

The prince of Novgorod Oleg occupied Kiev in 882. His successors, Prince Igor and Princess Olga, subdued a number of surrounding Slavic tribes to form the Kievan principality. Olga's son Svyatoslav was a warrior. He began his campaigns near the upper Volga and conquered Finnic and Bulgar tribes on his way down to the Volga delta. There he integrated into his principality the Slavic tribes who had been paying tribute to the Khazars. He was also involved in the warfare between Byzantium and the newly founded Bulgar state.

There was no law of primogeniture establishing the succession to governance by the oldest son. And when Svyatoslav died battling the latest nomadic invaders, the Turkic-speaking Pechenegs, the ensuing succession contest was won by Vladimir in 980. Because of his conversion to Christianity, he became known as St. Vladimir. This facilitated his efforts to unify the peoples of his vast territories, while his marriage to the sister of the Byzantine emperor Basil II gave him the authority and prestige to accomplish the task.

Vladimir's death in 1015 caused, as earlier with Svyatoslav, his sons to contest over the succession. After these earlier years of turbulence, Yaroslav, who had prevailed, presided over long years of stability, and became known as Yaroslav the Wise. He invited Greek architects to build churches and demonstrate the arts of icon painting. Greek clerics organized church parishes, monasteries and schools. Cyril and Methodius, the Bulgarian missionaries to the Slavs, had already created a special alphabet to transcribe the Slavonic language. By translating major passages of the Bible into that idiom, they made it immediately accessible to the people.

The inevitable conflict of succession between Yaroslav's five sons weakened the principality, as the vast territory was gradually subdivided into appanages or parcels. At the same time, the vital trade and cultural relations with Byzantium were also weakened. The sack of Constantinople by the Franks in 1204 redirected trade away from the Black Sea. The Pontic Steppe was abandoned to its nomadic conquerors, and its populations migrated to the South-West, West, North, and especially the forested region of the North-East.

In 1169 Prince Andrew of Rostov and Suzdal sacked Kiev and transferred the capital of Rus to the town of Vladimir in the Northeast. Thus, when the massive Mongol threat appeared on the horizon of the early 13 century, Kievan Rus was no longer a confederation, but a collection of independent city states. One by one they fell under the Mongol "yoke," which was to last for the next 250 years.

Historians credit the overwhelming success and far-reaching scope of the Mongol conquests to the outstanding abilities of their leader, Genghis Khan. He united the Mongol and Turkic tribes of Siberia, then in 1211 conquered northern China and Central Asia, and in 1223 defeated a joint army of Rus and Cumans. Genghis Khan's successors conquered the rest of China, Persia, and the Middle East. Crossing the frozen rivers in winter, they subdued the northern principalities of Vladimir and Ryazan. If a town resisted, its population was condemned to all-out massacre. The fate of Kiev, which offered fierce resistance, was to be raised to the ground in 1240.

The Mongols did not attempt outright occupation of the large former territory of Kievan Rus. Given their overwhelming military superiority, they made sure that tribute was paid by playing favorites among the local rulers in order to keep them divided and dependent on Mongol might. The Pontic Steppe, however, whose grassland they needed to feed their horses, was under direct Mongol occupation known as the Golden Horde.

Their capital of Sarai on the lower Volga became a large urban center. The Greek merchants on the shores of the Black Sea were replaced by Genoese and Venetian merchants. Some trade was re-established on the old river routes between Novgorod and the Caspian and Black Seas. A mixed population of Finno-Ugrians, Sarmato-Scythians and Slavs was governed by a Mongol-Turkic elite. The slave trade was booming, and some of the richest agricultural lands of Kievan Rus were lost for centuries.

The political and cultural achievements of Kievan Rus remained a treasured but much diminished inheritance. The rise of successor states happened elsewhere. Ukraine remained a borderland, now between the rising powers of Poland-Lithuania, Muscovy, and the continued Mongol-Tatar occupation of the Pontic Steppe. In 1362 the Lithuanian army defeated the Mongol Golden Horde, and recaptured Kiev. They annexed Volhynia while Poland annexed Galicia, the south-western territories of former Kievan Rus. However, the southern territories and Crimea were reorganized under the rule of an Islamic Tatar Khanate in 1441.

In 1380 it had been the turn of Moscow to win a decisive battle against the Mongols, which empowered its princes to claim suzerainty over the other principalities of the north and northeastern Rus. In 1471 the capture of Novgorod, which had been an independent mercantile republic associated with the Hanseatic League, continued the "gathering of lands" under the princes of Moscow.

Christianity, which had been a rallying point to organize Kievan Rus, was no longer a universal set of beliefs. Since 1054 there had occurred a schism between the bishop of Rome and the patriarch of Constantinople, and Christianity was now preached under two different names – Catholicism and Orthodoxy. Lithuania had been a pagan state until 1385. In that year the marriage between the Catholic princess of Poland and the pagan Grand Prince of Lithuania resulted in Lithuania's adopting the Catholic version of Christianity. The Orthodox metropolitan of Kiev had moved to Vladimir back in 1299, thus grounding the institutional roots of Byzantine or Orthodox Christianity in what was to become Muscovite Russia.

These religious differences will play themselves out in the devastated territory which will become known as Ukraine. A significant minority of the original Orthodox clergy, particularly in Galicia, turned to the pope's authority if allowed to retain their traditional practices and liturgy. They became known as Uniates or "Greek Catholics."

The installation of Lithuanian and Polish rule over areas that had been Orthodox, including White Russia or Belarus, also created class divisions between the Catholic nobility, often absentee landlords, and the Orthodox peasants and townspeople. The practice of delegating the day-to-day running of the Polish estates to Jewish managers caused long-standing resentment of Jews. Another problem was caused by the enterprising Crimean Muslim Khanate, which relied on the lucrative slave trade to fill its coffers. Their annual raids unto the sparsely settled lands caused perennial insecurity.

All these conflicts resulted in the organization of Cossack units. The Cossacks – the word means free in Turkic - were heirs and descendants of all the peoples who had passed through the Pontic Steppe. They had learned to assert their freedom by organizing themselves into disciplined military bands. They practiced popular democracy, gathering in assemblies and choosing their leaders by acclamation. These free ways attracted runaway peasants from Polish as well as Russian territories, where serfdom, or forced attachment to the land, was a common practice.

These Cossack communities organized themselves into loose confederations. One such community or Host settled beyond the rapids on the Dnieper river. Another Host settled further east on the Don river. The Cossacks engaged in mercenary service in the various conflicts between Poland, the Tatars and Muscovy. But they also repeatedly asserted their independence in rebellions, early on against the Polish, and later against the Russian conquest of Ukraine.

The main such event in the 17th century concerns the rebellion of the Cossack leader Bogdan Khmelnitsky against Polish rule and the imposition of the Catholic religion. This resulted in his capture of Kiev and the proclamation of a new Rus state. But as he was subsequently defeated by Polish forces, he turned to the Orthodox tsar Alexei of Moscow. The treaty of Pereiaslav granted, under Moscow's 'protection,' some of the privileges to the Cossack leaders and civic freedoms to the general population Poland had been unwilling to grant.

But persistent warfare between multiple parties led to the 1667 Treaty of Andrusovo between Russia and Poland, which divided Ukraine between them along the line of the Dnieper River, with Kiev remaining under Russian rule. This caused another Ukrainian rebellion, under the Cossack leadership of Mazeppa, this time against the Russians. But Mazeppa and his Swedish allies were defeated by Peter the Great at the battle of Poltava in 1709. As a result, Ukrainian autonomy was drastically reduced.

The 18th century witnessed a major expansion of Russia. It had reclaimed much of the Siberian territory from its ancient Mongol and Turkic foes. This culminated in the conquest of Crimea by Catherine the Great in 1772. The cities of Yekaterinoslav (now Dnipropetrovsk), Sevastopol and Odessa were founded. The Pontic Steppe was opened to agricultural colonization. However, the introduction of serfdom, unknown in Ukraine until then, also triggered repeated rebellions, not only by Ukrainian Dnieper, but also by Russian Don Cossacks.

Similarly, the long-standing contest between Poland and Russia resulted in the three partitions of Poland between Russia, Prussia, and Austria. Galicia, once part of Kieven Rus, then of Poland, came under Austrian rule. And in 1793 right-bank Ukraine, so long under Polish rule, was annexed by Russia. Much later, after the German invasion of Poland in 1939, Eastern Galicia and Volhynia, once part of Kievan Rus, were returned to what was now Ukraine.

The 19th century witnessed an increasing integration of Ukrainian gentry into the ranks of its Russian counterpart. And the once rebellious Cossacks, having been at the forefront of colonizing Siberia, now became elite units in Russia's imperial army.

However, just like with the historical movements toward nation-building in the rest of Europe, Ukrainian intellectuals sought to assert local varieties of culture, tradition, and political independence. Still, Ukrainian-born Nicolai Gogol wrote novels and stories, many of them taking place in Ukraine – in Russian. The poet Taras Shevchenko, on the other hand, used the local vernacular, which had slowly established itself in the 18th century, and thus became a symbol of national self-assertion.

All these complicated historical developments are operative to this day. As briefly described in an earlier chapter, Ukraine established an independent governing body or Rada during the turmoil of World War I and the Civil War. But after successive occupations by contesting armies, the victory of the Bolshevik Revolution resulted in Ukraine becoming one of the constituent republics of the Soviet Union.

As also referred to earlier, there was an initial support of the exercise of national cultural traditions by the various republics. And under NEP (New Economic Policy) individual economic initiative was also encouraged. But in the early '30s there was a general change of policy. There was a sense that agricultural recovery needed to be accelerated. To accomplish this, the new policy insisted that the ancient ways of family farming needed to be modernized and that the rural population needed to be redirected toward industrialization. The looming danger of German invasion created a sense of urgency and, in due course, intolerance and coercion. The niceties of cultural assertion were brushed aside as harboring seeds of rebellion.

And rebellion was indeed one of the traditional options, particularly in Ukraine. It was, after all, the most fertile territory of the Soviet Union, and its peasants - and especially the successful farmers who had been given their land by the Revolution - were not willing to be told their business by Moscow bureaucrats. Thus, the compulsory collectivization drive proved one of the most contested and tragic episodes of the Soviet history of the early '30s.

The statistics with regard to the number of deaths resulting from starvation or the transfer of populations are actively contested. The Russian dissident Roy Medvedev cites the deaths to be in the hundreds of thousands. Robert Conquest of the British MI 5 insists on millions. Grover Furr, an American professor of Medieval English Literature at Montclair State University, cites Mark Tauger of West Virginia University, an expert in the field, to contest the Robert Conquest figures.

Let me address, as a way of comparison, the problems of agricultural modernization as they are happening today. There is a prevailing view that the Bill and Melinda Gates foundation is a wealthy charitable organization concerned about the plight of the Global South, and that they have been leaders and major investors in the "Green Revolution." On the other hand, critical voices are being raised about the results of the foundation's activities.

An article by Robert Kennedy Jr. on *Global Research* cites a number of sources to that effect. Howard Viegler, an Iowa farmer who has worked as a crop and livestock consultant in the U.S and Canada since 1992, is quoted as follows: "Gates talks about farming as an archaic, quaint, dirty, dangerous, inefficient, barbarous relic from the past..." This sounds reminiscent of how Soviet modernizers saw the "archaic" farming practices of the Russian and Ukrainian farmers.

Christian Westbrook, an agricultural researcher, states: "We know who Bill Gates is, and we know the mischief he made for small farmers in Mexico, Africa and India..." According Robert Kennedy Jr., his claims are confirmed by the 2020 study, *False Promises: The Alliance for a Green Revolution in Africa (AGRA)*: "the investigation concludes that the number of Africans suffering extreme hunger has increased by 30% in the 18 countries that Gates targeted. Rural poverty has metastasized dramatically, and the number of hungry people in these nations has risen to 131 million..." In language reminiscent of the condemnation of Soviet collective farms, Robert Kennedy Jr. concludes: "Under Gates' plantation system, Africa's rural populations have become slaves on their own land to a tyrannical serfdom of high-tech inputs, mechanization, and rigid schedules..."

Dr. Vandana Shiva, an award-winning author of some 20 books, tells a similar story of disastrous consequences from the Gates' intervention to 'rescue' the poor Indian farmer. The effects of the NAFTA agreement under President Bill Clinton have also been described as utterly devastating to the Mexican subsistence farmer by the tax-supported American corn imports.

Now Christian Whitmore insists that a similar fate awaits us here at home. He states: "We know that his (Bill Gates') recent purchases here are just the start of the Green Revolution 3.0. He wants to suck out the democratic essence of America's pastoral landscapes and our farm families – to steal our livelihoods, our knowledge, our seeds, and our land." This sounds like the cry of the "kulaks" whose lands were nationalized in the Soviet Union. And when Gates is accused of megalomaniacal, even "messianic," faith in his calling to "save" the perishing world, this is reminiscent of those who castigated the Communists for promising to create heaven on earth?

Is modernization, then, always problematic? Or is it the case when modernization is sponsored under Capitalist auspices rather than Socialist ones, it should be supported? Or vice versa, presumably because in the latter case it is done for and by the people while in the former, primarily for profit? But then again, is this circular planet of ours not becoming overpopulated, and Mother Earth's bounty exhausted?

Unfortunately, instead of seeking peaceful solutions to very real problems, arms build-up and arms trafficking is still the obsession of those who run the world. In the past elections in this country, when Tulsi Gabbard even mentioned the word "peace," she was immediately reviled as "a Russian asset." Similarly, even in a respectable journal like the *New York Review of Books*, for some time now I have observed a slide toward "mainstream" trends unchecked by dialogue with countervailing positions. And by "mainstream," so strenuously proclaimed in the less respectable day-to-day media – I mean a full-blown Russia-gate.

I have struggled with Russian history and politics all my life, and have come to accept, among others, the work of Professor Stephen Cohen as thoroughly knowledgeable and eminently reasonable. But you will not find his voice in the NYR to challenge the vehemence of someone like Anne Applebaum. Well, no, I am being unfair. The NYR has been repeatedly offering its platform to a man of good will - George Soros. His Open Society Institute has been financing the good news of Capitalist salvation to the poor, benighted peoples of the Soviet Union and its "satellites."

And together with all the other missionaries from the West, he has succeeded! The Soviets admitted the error of their ways, converted, and were saved. Not so fast. What about beady-eyed Vlad who turned out, despite Bill

Clinton's expectations, NOT to be just another (but sober) Yeltsin? After the villains Milošević and Saddam Hussein and Osama Bin Laden and Muammar Gaddafi were disposed of, it was Putin's turn to be selected for ritual stoning. A new version of the Cold War is on.

What exactly are Putin's sins – other than riding horses bare-chested? It really doesn't matter. Our addiction to the military industrial complex, like any addiction, needs an excuse. As the Pentagon chief Chuck Hagel put it: "Let us remember that the biggest beneficiaries of American leadership and engagement in the world are the American people." True enough that we do enjoy cheap imports from Asia, Africa, Latin America, and of course, the Middle-East. But how long can we count on these life supports? As our leaders tell us in no uncertain terms, only as long as we are strong enough to enforce the status quo.

That's why NATO, after "Operation Gladio" implemented after World War II, has to keep doing its job. And it is doing just that: training volunteer soldiers, newly recruited from Croatia, Hungary, Bulgaria, Romania, Montenegro, Poland, Lithuania, Latvia, Estonia... also Kazakhs and all their neighbors from the former Soviet Stans... They are all joining the Brits and French and Italians and Spaniards and Turks – and Germans (why not?) to fight the good fight. Am I missing anyone? Oh yes, Ukraine.

Why Ukraine? As the title of Yale University Professor Timothy Snyder's article in the New Republic put it: "The Battle in Ukraine Means Everything." Maybe so, because the Orange Revolution of 2004 petered out. Instead of our friend Yushchenko, and the glamorous Yuliya Timoshenko (a natural brunette whose instant golden hair is woven in a braid around her head to symbolize fairytale days of yore) were not elected: Victor Yanukovych was.

And when faced with two different options, a trade agreement with the European Union or a deal with the Russian Federation to whom he was heavily indebted for gas use, Yanukovych vacillated. Implicit in the European Union offer was the imposition of austerity measures against loans from the IMF. If Putin could forgive some of the gas debt, which, apparently, he did, Yanukovych decided for the latter option.

REALLY? After the West's strenuous and costly (Victoria Nuland mentioned ten billion dollars) coaching in the ways of democracy? Actually, the Ukrainian people did get democracy. After Kravchuk, and Kuchma, and Yushchenko, and Yanukovych, every one of them duly elected, had presided over the distribution of public goods to newly-baked, mafia-protected, buddy oligarchs, the Ukrainian people were fed up. They gathered on the Maidan square and protested. And they did so peacefully.

But that was only the prelude - with the touching side show of Victoria Nuland distributing cookies and John McCain haranguing the crowd. The real show started when bullets started flying and people started dropping dead. The evidence that snipers were at work, trying to make it look like the attack came from the police, is incontrovertible. The main result was that a group of well-trained people, locals belonging to Nazi insignia-touting nationalists, as well as hired mercenaries, took over the government.

And whether expected or not, the regime change in Kyiv (Kiev) caused the country to descend into civil war. The law to ban the official use of the Russian language was not only experienced as an assault on the eastern and southern regions of Ukraine. The language divide coincides largely between the urban versus the rural population. The Russian-Ukrainian intermarriage of so many people – just as in the case of my own parents – is widespread. The Ukrainian economy is just as thoroughly intertwined with the Russian one – and always has been.

While most Ukrainians recognized this, but have been well "trained" to exercise the presumed options of "democracy," the demographically more dense and industrially more developed Donbass territory was prepared, instead, to fight it out. That region had owned its development to Soviet times, and they had fought against, not sided with, the German invasion of World War II. They ejected their Kyiv-appointed politicians and organized grassroots, popular militias.

But then "Socialist" Francois Hollande of France and angelic Angela Merkel of Germany tried to backpedal because civil war is hardly conducive to favorable trade deals. Even before, at the Geneva meeting, the concept of a federal Ukraine with elected regional governments and protection for regional interests had been proposed. They spearheaded two new meetings in Minsk, the capital of Belarus. But the ceasefires they agreed upon with their Russian counterparts were broken. Unsurprisingly, the Ukrainian government cannot control those to whom it owes its position.

Thus, while yet another Ukrainian president, the chocolate king Poroshenko, was duly elected, the right-wing putschists were still in charge. A law was passed to exonerate them from any suspicion of atrocities against the civilian population by officially recognizing them as "freedom fighters" – echoes of Oliver North and the Nicaraguan "freedom fighters?" And while statues of Lenin were systematically demolished everywhere (except in the Donbas and Lugansk territories) a statue of the Nazi collaborator in World War II, Stepan Bandera, was erected in Lviv (Lvov, Lemberg).

As for the rest of the people, nothing was undertaken to improve their lives. The fact that national needs were trumped by global priorities is exemplified by the installation of Hunter Biden, as well as the former president of Poland, on the board of directors of Burisma, the largest natural gas company of Ukraine. And when Ukraine's Attorney General was foolhardy enough to initiate an investigation into Burisma's tax-evading Cyprus registration, Hunter's daddy, the vice-president of the United States, reminded the locals who's boss. If the prosecutor did not cease and desist, his government better say good bye to the promised billion dollars they were counting on. Naturally, the prosecution was dropped.

Global interests in the fate of Ukraine are demonstrated by the careful planning behind the scene of the "spontaneous" events of Maidan in 2014. Diana Johnstone cites The Economist describing the meeting that took place in September of 2013 in Yalta, famous for the meeting that had decided the future of Europe back in 1945. Now the topic of discussion was DCFTA, or Deep and Comprehensive Free Trade Agreement. Participants included Bill and Hillary Clinton, former CIA head General David Petraeus, former US Treasury Secretary Lawrence Summers, former World Bank head Robert Zoellick, Swedish foreign minister Carl Bildt, Shimon Peres, Tony Blair, Gerhard Schroder, Dominique Strauss-Kahn, Mario Monti, Lithuanian president Dalia Grybauskaite, and Poland's foreign minister Radek Sikorski. The then President Viktor Yanukovich and future President Petro Poroshenko were also present. Former U.S. energy secretary Bill Richardson explained how the future of Ukrainian shale-gas extraction could counter Russian natural gas reserves.

As some commentators suggest, the assault on Ukraine was not about Ukraine, but about the Russian Federation. The winter Olympic games taking place in Sochi that same year were boycotted by Western heads of state. More importantly, Secretary of State John Kerry visited Riyadh in 2016 and this resulted in a drastic drop in the price of oil. Since oil and gas account for half of the Russian Federation's GDP, this caused a precipitous devaluation of the ruble.

Perhaps the underlying purpose of all these moves was to entice Putin to intervene in Ukraine, as Brezhnev had done in Afghanistan, which would have given NATO a chance to rescue the poor Ukrainians. But Putin did not fall for it. If he did help Donbass, now labelled as "separatists," it was surreptitiously so. The million, and still counting, refugees from the civil war were well received in Russia, and many have since been granted Russian citizenship.

Crimea, however, was another matter. Crimea had been "given" to Ukraine by Nikita Khrushchev in 1954. This was a purely administrative move, and Ukrainian Nikita, who was the premier of the Soviet Union the way the Texan Bushes, father and son, had been presidents of the United States, must twist and turn in his grave at the unexpected results.

Catherine the Great had fought the Turkish Empire over Crimea, Nicholas I had fought the British and the French over it, and Stalin had fought over it during World War II. Of course, Catherine and Alexander and Stalin were not the ones fighting and dying in Crimea: it was the Russian-Ukrainian people. That is why Sevastopol is known as "the city of glory." It is the vital port to the Black Sea landlocked Russia could not lose. After all, Putin had an agreement with Ukraine for a twenty-year lease for the Russian fleet: he had legal grounds to make his move.

And although nuclear-armed American submarines were present in the Black Sea at the time, they did not make the move that would have started World War III. Instead, the West denounced the Crimean referendum as "fake," and proceeded to punish the Russians with more economic sanctions. Congressman Denis Kucinich describes how the sanctions were passed on December 11, 2014: "Legislation brought forward before Congress under "unanimous consent" is usually not read by most members because copies of the bill are generally not available." ... "As a result, the Russian Sanctions bill was passed "unanimously," with no scheduled debate."

As to the Ukrainians, are they any better under yet another duly elected president, Volodymyr (note the Ukrainian version of the Russian name Vladimir, as in Vladimir Putin) Zelensky? He came to power thanks to peace-making slogans, and the usual promises to control street violence and battle corruption. Instead, he is reduced, as the presidents before him, to rely on paramilitary groups against his local competitors.

The election of Donald Trump put something of a freeze on the Ukrainian situation. As Secretary of State Mike Pompeo put it on Fox News: "Do you think that Americans care about Ukraine?" We are much too mesmerized by our own political soap operas. Trump wanted Zelensky to out Biden about Burisma, and the Democrats wanted Zelensky to out Trump. He was caught threatening Zelensky to withhold promised military hardware. However, Trump did underwrite the military hardware anyway, which is bound to perpetuate the civil war in Ukraine. Does that worry the American public?

Now that Joe Biden has won the United States presidency, the American public need worry no more. The U.S. Secretary of State Antony Blinken has been conferring with Ukrainian Foreign Minister Dmytro Kuleba. He assured Blinken that the prospect of a united front between Ukraine, Georgia, and Moldova may be counted upon in any future NATO plans. And if you have finally figured out where Ukraine is, and don't look for Georgia south of the Mason-Dixon line, you will still need a magnifying glass to find Moldova on the map.

I have inflicted much ancient history on my prospective readers because the ghosts of history are still haunting Ukraine today. After being a passageway for multiple nomadic invaders, even in the glory days of Kievan Rus, it became the borderland between the Catholic West and the Orthodox East. In time, new ideologies have come to clash on its territory. The residual contest between the Capitalism of the West and the Socialism of the East may be recognized today in the triumphalist positions of Western Ukraine and the dogged resistance of South-Eastern Ukraine.

The latest contest between the United States and the European Union against the Russian Federation over Ukraine reflects more basic power struggles. Even if Ukraine is not subject to literal invasion, it is, like in the days of the supreme Mongol power, expected to pay tribute. Are the Russians the dreaded "hordes" from the East, or are the rulers of NATO the new Mongols?

Thanks to my freedom ticket from the expectations and pitfalls of my academic career, I was able to resume my ventures into forbidden territories. But, to borrow Michael Parenti's self-definition as a "recovering academic," I found myself in a kind of double bind. OK, I didn't have to teach Russian to future spies anymore, but I had also lost my niche in a socially sanctioned position. But then again, what are the costs of such a position?

I began to identify with Peter Weir's movie The Truman Show. The perfectly staged life of an "everyday hero" (played by Jim Carey) is a kind of science-fiction vision of ordinary life. The setting, vaguely suggestive of a bucolic New England town, is large enough to also suggest a "universal" version of urban living. There are no skyscrapers, traffic is not intrusive, and people walk about and ride bicycles. An overhead camera shot presents a picture-perfect vista of a well-proportioned collection of white buildings ringed by the sea: the place is an island. The hero is surrounded by a friendly cast of characters, and his blue-eyed, permanently smiling wife, (played by Laura Linney) is a kind of distillation of the all-American girl next door.

But nothing is perfect. The hero is haunted by a childhood tragedy. His father, he believes, drowned during their father-and-son sailing outing. Also, it would seem that he had been in love with another girl, but circumstances caused him to find himself in the present situation with the forbearing, smile-ready wife. What are we to make of these anomalies? Truman himself, at any rate, begins to act suspicious. Little by little, the plot unravels. We become aware that Truman is but a captive player in a TV show. And the more "human" his dilemma, (his trust in his best friend, or his father's presumed death, or his longing for another woman) the more his faithful, world-wide audience is mesmerized by the show. And the puppet master who stages it all (played by Ed Harris) is quick to capitalize even on Truman's increasingly dramatic efforts to escape.

Is Peter Weir, in placing his hero in this "perfect" and perfectly sanitized environment thinking of his own "lucky country," Australia? Or is this an outsider's gaze at the model Western country, the United States?

I too had become an estranged American. I was increasingly irritated by the unavoidable, inane smiles when advertising the latest detergent or the latest potency pill - in vehement contrast to the lack of smiles in the "evil empire"? Well yes, there was some healthy pushback, but the actual bones of contention struck me as minor: all about a particular football team or political party. I had always found football boring – and the politics, eventually, boringly predictable: nothing changed no matter who won. What was wrong with me? Like the Truman character, I began to feel confined and restless and started looking for a way out.

And like the man who had been running the show in which Truman had been cast as the hero, my friends and family warned me about the dangers of the outside world. They were right. The ashen cross the young man in El Salvador traced on my forehead – while the American convoy was rumbling up above – weighed heavily on me ever after. And now when I drive my car, I know, as the man in Colombia had told us, that a body is burning in its exhaust fumes. And when I finally decided to recapture my life's journey by returning all the way to its beginnings in Yugoslavia, it was as if time had stood still: the country was devastated again as when I left it so long ago, and its people were in mourning again.

As the song goes, "when will we ever learn?" I guess we will never learn until we absolutely have to. The Occupy Movement has been trying to point to Wall Street, but who, except for the 0.01 percent, knows how to play that game? Surely, there is another way for the rest of us? In the meantime, there is always room for entertainment: we can keep poking the Russian bear in the eye over Ukraine - until we all die laughing in a nuclear meltdown.

But then again, young Truman in the *Truman Show*, after a number of escape attempts, finally makes it: there is a door in the invisible wall that surrounds the island. And he opens it and steps out. We, too, can look for that door.

***

POSTLUDE

"I am for those who walk abreast with the whole earth
Who inaugurate one to inaugurate all."

-Walt Whitman

We step out as usual. It is 6 a.m. Like Rick, John is a hiker. The upturned bowl of the sky rests on the mountaintops which surround Tucson... there isn't a wisp or shred of cloud to hitch one's thoughts to... instead, they churn and tumble in my head like clothes in a dryer.

If only... a jack rabbit, a young one, darts across our path. If only, if only Peter... if only he could hang in there...

Peter was so tense when he called last night... He has gone through some relationship disappointments again... who wants to put up with a crazy guy? He only spoke about this and that, but how well I know that strained, ever-so-"normal" voice, thin and brittle, and the sound of my own voice in reply, just as falsely calm, but swollen with helpless, useless grief... If only...

hank goodness Muriel's okay. This New York city girl grew up watching "Little House on the Prairie" on TV... and now she lives her dream. After Rick died and I sold the house, she and Rob have moved out of Tucson where land is cheaper, and now she has chickens, and goats, and plans to grow lavender...

We step out as usual. It is six a.m. The sky is blue. We walk at a good clip, and I am thinking of the girls. They've reached college age, but tuition is SO prohibitive these days... Chloe is working at it... Astrid decided to take time off... She is helping Muriel with the farm... and learning to train horses...

We step out as usual. It is 6 a.m. The sky is blue all around, resting lightly on the earth's rim. It really does look like an upturned bowl, but all the water has long since poured out and the sky now is clean and empty...

Even at this early hour the cactuses are beginning to look a faded, sickly green... something about the saguaros with their uplifted arms makes them look almost human with exhaustion...

I am looking forward to the holidays... There is so much I want to tell the girls, but they are absorbed in their own lives... Chloe is living her first love... He is a very handsome Hindu boy whose parents have come to the United States by way of Trinidad...

I love those girls with a fierce, protective love, and I worry about the kind of world we are leaving them... empires have been known to be as transient as tribal sand paintings...

All this is *déjà vu:* my parents' Russian generation has lived through the consequences of their denials... they too had God and all the decencies of well-fed good intentions on their side, but were swept away, the good as well as the bad and the ugly... gone with the wind...

And the same thing in Germany... the master race was finally subdued, their awesome weapons matched... and now it's our turn... I feel like Cassandra before the wall of Troy – no one will believe my sad prophesies...

There goes the sick coyote again... We see coyotes often, with fluffy fur and tail, but this one is mangy and emaciated, probably fed on some poisoned pack rat.

We step out as usual. It's 6 a.m. The sky still spotless blue, still untouched... nothing remains untouched... Nancy has been struggling with breast cancer... I've lost touch with Jane... And now Hélène, after a long struggle with lymphoma, has passed on... Irène called from Paris to tell me that she had left this earth peacefully...

Living peacefully, dying peacefully... a fool's dream... but we keep on keeping on... People I know and people I don't know – peaceniks, nuclear resisters, tree huggers, planned parenthood defenders, gay rights activist, black lives matter protesters, union advocates... they get arrested every day... and every rebellious, peaceful step they take blesses the earth.

Tribes used to meet in jungles and the word for "stranger" and "enemy" was the same ... so they fought each other, then ate the losers' livers to gain their spirit... It was Lahsen who had told me that a man's courage resides in his liver...

The people in the Middle East are showing plenty of "liver" right now all along "the axis of evil"... The way Hillary smirked when Gaddafi was sodomized...only the well-ensconced and well-fed dread change...

We step out as usual. It is 6 a.m. The backyard needs attention...We told Noé, but he had to take the day off to go see about his green card. He's been in the country twenty years now, he came from Guatemala when his best friend was dropped off a helicopter into the sea... He had walked all the way north... he is here under some legal amnesty, but lawyers stall for money and nothing happens...

What would we do without Noé? He trims the bushes, cleans the driveway, sprays for termites, fixes the tiles, rebuilds the steps, and deals with our antiquated electric system... what would we do without patient, smart, hard-working Noe?

Our nice houses... Frank and Francine gave us our first leg-up... and then the Coca Cola inheritance to keep it going... our proud inheritance now drains the well water away from whole communities somewhere in India... and hires killers to stop workers from unionizing in Colombia... The pause that refreshes? The drink that represses?

Ahead of us, a black turkey vulture tears away at road kill... we stop... the vulture keeps an eye on us as he puts away his dinner...

We step out as usual. It is 6 a.m. There's the red cardinal, our own local firebird... he sits among the gnarled mesquite branches, trilling "pizza, pizza, pizza..."

This unimpeachable sky gets to you after a while... yet this is the sky we loved so much in Morocco, just as true blue and constant... Australia too had blue skies, but there the blue of the sea blended in, blue on blue... California was like that - actually the Bay Area could be pretty murky... and Rick had been only too happy to leave Belgium's soggy skies behind... yet my parents had so missed the brooding skies of Russia, swollen with gathering storms... German skies went with the seasons: cold season, hungry season, war season, waiting for Godot season... I don't remember the color of Yugoslav skies, except that bombs fell out of them...

Ahead of us a family of quail, the mom and dad in front... with their quavering crests, and the little chicks following in solemn order...

I was family rich and didn't know it... thanks, Mom, for listening to your reproductive clock... thanks, Father, for conceiving me before your life was cut short... thanks, Dad, for staying put and seeing me through...and thank you Babushka for your pies and prayers and fairy tales...

And thanks to the larger family... to Frank and Francine and to all the strangers practicing random acts of kindness ...the Moulinous and the Mandrykas and the de Millers and the Benchemouls and the Mayranoffs and Frau Dopner...

And thank you, John, for taking care of me in my old age.

A hawk rises from our pine tree and heads straight for the blue...

***

Lightning Source UK Ltd.
Milton Keynes UK
UKHW021217010822
406675UK00009B/1909